Doing Time

THE SUNY SERIES

HORIZONS OF CINEMA

MURRAY POMERANCE | EDITOR

Also in the series

William Rothman, editor, *Cavell on Film*

J. David Slocum, editor, *Rebel Without a Cause*

Joe McElhaney, *The Death of Classical Cinema*

Kirsten Moana Thompson, *Apocalyptic Dread*

Frances Gateward, editor, *Seoul Searching*

Michael Atkinson, editor, *Exile Cinema*

Paul S. Moore, *Now Playing*

Robin L. Murray and Joseph K. Heumann, *Ecology and Popular Film*

William Rothman, editor, *Three Documentary Filmmakers*

Sean Griffin, editor, *Hetero*

Jean-Michel Frodon, editor, *Cinema and the Shoah*

Carolyn Jess-Cooke and Constantine Verevis, editors, *Second Takes*

Matthew Solomon, editor, *Fantastic Voyages of the Cinematic Imagination*

R. Barton Palmer and David Boyd, editors, *Hitchcock at the Source*

William Rothman, *Hitchcock: The Murderous Gaze, Second Edition*

Joanna Hearne, *Native Recognition*

Marc Raymond, *Hollywood's New Yorker*

Steven Rybin and Will Scheibel, editors, *Lonely Places, Dangerous Ground*

Claire Perkins and Constantine Verevis, editors, *B Is for Bad Cinema*

Dominic Lennard, *Bad Seeds and Holy Terrors*

Rosie Thomas, *Bombay before Bollywood*

Scott M. MacDonald, *Binghamton Babylon*

Sudhir Mahadevan, *A Very Old Machine*

David Greven, *Ghost Faces*

James S. Williams, *Encounters with Godard*

William H. Epstein and R. Barton Palmer, editors,
Invented Lives, Imagined Communities

Doing Time

Temporality, Hermeneutics, and Contemporary Cinema

Lee Carruthers

SUNY PRESS

Cover image: "Thanksgiving Chapel Window" courtesy of photographer Helen Powell.

Published by State University of New York Press, Albany

Printed in the United States of America

For information, contact State University of New York Press, Albany, NY
www.sunypress.edu

Production, Ryan Morris
Marketing, Anne M. Valentine

Library of Congress Cataloging-in-Publication Data

Names: Carruthers, Lee, [date]
Title: Doing time : temporality, hermeneutics, and contemporary cinema / Lee Carruthers.
Description: Albany : State University of New York Press, 2015. | Series: SUNY series, horizons of cinema | Based on the author's thesis (doctoral)—University of Chicago, 2008. | Includes bibliographical references and index.
Identifiers: LCCN 2015026348 | ISBN 9781438460857 (hardcover : alk. paper) | ISBN 9781438460864 (pbk. : alk. paper) | ISBN 9781438460871 (e-book)
Subjects: LCSH: Time in motion pictures.
Classification: LCC PN1995.9.T55 C38 2015 | DDC 791.43/684—dc23
LC record available at http://lccn.loc.gov/2015026348

10 9 8 7 6 5 4 3 2 1

For Charles and Laurel

Contents

Illustrations

Acknowledgments

I'm fortunate to have received many kinds of support while writing this book, which I will attempt to enumerate here. This project began as a dissertation at the University of Chicago, where I was delighted to work with Tom Gunning, whose intellectual generosity and friendship has been sustaining throughout this process. Tom's way of responding to films (and other texts) is inspiring—and remains the best hermeneutical model I've encountered. I'm grateful also to Jim Lastra, whose keen engagement improved this project in many ways in its early stages. I also wish to thank Yuri Tsivian for lending expertise at key moments; and of course Miriam Hansen, who insisted I come to Chicago in the first place. Thanks are due to Michael Forster for inviting me to sit in on his courses at Chicago, and to Kristin Gjesdal for sharing her early work on Gadamer with me. More recently, an early version of one of this book's chapters was delivered as a paper at the annual conference for the Society for Cinema and Media Studies: I'm indebted to Richard Neer for his considered response to that talk, and for his thoughts on Terrence Malick's cinema more generally.

In another way, my interest in this book's material is more long-standing, initiated in my master's degree with Charles O'Brien, who introduced me to hermeneutics, and Laura U. Marks, who showed me the value of good phenomenological description. Casting back even earlier, I'm grateful to Charlie Keil for setting the bar so high, and for his continued support. Thanks also to Bart Testa, who once told me that he reads hermeneutics in the dark, when no one is looking.

My research for this project was initiated with the support of Division of the Humanities at the University of Chicago, the Social Sciences and Humanities Research Council of Canada, and the Josephine De Kármán Fellowship Trust, and concluded with material support from the University Research Grants Committee at the University of Calgary. It was bolstered by my participation in the Cinematic Times Symposium at the University of California, Berkeley, in 2013; my thanks goes to Natalia Brizuela for her invitation, and to all who contributed to that lively event. The enthusiastic energies of Murray Pomerance have been instrumental to this book's publication, as well as James Peltz, Rafael Chaiken, Ryan Morris, and everyone at SUNY Press who facilitated the process. This book also benefits from the excellent advice provided by its anonymous readers, and from the talent of Helen Powell, who supplied the beautiful image on its cover.

A range of friends, colleagues, and like-minded individuals deserve mention here for their kindness and assistance. At the University of Calgary, I want to thank Charlene Elliot, James Ellis, Erina Harris, Dawn Johnston, Barbara Schneider, and Lisa Stowe. In other places, I'm grateful to know Courtney Augustine, Matt Hauske, Nathan Holmes, Alyson Hrynyk, Andrew Johnston, Brendan Kredell, Dan Morgan, Inga Pollman, Scott Richmond, and Allison Whitney. My long-standing friendships with Gillian Roberts and Theresa Scandiffio predate this book's formulation, and will outlast it. A special kind of acknowledgment goes to the students who have tested this book's ideas, in various forms, as participants in my senior seminar. My sincere thanks goes to this group for causing me to think though the material more concretely, and for responding to it so creatively. I cannot name everyone here, but will point to Val Baravi, Felicia Glatz, Voytek Jarmula, Pat Matthews, Dillan Newman, and Julien Testa as key contributors to this conversation.

Thanks also to my family for their support: my mother, Maureen, Scott, and Tanya—and on the other side, Lorne, Sandy, Ruth, Margie, and Heather for their help at many crucial moments.

Finally, Charles Tepperman has patiently endured this book's first formulation through to its completion, which is surely gift enough. But my gratitude for his intellectual and personal support is more extensive. Charles's research has always been a source of inspiration for my own, and his thoughts about this project at different stages have been invaluable. While he cannot be held accountable for the flaws in this work, in some sense he has facilitated all of its brightest moments. My profound thanks to Laurel, as well, who understands time better than any of us.

Some of the ideas developed in Chapter 1 appeared in "M. Bazin et le Temps: Reclaiming the Timeliness of Cinematic Time," *Screen* 52, no. 1, Spring 2011. A version of chapter 2 was published as "Biding Our Time: Rethinking the Familiar in Soderbergh's *The Limey*," *Film Studies: An International Review* 6, Winter 2006.

Introduction

> When you see a movie, try to guess the moment when a shot has given its all and must move on, end, be replaced either by changing the angle, the distance, or the field. You will get to know that constriction of the chest produced by an overlong shot which breaks the movement and that deliciously intimate acquiescence when a shot fades at the right moment.
>
> —Roger Leenhardt, "Le Rhythme Cinématographique" (1936)

This book is motivated not just by filmic images and sounds, but by their affective correlation. It's about the way images cling to each other in a lingering dissolve, are stretched across time by musical phrasing, or are palpably severed by a cut. It's about the situation that Roger Leenhardt described in the pages of *Esprit*, when a shot hangs around longer than it has a right to; it also concerns the bristling effects of shots and whole sequences that are fragmented and fleeting, moving faster than causal logics.

These are details that matter to us in film viewing by their mutual impact and implication: these articulations of cinematic time do more than merely mark it, standing in evocative alignment with sensations of regret, longing, loss, and laughter, among others. Viewers of American film noir, for example, or of the postwar European art cinema, will recognize aspects of this syntax, where time registers not just for itself, but as powerfully steeped in feeling. In this study, I pursue temporal forms and their consequences across contemporary cinema, scrutinizing the trends of recent film practice to discover the kinds of time we find there.

The title of this book suggests that cinematic time can be conceived as an active process of engagement—in other words, as something we *do*, as viewers. As will become clear, the resonance of this title is phenomenological: it names a way of understanding filmic temporality and motivates an approach to it. It follows from the idea that our experience of time is fundamental to film viewing and yet receives little theoretical scrutiny. We engage cinematic time with every film we watch, in ways that are spontaneous, complex, and endlessly variegated. Here a question arises: How should we understand this transaction between film and viewer? In this book, I trace this exchange across a range of case studies drawn from contemporary narrative cinema, offering intensely detailed assessments of their temporal logics. Each chapter uncovers the film's characteristic way of conditioning temporal experience for viewers, or what I will call its *timeliness*. In this context, the ambiguities of filmic time are powerful attractions as they modulate film viewing: such pauses, gaps, repetitions, and stretches of time illuminate a living field that extends from our viewing activity.

It may be easiest to see how cinematic time matters to us when we think of a familiar version of it, like narrative suspense. Suspense is evidently a temporal phenomenon: it is a carefully calibrated play of duration and alternation that is designed to manage the pleasurable fears of viewers. Its tensions are assiduously structured, beginning as a deliberately decelerated action before rising to a dramatic peak; with suspense, we cannot help but notice that a film's temporal forms continuously shape our viewing experience.[1] We may also recognize that this experience occurs in an embodied way, as time told in sensation, and as a delimited event that binds uncertainty with pleasure. This kind of experience is the subject of this study, but is perused in its less emblematic permutations, exploring a variety of temporal modalities across recent film practice.

Underlying my approach is an idea that may at first seem idiosyncratic: this book assumes that films *know* about time, and can teach us something about it. Except that films do not essentially operate by means that are verbal, or propositional, I want to say that cinema forges arguments about temporality by diverse aesthetic means. Or more accurately, I want to say that the temporal forms of cinema are profoundly insightful: they can disclose subtle permeations of past and present, capturing both the pleasure and the pain of time in ways that reflect lived experience. Think here of an image that appears more than once in a film, evoking not just the stirrings of memory, but a deeper redundancy, perhaps marking the way that old routines still animate the present. Or consider the more elusive image, flashing before us but for a second, highlighting the passing of time and the hallucinatory edges of perception. To borrow a significant phrase from David Couzens Hoy, such filmic moments may help us to reconcile ourselves to the "time of our lives" by their dynamic mediation of temporality.[2] Not every film proves instructive in this way, of course, but certain titles are exemplary. I focus on recent films that frame their temporal insights most clearly, analyzing titles that in some sense embody Merleau-Ponty's vision of a future cinema, standing as "filmic films," more richly perceived through their cinematographical rhythms.[3]

This kind of temporality is not just presented by a film, nor is it gleaned at a distance. To bring out the richness of filmic temporality, the analyses collected here are grounded in phenomenological hermeneutics, engaging the fray of time as we negotiate it in film viewing. Drawing on philosophical sources, such as the writings of Martin Heidegger and Hans-Georg Gadamer, hermeneutics allows us to discern the temporal event that a film opens up, in which we actively participate. In its overlap with phenomenology, particularly that of Maurice Merleau-Ponty and André Bazin, this approach invites us to see our participation as sensuous and significant, and thus to plausibly relate the temporal terms of recent cinema to wider spheres of experience.[4]

Hermeneutics has at times held a prominent place in academic film study, cited for example, as a key theoretical valence by Dudley Andrew's mid-eighties text, *Concepts in Film Theory*.[5] More generally, film interpretation has long stood at the center of discussion and debate, whether as fodder for the generative commentaries that emerged from film journals in the 1970s, theorizing filmic systems, or in opposition to such activity, as the contested ground of a historical poetics the following decade. This tension has in fact been determining: while familiarly framed as a disagreement about the pertinence of film theory for the future of film scholarship, an unintended consequence of this debate has been to foreclose the potentialities of film hermeneutics before they can be taken up.[6] My priority is not to renew this discussion, but to retrieve hermeneutics from it, making a distinction between the closed practice that David Bordwell critiques and the phenomenologically inflected and historically informed mode of receptivity that motivates this study.[7] Along the way, we may discern some common ground spanning these perspectives: imagine Bordwell's poetics conceived not as the enemy of theory, but of the indifferent discourse that Merleau-Ponty calls "high-altitude thinking."[8] So this book is also a work of methodological retrieval, reappropriating and augmenting a piece of our disciplinary past that sharpens our view of the present.

The hermeneutical approach that serves this book endeavors to retain something of the spirit of Hermes the messenger, that trickster figure allied with a kind of play that is always susceptible to mischief, prevarication, and transformation. The movement of hermeneutics is therefore perpetual and polytropic, advancing a relation to the text that is continually reconfigured because it turns many ways.[9] Adopted as a textual practice, this stance does not project the semantic or conceptual possibilities of a film in advance, but rather awaits their temporal unfolding. As a hermeneutics of cinematic time, it exhibits an unusual sensitivity to imbrications of past and present, carefully observing the ways that recent films combine established and innovative filmic forms. Held against the contours of contemporary cinema, hermeneutics has much to offer us, affording a theoretical engagement with the films that continually mediates their history.

Bringing phenomenological hermeneutics to issues of cinematic time is far from an arbitrary choice for this study, and in fact relates integrally to its arguments. My approach in these pages reflects a doubled correspondence that can be discerned between a film's temporal articulations and our efforts to interpret them: I take it that our engagement with a film's time structures powerfully modulates our understanding of the work, and reciprocally, that thinking about our interpretive stance toward the cinema renews our contact with its temporal character.

Though directed to a different topic, Lesley Stern and George Kouvaros's essay collection, *Falling For You: Essays on Film and Performance*, provides an eloquent argument for the practice of close film description that is a source of inspiration for the hermeneutical model developed here. Drawing attention to a deficit in the literature related to the rhetorics of film-critical writing, the authors address a rift that occurs between film viewing and film analysis, resulting in a second-order description of experience that retains none of its affective potency. For Stern and Kouvaros, this is a problem that concerns

> the role of persuasion and communication in film writing. If we are concerned not simply with how films communicate with audiences, but with how theoretical and analytic writings communicate with readers who are also film viewers, then we would stress that they are constituted to some extent as film viewers by the very fact of writing/reading. Ideally we would like to write in such a way as to bring the film into imaginative being for the reader, so that she views it in the process of reading. But we would also like to offer a persuasive interpretation based on attentiveness to the object, on detailed and accurate rendition.[10]

How deftly these lines speak to the fruitful interconnections of film analysis and film theory, and of reading and writing, brought together in the event of film viewing. We should also mark the authors' insistence that the effort to bring a film "into imaginative being" relates fundamentally to the medium's temporal basis. Film challenges us not just to describe its visual qualities, but also to "capture its movement, its temporalisation."[11] As Stern and Kouvaros suggest, there is a way in which such descriptions aspire to ekphrasis, the ancient practice of calling to mind the visual by skillful verbal discourse.[12] For an approach to cinematic time that is informed by phenomenological hermeneutics, we might put things a little differently: what is required is not just an evocative description of the work, though that is ambitious enough, but one that acknowledges our traffic with its temporal forms, forging a kind of analysis that in some sense begins from *within* the time we seek to interpret.[13]

This call for a renewed practice of close textual reading has other allies, too; it can be discerned across varied analyses of film stylistics, including David Bordwell's trenchant assessments, and at the other end of the spectrum, in studies that describe the fascination of the filmic detail via cinephilia.[14] While my subject in these pages is more particular, and proceeds as a mode of film theory, its enframing movement toward textual understanding is a concern that is more widely shared.

Most evidently, this study merges with contemporary film-phenomenological investigations as they attempt to bridge, in Vivian Sobchack's terms, "the gap that exists between our actual experience of cinema and the theory that we . . . construct to explain it."[15] Sobchack's work has been influential for phenomenological elaborations of film experience, inspiring the haptic critical practice of Laura U. Marks, for example, as well as more recent theorizations of embodiment, corporeality, and materiality offered by Jennifer M. Barker, and others.[16] It seems right to say that Sobchack's efforts to recover the experiential dimension of cinema through existential phenomenology, particularly as dominant theoretical practices have tended to obscure the "dynamic, synoptic, and lived-body situation of both spectator and film," her research prepares the ground for this study, making it much easier to pose its central questions.[17] With the benefit of this literature, this book's blend of phenomenology with hermeneutics assumes the embodied nature of film viewing—and more specifically, the sensuous impact of a film's temporal forms—but directs these premises toward matters of interpretation. Because I mean to address a gap in the literature that concerns not just the perceiver, but the thing perceived: close readings of film texts have largely fallen out of fashion in recent years, to the detriment of renewed theoretical inquiry and our understanding of contemporary works.

For some readers, a conspicuous absence of this text is the work of Gilles Deleuze, whose theorization of cinematic time has suffused the terms of this topic for Anglo-American film study since its appearance in translation.[18] Deleuze's two-volume consideration of the cinema, and the analyses of *Cinema 2: The Time-Image* in particular, is arguably the most salient theorization of filmic temporality to emerge in the contemporary context.[19] Deleuze's study stands as a complex assessment of the medium's philosophical character and as a historiographical mapping of its transformation over time. Most familiar is the key distinction between the movement-image of classical cinema and the modernist cinema of the time-image; while the former subordinates time to narrative action, the latter is said to yield a direct image of time that presents itself in a pure state.[20]

Notably, Deleuze's analysis of the cinema responds to and bears important affinities of argumentation with André Bazin. Both thinkers identify a shift in the history of cinema that occurs at World War II, and is evidenced by exemplary directors (such as Orson Welles), film movements (Italian neorealism), and filmic devices (the long take). But the more urgent point of connection for my purposes is their shared commitment to the phenomenon of filmic duration.[21] Like Bazin, Deleuze does not aim to "fix" the image as a static indexical marker; rather, he is concerned with engaging the movement of cinema in a manner that sustains its characteristic difficulty and flux. Yet for readers, engaging Deleuze surely entails a kind of conceptual fixing; filmic temporality does not open up as an embodied viewing experience, but instead serves as generative material for the articulation of philosophical concepts. Thus, the rich elaboration of the time-image, and the extensive classificatory vocabulary that it subtends, does not elucidate the experiential dimension of filmic temporality because it does not seek to: in Deleuze's formulation, the viewing subject is dissolved into a flow of images, refusing both the rigid spectatorial positioning of psychoanalytic film theory and also the anchored, "perceiving subject in the world" of Merleau-Ponty's phenomenology.[22]

But this book focuses on different issues. Engaging Merleau-Ponty's writings, and modeled quite explicitly after Bazin's phenomenological outlook, I try to understand how cinematic time matters to us in film viewing. Though working to upend certain assumptions of analytical mastery, and the notion that filmic temporality occurs only "for" a subject, this study is concerned with viewing experience as a rich rapport between film and viewer. Clearing this middle ground proves extremely valuable: it means that watching a film is doubly illuminating, clarifying not only the vagaries of temporal flow but also the ways we actively endure it. Deleuze's thought, which relates filmic time to abstract material flows rather than the activity of viewers, pursues a fundamentally different project.[23]

While the films that I analyze might furnish versions of a "time-image" in Deleuze's sense, so far as they raise the fluctuations of temporal exchange to greater visibility, this designation is avoided for another reason. I'm mindful of a potential reduction that occurs by piecemeal appropriations of Deleuze's terminology: the fluid and refractory quality of his thought is readily suppressed in instrumental usages, narrowing the cinema books to a rigid semiology of the cinema that removes the image from both movement and time, in contradistinction to his arguments. Rather than pointing to a "time-image," then, I attempt to hold open the question of what else the image offers: this is to keep it "in time" a little longer, sustaining its interpretive prospects beyond the reach of received film-theoretical categories. Thus, Deleuze's descriptions of cinematic flux motivate the spirit of my inquiry, but not its conceptual vocabulary, which endeavors to lay bare the experience of cinematic time rather than a system of image classifications that may be derived from it. On these grounds, the present study offers itself as a work of hermeneutics and film-phenomenology rather than of Deleuzian discourse.

Another prominent association for the topic of cinematic time, this one related more closely to film practice, deserves mention. A descriptor has emerged in recent years to characterize the long take aesthetic that has dominated the global art cinema of the last two decades: slow cinema. Initially circulating on the blogs, and now finding currency in scholarly writings, the term identifies a mode of film practice with a set of distinctive features we have come to identify with the contemporary festival film, and which differ in apparent ways from mainstream commercial fare. Besides the use of long (often extremely long) takes, the films' protracted pace may be enhanced by the use of an unhurried mobile camera; on other occasions, a static frame is deployed to deepen their sense of lassitude. Compositions are studied, built to accommodate the lingering scrutiny of extended duration; narrative and dramatic actions are typically diminished, instead foregrounding the quiet unfolding of quotidian routines. Taken in combination, these effects produce an aesthetic that may be called contemplative—or at a minimum, that emphatically calls attention to the temporalization of the viewing experience. Recent practitioners of this mode include filmmakers such as Lisandro Alonso, Theo Angelopoulos, Sharunas Bartas, Pedro Costa, Philippe Garrel, Hou Hsiao-hsien, Jia Zhang-ke, Abbas Kiarostami, Carlos Reygadas, Aleksandr Sokurov, Béla Tarr, Tsai Ming-liang, Gus Van Sant, Albert Serra, and Apichatpong Weerasethakul. This list is not exhaustive.

The idea of a slow cinema obviously stands in opposition to a fast one, and is often cast as a thoughtful alternative to the accelerated pace of recent Hollywood production as well as international action cinemas of the same period. David Bordwell has termed the latter style of filmmaking as “intensified continuity,” combining abbreviated shot lengths, continual camera movement, and a reliance on close framings and single shots.[24] By comparison, the deliberative pace of slow cinema retains a spatiotemporal fullness that engages the viewer in a different kind of dialogue: an example of this interpretive cadence is detailed as one of this book’s case studies, in the context of Tsai Ming-liang’s cinema. Slow cinema has also been proposed as an aesthetic practice whose rigors articulate the pressures of a lived history and its politics. One thinks of Jacques Rancière’s eloquent response to Béla Tarr’s cinema, and in particular to *The Turin Horse* (Hungary, 2011), finding within the film’s interplay of expectation and repetition a temporal continuum that powerfully sustains the textures of lived duration.[25] In other contexts, scholars have suggested that the work of engaging slow films might be read as a form of labor, a point that opens up productive avenues for thinking about their political address.[26]

The formulation of slow cinema as a considered category has meaningful implications for our hermeneutic practice. It announces a mode of filmmaking that demands a comparable critical response, such as a “slowed” style of interpreting modeled after the patient progress of the films themselves.[27] It’s important to tread carefully here, in order to balance the broad explanatory power of a new classification with the particularities of our viewing engagement. Generalizing about slow cinema, as with any phenomenon, always runs the risk of subsuming its specificities, or what I will call its *timeliness*, and thus the work’s power to surprise us. In fixing these films to a preconceived routine or idea, we may preempt their individual possibility—which includes, of course, the possibility that a film may not be profound at all. An adjacent issue concerns the temptation to conflate this recent practice with André Bazin’s stated preference for duration.[28] While the postwar art cinema that Bazin admired is surely a crucial antecedent, his interest there was stirred by the light hand of filmmakers like De Sica and Rossellini, and by their inclination in that context toward stylistic transparency, which does not easily square with the weightiness we associate with slow cinema, nor with its marked self-consciousness. We should also recall that extended shot duration does not cultivate ambiguity, but simply foregrounds it. (Or, as it becomes fully conventionalized, it may simply signal “ambiguity” as an effect of style.) In any case, with Bazin we are reminded that film history is constituted by a diversity of stylistic practices and not by their rigid consolidation: this is to discern resemblances across filmic modes, but also to see what is distinctive, and particularly as such features yield a different sort of temporal experience. For this book, slow cinema is one way that contemporary cinema does time, among others. As we shall see, each temporal mode exerts a claim that rewards our attentiveness.

The wish to formulate a felicitous description of cinematic time, one that penetrates the viewer's experience of it, is a peculiar sort of ambition. It needs a language that balances lucidity with pliancy, speaking clearly to the mechanisms of filmic time that are regulated and recognizable, but also to those that implicate us more deeply by their ambiguity and difficulty. The thought occurs that filmic time is most instructive as it gets away from us, exposing the limits of academic language and approved discourse. This is an argument that this book's case studies extrapolate with more grace than I can summon here.

Dudley Andrew's exuberant manifesto, *What Cinema Is!* insists on the value of this film-critical work, calling it "precious."[29] Hence our obligation to the films we watch endures beyond disciplinary and technological transformation, and proceeds best as a focused fusion of theory and history. This book is an effort to answer to such appeals in a language that can be shared, attending closely to the sounds and images of recent films as they make time for us.

This book begins with an overview of its theoretical premises before setting these to work in four contemporary case studies drawn from American and international film contexts. Chapter 1 fleshes out the idea of cinematic time as timeliness, sketched as a hermeneutical and film-phenomenological concept, and as an intervention for film studies scholarship. The chapters that follow focus on individual titles, taking the film as an unfolding totality whose formal structures orchestrate a particular experience of time. Each film can be seen to operate distinctively; thus, each chapter uncovers a unique temporal mode of contemporary cinema that is intended to be exemplary, standing as a model for what the timeliness of cinematic time can teach us, and perhaps inspiring related commentaries for other films and viewers. The guiding principle for the case studies is to allow each film to more or less "run its course," so as to capture the working through of time that it uniquely frames. As such, the discussion entertains a dialogue with the work itself, rather than with the criticism it has inspired, though I have sought to direct the reader to other scholarly perspectives, where appropriate.[30]

Chapter 2 addresses the ways that time is complexified in contemporary cinema via intertwined strategies of editing and filmic appropriation. Specifically, the chapter probes the intricate temporal workings of Steven Soderbergh's *The Limey* (USA, 1999) to uncover a thoughtful system of temporal flashbacks, flashforwards, and borrowed images. From this a different understanding of the film emerges that shatters limited conceptions of filmic temporality: I argue that *The Limey* observes a mode of defamiliarized time that encourages us to discern—and to reflect on—rich intersections of past and present, with an eye to the future. This perspective discovers greater depth within *The Limey* than a cursory assessment would indicate, and yields a more comprehensive picture of Soderbergh's contribution to American independent cinema.

Chapter 3 departs from Hollywood to assess François Ozon's experiment in narrative form, *5x2* (France, 2004), observing the phenomenon of temporal reversal. Here, the expectation that reversed chronology should operate as a kind of narrative hindsight, revealing underlying motivations and causes with special clarity, is turned on its head. By a detailed analysis of its temporal logics, the chapter suggests that Ozon's film operates with surprising subtlety. The film's silences and opacities are deepened by an elliptical temporal structure: as a result, the sense of time that *5x2* evokes is aligned with ambiguity, rather than its opposite.

Chapter 4 engages the slowed cadence of Tsai Ming-liang's *What Time Is It There?* (Taiwan, 2001), examining the film's calculated use of temporal duration. Deploying static framings and long take structures, Tsai's film makes us aware of time by asking us to endure it, while remaining receptive to the terms of its protracted unfolding. In place of conventional causal structures, *What Time Is It There?* forges more oblique connections across time and space. I argue that the film offers an experience of temporality that is difficult and drawn-out, but finally revelatory, and forwards a wider, existential claim.

Finally, in chapter 5 I suggest that Terrence Malick's large-scaled and ambitious work, *The Tree of Life* (USA, 2011), discloses the profoundly immersive character of temporal experience through a formal design that is driven by montage. My assessment of the film finds within it an in-between temporality of self and world that may be claimed by yielding to it. In this way, the chapter proposes that the speed of cinema may be as profound as its capacity for duration.

1

Timeliness and Contemporary Cinema

[T]emporality is not some half-hearted existence.

—Maurice Merleau-Ponty, *The Phenomenology of Perception*

In this book, I offer a hermeneutics of cinematic time, aiming to clarify some of the ways that we interpret temporality as viewers of contemporary cinema. This is to look closely at the specificities of slow cinema, for example, noticing how we cope with filmic delay and drawn-out duration. Alternately, it is to examine our engagement with filmic "tricks" of time, in our contact with the convoluted temporalities of cinema in recent years.[1] One payoff for these inquiries is to be able to say something precise about our experience of contemporary cinema that recognizes its inclination toward temporal rift and rumination. Given the distinctive time scales of films from Hollywood and the international art cinema in the last two decades, as well as the shift in film's status as an enduring medium brought about by digital technologies, cinema's temporal inflection is a live issue.

My focus on the temporal modulations of contemporary cinema does not construe the films as a radical break from older practices, however, but as performing fresh variations on an enduring tendency of the medium. These temporal effects, whether operating as time slowed, reversed, or profoundly fractured, belong to film's long-standing traditions of temporal play. We need only think of the attractions of accelerated and reversed motion offered by early cinema; the appeal of time lapse effects in science films; the forthright temporal experimentation of cinema's avant-gardes; the moody time zones of film noir; or the decentered temporalities of the postwar European art cinema. These are not exceptional cases, but integral ones: playing with time is what cinema does—and these days, from an altered technological base.[2] The question to ask of recent film practice concerns how we receive its possibility. What kinds of time does contemporary cinema extend to us?

So this book is neither an elegy for cinema, nor for an experience of time that film technologies regulate or refuse. Instead, it is an effort to be attentive to the kinds of time that recent films actually generate, to name and describe the temporal possibilities that cinema enframes for its viewer. Attentiveness, as practiced here, is a viewing (and listening) stance that demands patience and participation. It involves staying close to filmic detail and nuance, observing not just from the sidelines but from a place of proximity, so as to preserve the unique temporal conditions that a film initiates, and to acknowledge that such conditions are experientially immersive and embracing. The idea of standing *open* to a film in this way—of engaging the encompassing structures of narrative cinema, for example, rather than critically curtailing them—may seem a naive proposition, as though to disregard the formative influence of the apparatus and of filmic representation. But the kind of stance that I am proposing remains alert to such tensions, analyzing both cinematic time and the ways we are implicated by it.

This approach to cinematic time also facilitates a claim about its value for thinking. I will argue throughout this book that filmic temporality is richly insightful—and more pointedly—that what is insightful about it is conveyed in our experience of time, as film viewers. It is sometimes assumed that the significance of filmic temporality is adjacent to the work itself, contained in an idea of time that the film references, for example, or in a temporal principle that it demonstrates. This discussion puts pressure on such assumptions to suggest that the meaning of filmic temporality lies much closer than this, conceiving it as a phenomenon that is conditioned by filmic form, and released through our viewing engagement. Attending closely to the ways we interpret a film's temporal cues, or negotiate its chronological uncertainties, proves strongly suggestive, reflecting means of coping with time that belong to and extend beyond the viewing situation. We learn much about the films themselves as we carefully observe the terms of their temporal unfolding; more provocatively, however, we may discover what it means to exist "in time," as we participate in the temporal event that a film sets up. This special receptivity to cinematic time is the center point of this book's arguments—and discloses what I will call cinema's *timeliness*.

A related goal of this study is to offer a phenomenological account of our viewing experience, producing a thick description of the contours of filmic time as we endure it. Attentiveness proceeds from the assumption that cinematic time is something we actively interpret, that draws on our familiarity with film language acquired by watching other films, and by this, our situatedness in film history. A corollary of this idea is to emphasize that our interpretive activity is also temporal. Focusing on cinematic time is meant as an occasion to reflect on the ongoing work of interpretation that we pursue as film viewers. As I have remarked already, this kind of discourse has gone quiet in recent academic film study, but I hope to restore it to vigorous consideration. Contemporary cinema particularly invites close assessment for its inherent interest and because its emergence coincides with the diminishment of textual analysis as a scholarly practice. So the work of interpretation is equally the subject of this book, as film's complex temporal structures enable it.

These are matters that require fuller elaboration. Let me begin to situate this study and its objectives by outlining the arguments to be presented in this chapter. First is the matter of filmic temporality itself, construed generally, and then hermeneutically, to frame an idea of cinematic time as timeliness. Next is a discussion of the kindred idea of ambiguity, relating André Bazin's filmic concept back to the phenomenology of Merleau-Ponty. Along the way, the discussion pauses to observe the extent to which Bazin's thought has been reconfigured in film-theoretical work. Finally, the chapter concludes with a consideration of the ways that timeliness speaks to issues of film history.

Toward a Hermeneutics of Cinematic Time

Cinematic time begins with the ontological character of film itself. In its origins as mobile filmstrip, usually projected at a rate of twenty-four frames per second, film's movement necessarily occurs in time. With digital cinema, which encodes its data numerically, allowing it to be transferred and manipulated with greater ease, the medium's basis in time remains its salient feature. Watching a film is to participate in a delimited temporal event: it is, at its most basic, an experience of temporal duration. The precise terms of this filmic event, however, are somewhat more complex: founded in photography, cinema "makes the past" when it captures a temporal instant, yet is experienced "now," as a succession of images unfolding before us in the present.

But cinematic time is probably more familiar to us in other ways. Whether we think of an image that flickers onscreen for mere moments, or one that presents an action or event unfolding in its entirety, every shot, as an individual filmic unit, is temporal. Films also generate temporal experience more actively via editing procedures across shots. To this end, narrative film, which this book examines, rarely presents time "for itself," as sheer duration—although, as we shall see, certain films do foreground this aspect of their operations. Instead, narrative films typically engage in a dynamic shaping of time to accommodate the stories they tell: this process is strongly selective, honing and recombining filmed materials to institute new temporal coordinates. This produces a range of temporal structures that we readily assimilate in film viewing, organizing narrative activity into meaningful units of time.

Consider, for instance, the way a pair of shots, or a shot series, creates distinct relations of "before" and "after," or by implication, the idea of "cause" and "effect." Similarly, shots may be structured to convey different perspectives on a single time (temporal simultaneity; the "meanwhile" effect), reflexive relations between one time and another (the logics of temporal flashback or flash-forward), transitions between different times (the bridging devices of fades and dissolves), or suggestive temporal gaps (ellipses). These kinds of temporal structures and their many permutations—deployed to varying degrees of legibility and expressivity, and accompanied by other aesthetic forms that enrich their effects—are the specific temporal terms that each film sets up to condition our experience of time, as viewers. I take these structures seriously as constitutive elements that facilitate a productive exchange between film and viewer. Thus, cinematic time is here conceived as a reciprocal mode of engagement: it is an experience of temporality that arises in our encounter with the work, as we respond to its call to interpret it.

Hermeneutics is something more precise than a loose theory, or method, of interpretation. To approach cinematic time hermeneutically is, in an important sense, to *enter into it.* It is to assume that filmic temporality demands sustained attention and reflection, and a special self-consciousness about the way we respond to it. In other words, it is a way of being thoughtful about our contact with cinema's temporal forms, and the time we take to interpret them.

One shouldn't mistake this perspective for a kind of vagueness about filmic structures, or a species of naiveté. If anything, it is a mindful blend of concreteness and abstraction, continually moving between the details of the filmic text and the interpretive fields they open up. Hermeneutics counts on all the knowledge we bring to a text, including our expertise in its aesthetic forms; our familiarity with the stories it tells; our sense of its historical placement and its political urgency. But it also depends on our willingness to stand open to it, weathering these competing considerations. Paul Ricoeur's well-known distinction between a hermeneutics of suspicion and a hermeneutics of faith is one way of positioning these issues, holding the demystification of texts against a counterperspective that welcomes textual irreducibility. The chapters to follow trace a dialogical movement between interpretive modalities that acknowledges the claims of both suspicion and trust, probing instances of filmic time that are assumed to operate conventionally, or transparently, in order to uncover the alternate understandings that such assumptions suppress.

Aspects of Ricoeur's interpretive theory, crystallized in acts of understanding, explanation, and comprehension can be mobilized to permit a freer focus on the ambiguities encountered on the way to appropriation, or more precisely, on those instances where a film's time scales begin to shape a world that may shed light on our own.[3] Likewise, Ricoeur's premise that narrative acquires its fullest significance in its articulations of temporal experience is here reconfigured for cinema, advancing the idea that as narrative film generates time for its viewer, it may reflect something of lived temporality, as well.[4] Thus the project of "doing time" aspires to an active comprehension, bringing together our initial rapport with texts and the work of analysis, to arrive at a fuller understanding of filmic temporality that admits future revision.

This project locates its conceptual support in the tradition of philosophical hermeneutics that informs Ricoeur's thought, as developed by Martin Heidegger and Hans-Georg Gadamer. Crucial in this context is Heidegger's insistence on the immersiveness of lived experience and the idea that understanding occurs within this situation, and not in abstraction from it. On this view, interpretation cannot be limited to a theoretical assessment, achieved at a distance. Instead, it arises from conditions of continual contact: more fundamentally, it is the way this contact occurs. These are energizing terms for thinking about the immersiveness of film viewing while seeking to close the gap between experience and theory.

Let me bring these ideas into sharper focus. What Heidegger's thinking specifically contributes to a consideration of cinematic time is twofold: first, by its analysis in *Being and Time*, it forwards an urgent claim for the temporal character of existence. Second, it proposes that lived experience, as the meaningful grounding of temporality, is the appropriate basis for our understanding of it. Whether or not we accept Heidegger's analyses as they intervene in the history of philosophy, his claim is a powerful incentive for thinking: it invites us to consider temporality in terms of proximity and involvement; correspondingly, it proposes that we might know temporality better by attending to our concrete experiences of it. My point here is simple: Where better to start than with our experiences of time, as film viewers?

Cinematic Time as *Timeliness*

This question reaches to the very heart of this book, motivating its proposal that we think of filmic temporality as a dynamic situation, or as an unfolding exchange worked out in time between films and viewers. Within this situation, we encounter a film's distinctive temporal character, engaging its timeliness. This term draws on Martin Heidegger's thought, but also converges with a more standard usage: it is in this hybrid sense that I offer it as a descriptor for our engagement with cinematic time.

In *Being and Time*, we encounter the German word, *Zeitlichkeit*, usually translated to mean *temporality*—but its more literal rendering is timeliness.[5] For Heidegger, this is not equivalent to "time" taken as an entity or object: it is not, for instance, the kind of time that we have or lack for a particular task. Rather, *Zeitlichkeit* is less a static concept than it is an activity: it is Dasein's way of being temporal, as a dynamic structuring of past, present, and future.[6] Clearly this differs from our accustomed sense of this word. When we refer to something as "timely," we simply mean that it comes at a moment that is suitable: a timely action, for instance, is one that is appropriate or relevant for our present situation. But something new emerges when we combine these divergent significations to describe our experience of cinematic time. Retaining Heidegger's emphasis on the active, "how" of time as it mediates experience, and pairing it with the more everyday sense of responsiveness to the current context, we arrive at a broader term that ably characterizes temporal experience in film viewing.[7]

Timeliness, in this combined sense, emphasizes that time is actively mediated by films and viewers: on the one hand, there is the way that films continually occasion time by their unfolding temporal structures; on the other hand, there is the way these details solicit our engagement, making their acceptance and assessment a meaningful feature of viewing activity. This dynamic framework encompasses our encounters with filmic ambiguity, as we read and respond to shifting temporal cues, and it retains the immersive appeal of cinematic time as we acknowledge our ongoing investment in it, as viewers.

The hermeneutics of Hans-Georg Gadamer also shape this intervention, particularly as he conceptualizes art experience. Gadamer speaks of art in terms of a dynamics of play, as in the playing of a game (*Spiel*).

He observes that in play, we join in the game: it is an event that we share in and help to constitute, as players. Play is characterized by proximity and participation, not by distance and detachment; it is not opposed to seriousness, but rather requires it. Most importantly, play is not limited by subjectivity, but in fact attains "primacy . . . over the consciousness of the player." Thus, the appeal of play—or otherwise, the reason we are compelled to participate—lies in its ascendancy over us: the event of play is one in which the game masters the players.[8]

Gadamer's dynamics of play highlights our active contribution to art experience, framed as a dynamic exchange between work and perceiver. Moreover, it suggests that we know art only in a diminished sense when we pass over this exchange to reflect ourselves out of it.[9] These considerations are apposite for the case of film, and film viewing, where the "event" in question is, like music, a sustained performance that stretches out in time. Although film analysis will necessarily involve pausing this event, or repeating it, Gadamer's commentary underscores the essential task of restoring these findings to the perpetual flux of film viewing, where our relation to filmic images and sounds is not one of mastery, or distance, but more often assumes an attitude of open receptivity.

Finally, timeliness finds additional support in the work of Maurice Merleau-Ponty, especially as his early writings echo and extend Heidegger's thought. But Merleau-Ponty's arguments make a separate contribution in this context, as well. the discussion below retrieves his understanding of ambiguity so as to situate it first as a background for the writings of André Bazin, and then as a more independent idea that can be seen as intrinsic to film-temporal experience. This initiative hopes to revitalize ambiguity as working notion, specifying the terms of its phenomenological inflection—and more specifically, its utility as a temporal concept.

Cinematic Time: A Bazinian Background

The topic of cinematic time often circles back to the work of André Bazin, though this correspondence has been understood in different ways. Bazin's writings offer an important critical model by their balance of priorities. While his commentaries assume an attitude of openness to cinema, rather than a desire to reduce it by the application of limiting categories, the quality of his observations is unwaveringly precise, speaking lucidly to the finest filmic detail and also to broader dialectics of the medium's history. This receptive stance is also an integral valence of Bazin's ontology, describing not just the status of images, but implicitly, the way we stand (or ought to stand) with respect to them. In this context, the ambiguities of cinema are held as meaningful details because they mark a genuine exchange between film and viewer.

But Bazin's thought truly lights up for us when we recognize the extent to which his concern with filmic ambiguity is bound up with experiences of cinematic time. This connection may require a little unpacking. For Bazin, photography is a singular innovation in the history of representation because it operates by a new objectivity; as such, the photograph is something like an imprint, reflecting and confirming the actuality of things, as they exist in space and time. Concerning the ontology of the photograph, Bazin tells us that that the automatic nature of photographic processes lends them unprecedented objectivity; unlike painting, where the artist's hand produces a subjective rendering, filmic images are an indifferent inscription facilitated by the camera's lens. When these principles are extended to cinema, as a "moving picture," the phenomenon of photographic credibility is temporalized.[10]

An especially salient formulation in this regard is Bazin's description of the cinema as "objectivity in time."[11] For Bazin, this is the unique capacity of filmic representation: it conveys not just the instantaneous appearance of things, but also the continuum of space and time that this appearance entails. By this, filmic images reveal the world as we could not perceive it otherwise: they disclose it in its freestanding fullness as a spatiotemporal unity, as a reality that is distinct from our subjective claims on it. It is worth perusing an extended stretch of commentary on this point that brings out the phenomenological cast of Bazin's argumentation most clearly. He writes,

> It is not for me to separate off, in the complex fabric of the objective world, here a reflection on a damp sidewalk, there the gesture of a child. Only the impassive lens, stripping its object of all those ways of seeing it, those piled-up preconceptions, that spiritual dust and grime with which my eyes have covered it, is able to present it in all its virginal purity to my attention and consequently to my love.[12]

Thus, cinema's disclosure of the world breaks up our accustomed ways of seeing it: rather than simply retracing familiar patterns of understanding, filmic images make it possible to encounter the world anew, and perhaps not as we would make it. What accompanies this special capacity of cinema—what makes it truly "realistic," in Bazin's sense, and therefore profound—is its preservation of ambiguity: by picturing events holistically, in their autonomous unfolding, cinema also reflects the opacities that these conditions sustain.

In exemplary cases, such as Italian Neo-Realism, and in the films of Renoir, Welles, and Wyler, ambiguity occurs as a deepening of cinema's possibilities that is facilitated by the techniques of deep space and the long take. One thinks, for example, of Bazin's admiration for *La règle du jeu* (Renoir, France, 1939), which stems from the way the film's formal arrangements reveal "the hidden meanings in people and things without disturbing the unity natural to them."[13] Further, ambiguity relates to the filmic phenomenon of ellipses, as evidenced in Bazin's appreciative descriptions of Rossellini's cinema as it includes "the empty gaps, the white spaces, the parts of the event that we are not given."[14] Looking elsewhere, ambiguity arises even in the cinema of John Huston, a filmmaker sometimes disdained at *Cahiers du Cinéma*. Bazin finds in *The Red Badge of Courage* (USA, 1951) a lack of formal embellishment whose implications are metaphysical, manifest as a "respect for people, objects, and events, in and of themselves." By the deliberate understatement of its editing and mise-en-scène—essentially, a refusal to articulate the scene dramatically by cutting in to closer views of significant details—the film places special demands on its viewer. For Bazin, Huston's film "doesn't make sense if we don't contribute some insight of our own, the discerning fruit of an intellectual complicity."[15] Thus, filmic ambiguity does not derive from the application of limited techniques, but from the attitude of restraint that accompanies them, and an acceptance of uncertainty underlying their use. This is what binds the cinema of De Sica to that of Wyler and Huston: by differing formal means, their films permit a flowering of ambiguity that launches a productive interplay between film and viewer. To see this exchange most clearly, we can look to the film's temporal syntax: long take and ellipses, for example, mark these occasions strongly, as though encapsulating an interpretive process within their own structures.

This last point is critical for my purposes. Ambiguity is central to Bazin's reflections on the cinema, but is rarely treated as a self-standing term that might reward theoretical extrapolation. This relates, I presume, to its quality of approximation, or the way that "ambiguity" necessarily designates a space between concepts rather than a concept itself. Yet its utility for questions of filmic temporality is quite precise. I want to propose that we consider ambiguity a valuable ally for theoretical inquiry, and specifically, as an essential modulator of cinematic time. Ambiguity already inclines in this direction when we notice how often it is aligned in Bazin's thought with cinema's temporal movement, or in

Dudley Andrew's phrase, with cinema's "ongoingness, its registration of time flowing."[16] Likewise, it may emerge in instances of elliptical cutting, reminding us of our epistemological and temporal finitude. These are reasons to spend time with the temporal forms of cinema, observing the ambiguities that potentially spring from their operation. For Bazin, filmic temporality is a meaningful opportunity: it shows us time, not as something we know in advance, or master retrospectively, but as an ambiguous event that is opened up in experience and solicits our continued questioning.

Bazin Reconfigured: Indexical Time

Given Bazin's interest in the ambiguities of temporal experience, one might expect a convergence of scholarly interest around this facet of his thought, particularly within contemporary analyses of cinematic time. But this has not been the case. While seeking to renew Bazin's thought for the contemporary context, the significant theorizations that have emerged in recent years have little to say about ambiguity, in Bazin's sense, or its implications for conceptualizing filmic temporality. Instead, scholars have tended to stress a concept that Bazin himself did not deploy: namely, the index.[17]

Derived from the semiotic categories of C. S. Peirce, and directly applied to Bazin's writings by film theorist Peter Wollen, the indexicality of filmic images refers to the way they point to, and are an effect of, the objects they represent.[18] However, the index is conceptually at odds with Bazin's notion of ambiguity: it emphasizes the extent to which filmic images are structured in certainty, functioning as signs within a determining sign system. As we shall see, its prioritization in relation to Bazin's arguments is actually a substantive transposition that limits the ways that filmic temporality can be conceived.[19]

Philip Rosen's study, *Change Mummified: Cinema, Historicity, Theory*, revisits Bazin's work so as to recuperate aspects of his ontology for contemporary critical culture. In this context, Bazin's phrase, "change mummified," signals a special concern with temporality, and specifically, with dichotomies of temporal flux and preservation. Situating the indexical character of filmic images as the center of Bazin's thought, Rosen shifts the terms of Bazin's ontology to distill from it a certain understanding of subjectivity. On this reading, what is most salient about the filmic image is the way it serves the subject: by its reassuring indication of "the real," the image works to allay subjective insecurity.[20] Notably, this formulation does not just say that cinema "has" a subject, or that its indexical gesture toward the real is an appeal to subjectivity. Rather, it expresses what cinema *is* as a matter of epistemological utility, and thus sets aside such issues as the specificity of filmic images and the range of viewing experiences that this specificity might engender. Yet this emphasis sits uneasily alongside Bazin's repeated claim for cinema's revelatory capacities: recalling, in particular, his suggestion that cinema can convey the world stripped of "piled-up preconceptions," as released from the "spiritual dust and grime with which my eyes have covered it," we do not find an abstracting subject but one eager for experience, who receives cinema's reflection of the world in a spirit of joyful discovery.[21] As I will argue, Bazin's writings are persuasively read in other ways.

Laura Mulvey's recent work on cinematic time draws nearer to the premises of this book, drawing on Bazin while thinking through the ways we respond to filmic temporality as contemporary viewers. But by emphasizing issues of indexicality, rather than the potentialities of ambiguity, she ultimately charts a very different course. *Death 24x a Second: Stillness and the Moving Image* addresses the paradoxical nature of the film medium, as a moving picture comprised of still images. Mulvey understands this paradox as a process of profound mystification, emphasizing the ways that film's basis in the inanimate—the film still—is blurred, and thus covered over, by the regulated movement of the filmstrip. That this dynamic produces "conceptual uncertainty" initially sustains the possibility that ambiguity might serve as a generative mechanism for the analysis. But Mulvey's study is a hermeneutics of suspicion that regards the elusiveness of cinema as an obstacle to be overcome: its aim is to show how new technologies offer unprecedented control over moving images, allowing us to pause or delay them, so as to disclose the "hidden stillness" that such images conceal.[22] The way to cope with filmic time, then, is to disengage from it, refusing its powers of narrative absorption.[23] Having disclosed the "secret stillness" of filmic images, then, we are in a position to control them, exempt from their implicating force.

This systematic shattering of narrative time calls to mind Christian Marclay's celebrated art installation, *The Clock* (2010), the twenty-four-hour compendium of filmed images designed to be screened in, and as, "real time." Marclay's work is a meticulous collage of diverse materials, culled from both film and television, which directly or obliquely reference time; by their careful assembly, the piece functions as a working clock, with time told in images.[24] The broad appeal of Marclay's project for galleries and the viewing public is obvious: its democratic blend of footage, comprising thousands of images from television, Hollywood, and the art cinema, often affords the pleasure of recognition. In the time one spends with *The Clock*, it is fun to spot these cultural references, sharing with other viewers, and with the personae onscreen, a common concern with clock-watching. At 1:15, for example, the discoursing of Orson Welles overlaps with a characteristic composition from Wes Anderson; though nearly fifty years separates these titles, this distance is dissolved by *The Clock*'s governing structure, registered only in the contrasts of monochrome and color.[25]

By its continual referencing of time, *The Clock* causes us to notice the temporal markers of narrative cinema as oddly detached from the energies of their diegetic contexts. Within these workings, time rises to the surface, and narrative motivation withdraws. Beyond its intricate orchestration, however, it is hard to say what Marclay's installation finally means. Certainly it shows us that the stories told by cinema, and other media, are "made of time"; it also raises the temporalized nature of film viewing to perfect visibility. But in bending these materials to its own aesthetic structure, *The Clock* does not propose a particular significance for the new continuities that it traces: its work is accessible, not analytical. For the aims of this discussion, neither is it ambiguous: curtailing narrative development with cutaways to new situations, *The Clock*'s temporal movement is perpetually preemptive.[26]

But here we should return to the literature. Rosen and Mulvey's studies are valuable theorizations of cinematic time, which invite us, in different ways, to consider how Bazin's commentaries might speak to the medium's transformation by new technologies. But we should also notice that these formulations are particular, rather than general, so as to recover the significant terrain that they displace. This requires drawing on Bazin's critical sensibility, with its affection for open-ended experience; more precisely, it involves restoring these ambiguities of experience to his understanding of cinematic time. What would it be to envision a receptive viewing subject who engages both the rewards and resistances of filmic temporality, deriving pleasure and insight? More to the point, what would it mean to *be* that viewing subject? Before taking up these queries, there is more to say about the concept of ambiguity, placing it in its phenomenological context.

Merleau-Ponty's Philosophy of Ambiguity

Highlighting the period through the late-1940s when Bazin contributed to the literary magazine *Esprit*, Dudley Andrew has detailed the shared intellectual terrain of Bazin and Maurice Merleau-Ponty. In a recent piece, Andrew identifies direct linkages across their writings.[27] These are exciting connections, and for the topic of cinematic time, they are conceptually clarifying as they highlight the temporal inflection of Bazin's ontology. But these correspondences are most revealing when focused on the idea of ambiguity—developed as a filmic concept by Bazin, and as an informing principle of Merleau-Ponty's analyses. Fleshing out what ambiguity might mean for Bazin, in an intriguing interface with Merleau-Ponty's early writings, recalibrates ambiguity as a surprisingly sturdy term with which to address film-temporal experience.

Merleau-Ponty's work has sometimes been called a "philosophy of ambiguity"; while this designation is in certain ways imperfect, it reflects an essential preoccupation of his thought, particularly across the early writings.[28] As developed in *The Phenomenology of Perception*, ambiguity infuses lived experience: once the polarization of subject and object is rejected, and the detached stance that this framework supposes, ambiguity is disclosed as a basic condition of our situated being. It registers in perceptual indeterminacy, as when the length of a line appears to shift, depending on its context, and across the robust synergies of sense experience.[29] More emphatically, it springs from the deep reciprocity of subject and world, of perceiver and perceived, that the body mediates; indeed, it may be useful to think of ambiguity as an ongoing movement between these terms, assuring that our existence is never centered completely.[30] Merleau-Ponty tells us that humankind possesses "a genius for ambiguity" as its defining feature, pervading perception, sense experience, the body—and as we shall see, lived temporality.[31]

Thus, ambiguity is not to be "gotten around," or dissolved, but is something more integral: it is a binding condition of experience that might lead us to an improved understanding of it. Conceived in this way, it is remarkable that Bazin should locate ambiguity in the context of film technologies: we should mark the scale of Bazin's claim when he proposes that under certain conditions, cinema reveals the objective world and also our ambiguous relation to it. But a descriptor that is sometimes joined to ambiguity—the idea that it signals the presence of a mystery—is unhelpful in this context while it imports an idea of mystification.

Ambiguity, as Merleau-Ponty describes it, does not intervene between subject and object, as though willfully obscuring one from the other; in fact, this kind of thinking can only displace it. Instead, we should think of ambiguity as opening out in situations where two or more options are simultaneously possible—not as either/or, but taken together, with *and*—in this way testifying to the complexity of experience. A phantom limb is both absent and meaningfully present because the body remains open to all its past possibility; likewise, my body is an ambiguous form that both distinguishes me from others and facilitates my contact with them. Ambiguity permeates all these events, insisting on a multiplicity of copresent meanings. We might think of this multiplicity as an event in time: it happens spontaneously, and "at once."

Merleau-Ponty's formulation is temporal in other ways. The fundamental ambiguity of existence, as conveyed by the body, is discerned through the ambiguity of time.[32] That is to say, the ambiguity of our being in the world stems from its temporal character: time characterizes our being while also eluding our grasp—and this continual, ambiguous movement is existentially constitutive. He writes,

> My hold on the past and my hold on the future are precarious, and my possession of my own time is always deferred until the moment when I fully understand myself, but that moment can never arrive, since it would again be a moment, bordered by the horizon of its future, and would in turn require further developments in order to be understood.[33]

So to acknowledge the ambiguity of being—that is, the way it is never fully accessible to understanding, yet is always at issue for us—is to accept its temporal movement, and to see this movement not as an obstacle to thinking but as a source of its profundity. Likewise, we learn something about time, as it matters to us, when we recognize the ways in which it conditions our lived situation. Merleau-Ponty writes,

> Time only exists for me because I am situated in it, that is, because I discover myself already engaged in it, because all of being is not given to me in person, and finally because a sector of being is so close to me that it does not even sketch out a scene in front of me and because I cannot *see* it, just as I cannot see my face.[34]

As these lines indicate, our experience of time, as an ongoing temporal investment, is fundamentally ambiguous: like the event of being, time must be reckoned with as an immersive movement, not as an object represented to ourselves, or as a scene "sketched out" before us. These lines may help us to be better readers of Bazin, supplying a compelling context for the privileging of ambiguity we find in his writings. With this background in view, Bazin's ontology may be read as a set of arguments about the medium *and* the engagement of viewers. In particular, this perspective clarifies Bazin's sense that filmic ambiguity traces an existential arc, and potentially yields profound experience. In other words, cinema is uniquely equipped to show us our ambiguity, picturing an entanglement in space and time that speaks to our lived situation.[35]

Thus, the phenomenology of Merleau-Ponty lights the way for a new approach to filmic temporality that focuses on the ways we experience it, and the value of this experience for thinking. The time that matters here is necessarily ambiguous: there is no pulling apart these terms to shatter their deep imbrication, leaving our engagement with time out of the equation. This is why when we talk about ambiguity in a film, we are so often brought up against the temporal terms that condition it, referring to filmic episodes that are too fleeting to assess, or perhaps dwell so long as to grow opaque. For the purposes of this study, ambiguity is an essential feature of temporality because it signals our investment: put simply, it shows us how we are situated in time, as viewers.

So far our examination of Merleau-Ponty has emphasized an overlap with Bazin's thought, sketching some key affinities. But his writings extend to cinematic time in more direct ways as well, as evidenced by the arguments presented in an early lecture, "The Film and the New Psychology." While this text has received detailed elucidation by other scholars, most notably Vivian Sobchack, its potential for thinking about the temporal character of film experience remains untapped. Specifically, Merleau-Ponty's discussion serves as an essential complement to this study because it encourages us to look beyond the most familiar framework for Bazinian ambiguity: the unfolding time of the long take. Indeed, it foregrounds the timeliness of other temporal forms, allowing us to contemplate what we might call a *phenomenology of montage*.

"The Film and the New Psychology" was delivered as a talk at France's state-sponsored film academy, L'Institut des hautes études cinématographiques (IDHEC), the same year that *The Phenomenology of Perception* was published, and as such, it shares that investigation's concern with describing an embodied subject's relation to the world. But here film is taken up as a medium that is exemplary because it tutors us in perception. Merleau-Ponty indicates that perception allows us to understand the meaning of the cinema—but characteristically, the reverse is also true: cinema discloses the world, not as a mental construct, but as given in perceptual experience. Thus, the medium possesses a unique capacity to animate the insights of Gestalt psychology: it shows us that we are in continual contact with the world, joined to it by a natural bond.[36] This convergence of subject and world is consequential for the way we perceive others, as well: it suggests that emotional states, like love or anger, are not veiled, "inner realities," but observable behaviors contouring the body's sentient surface.[37] Crucially, these features of experience are raised to special legibility by filmic processes.

Moreover, what makes film an exemplary perceptual object is its temporal character: it is, as Merleau-Ponty insists, not a "a sum total of images but a temporal *gestalt*." As this formulation suggests, our engagement with cinema is always an experience of time, occurring in "a total way" that speaks to all our senses at once.[38] Whether in terms of individual shots, or longer temporal units like sequences, film editing shapes a new reality that always exceeds the sum of its parts. Phrased another way, film is not equivalent to the discrete, static elements from which it is composed: to be grasped in its significance, film must be held as a constellation of effects experienced bodily and unfolded in time.[39]

But Merleau-Ponty's claim for filmic temporality is also more precise. In a subsequent passage, he writes,

> The meaning of a film is incorporated into its rhythm just as the meaning of a gesture may immediately be read in that gesture: the film does not mean anything but itself. The idea is presented in a nascent state and emerges from the temporal structure of the film as it does from the coexistence of the parts of a painting.[40]

We should pause over these lines to notice just how purposeful they are. First, there is an idea that this book takes as its governing premise: the meaning of cinema is built into its rhythms; it "happens" through these temporal structures and not otherwise. But what about the latter statement that Merleau-Ponty makes—here, and at other moments in the lecture, repeatedly—that "film does not mean anything but itself"? In one way, this claim is necessary rhetorically. If cinema is to serve as a kind of perceptual analogue, as the author intends, we must appreciate that, like perception, the medium is not merely derivative: it does not follow on, or operate in service of, something else. While film possesses an essential realism, it is not bound to reproduce it; rather, like poetry, cinematic syntax can operate as a "machine of language" that induces "a certain poetic state."[41]

There is more here that is clarifying for matters of cinematic time. By their temporal orchestration, films create something *new*; they formulate fresh events of perception. This means that films aren't reducible to representations of a particular content: they do not simply stand in for something else. Likewise, filmic temporality does not just reference time, but activates it; it does not look to external phenomena for its significance, but *is that significance at every moment*. Merleau-Ponty puts this point strongly, stating that the medium's complex of effects "tells us something very precise which is neither a thought nor a reminder of sentiments we have felt in our own lives."[42] We should read him here as making a firm distinction: of course, a film may inspire such recollections, encouraging us to ponder a past event, or a comparable moment, but this is a secondary effect of film experience, not a primary function. Cinema's meaning arises out of our active engagement with its temporal forms, to touch us "at every point of our being"; in this event, it may disclose *our* meanings, as well.[43] This idea forms the crux of cinema's timeliness.

On this view, the ambiguities of cinema, which arise spontaneously from its temporal character, may be rendered as palpably by the rhythms of montage as by extended shot duration. This qualification is relevant for the case studies detailed here, which are not limited to slow cinema, but also focus on temporal fragmentation. Broadening the scope of filmic ambiguity in this way is uncontroversial: if anything, this return to Merleau-Ponty's writings foregrounds proclivities already present in Bazin's thought, such as his genuine regard for montage technique. As I have noted already, Bazin's call for a restrained approach to editing has always admitted other options: the long take, while exemplary, is situated within a comprehensive history of film style as one creative choice among others.[44] We should think particularly of Bazin's interest in Welles—assuredly an artist of the long take, but also one associated with a self-conscious cinematic optics. In a similar vein, to his claim that "analytical cutting tends to destroy . . . the ambiguity inherent in reality" by unduly subjectivizing it, Bazin appends this corresponding note:

> [I]t is nevertheless possible to use this technique in such a way that it compensates for the psychological mutilation implied in its principle. Hitchcock, for instance, excels in suggesting the ambiguity of an event while decomposing it into a series of close-ups.[45]

As these lines suggest, Bazin's arguments are consistently conditioned by their alternatives, receptive to variation and innovation. But there is another set of texts that convey Bazin's acute interest in editing technique more plainly. I'm thinking here of a series of lively reviews, written late in Bazin's life, on the cinema of Chris Marker.

In his assessment of Marker's documentary short, *Dimanche à Pékin* (1956), Bazin likens the work to a precisely cut diamond that leaves viewers dazzled, detecting within the film an approach to montage that gives the term a radically new meaning.[46] Subsequently, in Marker's *Letter from Siberia* (1957), Bazin sees montage reinvented, generating within this longer work newly dynamized relations of sound and image. He writes,

> Chris Marker brings to his films an absolutely new notion of montage that I will call "horizontal," as opposed to traditional montage that plays with the sense of duration through the relationship of shot to shot. Here, a given image doesn't refer

> to the one that preceded it or the one that will follow, but rather it refers laterally, in some way, to what is said. Better, it might be said that the basic element is the beauty of what is said and heard, that intelligence flows from the audio element to the visual. The montage has been forged from ear to eye.[47]

While these remarks speak to the operations of documentary rather than fiction, they evidence Bazin's characteristic receptivity to new creative and technical developments, especially as these potentially renew perception. But one wonders what this kind of reinvigorated montage might look like in the context of narrative cinema—not as something directly applied, but in its conceptual possibility.

To approach this question, we need to get clear aboutwhat this idea of editing involves. Horizontal montage, as Bazin explains it, poses two basic innovations: first, it deprioritizes the visual basis of cinema, that is, the primacy of the single image, to emphasize its mobile contact with other elements, like spoken text and competing images. It is a cutting procedure that moves "laterally," forging additions and fresh associations. Second, it is a method that disrupts the usual sequencing of shots, or at least the way we conventionally think of them; image relations do not work to secure a temporal progression, advancing from one shot to the next, but perhaps propose a mode of time that seems to "widen" it, increasing an image's available surfaces and points of contact in a kind of visceral interpolation.

As Bazin repeatedly emphasizes, this method proceeds dialectically, for instance, "placing the same image in three different contexts and following the results."[48] We might imagine here an effect of Kuleshov that does not tamp down meaning, but instead loosens it, to produce an open-ended and unsteady synthesis. In the context of Marker's cinema, these dialectics are palpable, producing sparks, shocks, and conflagrations.[49] As a thought experiment for narrative cinema, then, horizontal montage specifies a kind of cutting that preserves ambiguity rather than reducing it by setting the image in time with a plenitude of possibilities. Here Bazin's thought draws even nearer to Merleau-Ponty's than before.

So the concept of horizontal montage confirms the diversity of Bazin's thought, and its phenomenological inflection, providing an excellent justification for seeking ambiguity across different temporal modes. The benefit of Bazin's term is not as something newly affixed to narrative cinema, but as a way of acknowledging its temporal range. If the long take is understood to preserve ambiguity as it presents a situation holistically, certain applications of the cut, while structuring time very differently, may effect a comparable gestalt. This possibility registers, for instance, when a sudden spray of images conveys the fullness of experience by concentrating its shimmering energies; or alternately, when moments that are widely spaced in time are made to answer to each other, speaking quiet alignments of past and present. Thinking about *the cut* as a unit of filmic time that is susceptible to phenomenological inquiry is a fascinating proposition: in chapter 5, Terrence Malick's cinema gives us a way of situating this idea more concretely.

But here I should say something more about my approach before it is taken up in subsequent chapters. Most obviously, this book is concerned with ambiguity as facilitated by the temporal forms of cinema, where a film's way of doing time, and a viewer's way of engaging it, mediates an interpretive situation that constitutes cinema's timeliness. In this event, filmic temporality is not foreclosed by arbitrary creative choices, per Bazin's interdictions; along with Merleau-Ponty, we are concerned with a kind of time that carries the complex rhythms of lived experience.

For the titles analyzed in this study, the experience of time that a film offers leads us to its meaning, but does not still it: instead, our contact with a film's temporal forms conditions us to its ideas, preparing the ground for their potential recognition. As I have emphasized through Bazin, the temporal form in question—be it the long take or the transient image—does not guarantee a certain result, a priori. Rather, we can say that the form goes to work, in concert with other aesthetic elements, to create an encompassing temporal situation; as we shall see, the significance of this situation is held open to viewers, and mobilized by our engagement.

Ambiguity, Analysis, Attentiveness

If the interpretive activity of viewers has received scant attention in recent film-theoretical work outside of cognitivist frameworks, this silence extends from an earlier moment in the discipline, and in particular, from received theorizations of the film spectator. The insights of apparatus theory, and the significant critiques that followed from it, have had lingering consequences for contemporary film scholarship. One important, and intended, effect is the self-conscious questioning brought to any idealized notion of the film viewer and of viewing activity. In itself, this is a beneficial corrective. But in some contexts, it has fostered the idea that film viewing is conceivable only in terms of a binary opposition, committed either to a fixed formulation of the viewing subject, who always receives the film the same way, or to a kind of relativism by which all experiences are possible, and therefore unconceptualizable. A version of this claim surfaces in Matilda Mroz's recent study of film analysis and temporality, as follows:

> Although I suggest various possibilities for watching the films, and cite other critics' experiences of viewing and analyzing them, it is clear that to speak of a homogenous process of film viewing is impossible. Whether a shot is held for 'too long' or 'not enough' is dependent upon each viewer and each screening, the conditions of which will vary greatly.[50]

We should linger over these lines to recognize their operative assumptions. This passage conflates the task of analyzing a film with offering evaluative judgments of it, as though the assessment involved deciding whether the film's stylistic construction were more or less appealing. Conceived in this way, there is nowhere for the analysis to go, because it construes its task as a reading of the viewer rather than the details of the film itself. This is a curious picture of what film analysis and interpretation entails that needs to be dismantled in order to move forward with the work.

Film analysis and interpretation need not assume a "one size fits all" picture of the viewer, nor does it concede to an imagined conceptual impasse. It does not insist on a single, monolithic meaning once and for all; neither does it seek an underlying code that is indifferent to the situated play of interpretive activity. While giving priority to some interpretations over others—usually, the ones most responsive to complexes of textual detail, and to the overlapped contexts that shape them—this practice also stands open to future revision. In this respect, the work of interpretation is not so different from that of film-historical and cultural analyses, or those concerned with technological transformation, so far as each line of inquiry seeks to delimit, and explain, the conditions that make our understanding of cinema possible at a given moment. Of course, when we read a film, the terrain in question relates to its particular aesthetic configurations, but the movement toward understanding is compatible. This may be the best way to situate film analysis and interpretation within the shifting topographies of the discipline.

A further counterpoint may be helpful here, this time with reference to Garrett Stewart's *Framed Time: Toward a Postfilmic Cinema*. Stewart's account has certain features in common with the present discussion, but does not actually share its commitment to an open hermeneutic practice. Pairing theoretical discussion with a close analysis of contemporary examples, Stewart designates films produced since 1995 as a "postfilmic" cinema, where an image might "allude to its own optical conditions."[51] Sensing a correspondence between the context of medial transition and the preoccupations of contemporary European and American cinemas, Stewart reads Hollywood's "recent time-warp plots," for example, as "an implicit digitime."[52] Thus, the study marshals a selection of titles that serve as nimble demonstrations of the author's thesis; indeed, one sometimes wonders what the films might offer without Stewart's scintillating heuristic support. This is a basic difference of approach that looks to recent cinema for figurations of time, rather than experiences of it. Yet even with these differences, the book's frame-by-frame analyses reflect a lively investment in the task of working through filmic detail, though to different ends. Something of this shared spirit is reflected in Stewart's question: "Why should we think that trying to analyze, with our eyes open, the often contradictory message of contemporary screen fantasies doesn't put us more directly in touch than otherwise with the medium they manipulate?"[53]

Yet surely a gulf remains between the practice of film analysis and the phenomenon of ambiguity, at least as commonly conceived. These terms are typically figured as antagonists in both film practice and theory: after all, aren't the procedures of analytical cutting, and of formal-analytical assessment, rigorous efforts to *quench* ambiguity, from which it should be preserved? Or so a narrow understanding of Bazin, or of aesthetic analysis, might contend. But if we allow, with Bazin and Merleau-Ponty, that ambiguity may be raised to special visibility by different temporal forms, arising from the duration of the long take, and also out of the encompassing energies of montage, our project finds new purpose.

For one thing, we're freed of the faulty assumption that filmic ambiguity results from an absence of technique, rather than from considered applications of it. In the context of cinema, ambiguity is a kind of complexity that is facilitated by film technique even when the style in question operates unobtrusively, as in the transparencies of classical style, or of neorealism. As we have observed already, that cinema reflects "the ambiguities of reality," as Bazin maintains, does not mean that it is artless. Second, against the idea that analysis destroys ambiguity, we should recognize that good analysis in fact takes care to preserve it. Certainly analytical (and other species of) reflection places us at a distance from the work, but this rupture need not be absolute; the problem concerns a kind of reflection that is made to stand in for experience, rather than answering to it. So the pervasive notion that the pleasure of the text is eradicated by knowing too much about it only holds when we think of pleasure as a refuge from reason. Only a very limited kind of analysis curtails our pleasure in a work, because it has learned so little about it;

conversely, a robust analysis submits itself to the work more fully, and is once more enveloped in its appeals.[54]

Thus, the real objective is to discover as much as we can about a film, and the meanings that can be gleaned from it over time, sustaining the dialogue that it initiates. Here analysis unfolds as a mode of phenomenological attentiveness because it does not always assume the viewer's ascendancy. Ambiguity serves as incentive and reward for keeping this dialogue going; it reminds us that our work as film viewers and scholars always stands as an unfinished project. This idea is one of the ways that ambiguity matters for this study, and motivates it; the other concerns ambiguity's reach into the world, disclosing our ongoing involvements in it.

Timeliness and Film History

In the Introduction, I made some brief remarks about narrative suspense, positioning it as a particularly apt case for cinema's timeliness. I want to return to this idea briefly, though steering it in a different direction, toward matters of film history. Noel Carroll's oft-cited analysis of suspense centers on a paradox related to the engagement of the repeat viewer; he asks how it is possible for someone who has already seen a film, and therefore knows its outcome, to be gripped by it again in return viewings. Carroll's answer to this question identifies certain features internal to the text that are necessary to suspense, but ultimately rests on a key distinction: suspense does not derive from our belief in a situation, but from the thoughts we entertain about it. Such thoughts are shaped by the text's operations, provoking the feeling of suspense. This dynamic has a striking consequence: knowing the outcome of a scene, or of the film as a whole, does not quell such feelings while the film continues to guide our thoughts about it.[55]

What interests me here is the way suspense exerts a temporal tension that is infinitely renewable. Its pleasure is undiminished by the knowledge we have of a film because it draws on our imaginative engagement with it; as long as we remain receptive to the film's time structures, the sensation of suspense is rekindled across multiple viewings. Conversely, it follows that the surest way to mute suspense is to abridge the temporal structures that facilitate it: anyone who has attempted to select a "representative" excerpt from a suspenseful film knows how much its tensions depend on the stretches of time that surround it. At this juncture, we start to see the reach of timeliness as a concept, conjoining the activity of film viewing to wider horizons of film experience. Our engagement with filmic temporality underscores the localized effects of time as we watch a film, and the reasons we return to it. In this way, it opens a door to thinking about film history.

Being attentive to our encounters with cinematic time as viewers may highlight a film's historical situation, and by this, the way viewing experience also belongs to the movement of film history. Or, deploying the term that Hans Robert Jauss adapts from Gadamer's hermeneutics, it is to see the film as it belongs to a horizon of expectations.[56] This occurs as a foregrounding of the ways certain filmic forms are familiar to us, while others call for fresh thinking, engaging conventional articulations of cinematic time as well as those instances that register difference through formal innovation or obscurity.

Gilberto Perez has offered an anecdote about the reception of *Vertigo* that may help us to see this situation more clearly. Upon its release in 1958, American critics uniformly panned Hitchcock's film for its sheer implausibility; at the same time, it was hailed by a masterpiece by a lone critic in Havana—the novelist and critic, Guillermo Cabrera Infante (also a source of inspiration to Perez personally).[57] Of course, Infante's assessment now seems wonderfully prescient: if critics' polls can be taken as a barometer of mainstream taste, *Vertigo* has achieved total ascendency, toppling even Welles's *Citizen Kane*.[58] It seems that we are better prepared these days to accept all of *Vertigo*'s artificialities, finally recognizing them as the film's considered project. Thus, our shifting sense of what is "familiar" and what is "unfamiliar" as viewers reflects the historical life of the film by its modification over time: our expectations of contemporary cinema, for example, are continually transformed by new films and across subsequent viewings. So a film's way of doing time is also *historical*, as it draws on the past while remaining open to the future.

But there is another way that our attentiveness may disclose the historical character of cinematic time. This occurs when it uncovers textual details that refer to, or reiterate, some aspect of the cinematic past. Such elements may appear very vividly, as in the privileged case of films-within-films, or in discernible allusions to prior works. But more often, these details register as fleeting gestures, more on the order of a passing remark, or a momentary glimpse of a familiar face. Details of this kind surface frequently across this book's case studies, but as Jauss advises, they are not treated as isolated "facts" that stand apart from the textual fabric.[59] Instead, they are received as occasions in which our experience of cinematic time is suddenly saturated, or intruded on, by the claims of film history. For this study, the point is to make sense of these moments not simply as they reward specialized knowledge, but rather as they reinflect the unfolding experience of temporality that is at issue for us. For the specific situation of recent cinema, which this book takes as its focus, these intersections are a crucial feature of timeliness, and allow us to see older cinematic forms renewed, and made productive, within contemporary contexts.

Doing Time: A User's Guide

Before proceeding to the case studies, let me say a word or two about method. While I have detailed a rationale for engaging timeliness, contrasting it with other understandings of filmic temporality, and designating its philosophical affinities, a basic aspect of this book's approach remains unanswered: How exactly do we *take it up*? With Merleau-Ponty's emphasis on the "I can" of experience, this seems an apposite question.[60]

A basic principle of timeliness is that the experience of time that a film generates is a meaningful event for both film and viewer. It tells us something valuable about the film's concerns; correspondingly, it creates temporal conditions that may prove illuminating for our own lives. Deployed as an interpretive practice, then, a consideration of timeliness begins with a close analysis of filmic form that is focused on the conditions of time they generate. As David Bordwell has shown, the opening sequence of a film is particularly ripe for assessment as it establishes broad parameters of narrative time and space; often enough, the temporal cadence of a film shows itself most emphatically here, disclosing a technique and tone that proves characteristic.[61] For this book's analyses, opening sequences teach us much about each film's overarching prerogatives, framing an experience of time that is captivating, and shapes our expectations of the work to follow.

Timeliness also emphasizes the need to follow a film's course, remaining alert to its temporal patterning as the film presents it. This forms a different approach to temporality than Laura Mulvey advocates, seeking to sustain, rather than disrupt, narrative logics. Indeed, timeliness frames the effort to enter into the temporal event that the film generates—because enduring that event, from start to finish, is itself a meaningful issue. So the insights gained from the pauses and repetitions entailed by film analysis, which work to confirm the correctness of our observations, are redirected toward the work as a whole, enlarging its possibilities. While certain images, sounds, and sequences of a film are of greater interest than others, and receive more intensive analytical attention, the prevailing aim is to read them for their contribution to the film's overall temporal structure, restoring them to their constitutive place there.

Finally, this approach is sensitive to other filmic elements related to narrative content and theme. As we shall see, story events, character action, and lines of dialogue are meaningful markers of the film's temporal priorities, operating synergistically with aesthetic strategies. Thinking about the ways that characters cope with time, and discuss it, is frequently instructive; even the placement of clocks and watches within the mise-en-scène may prove expressive. Other kinds of temporal markers, such as pointed references to films from a different era, can lend a historical texture to the work that augments its force; they show us the long reach of filmic temporality, and the way it exposes both our connection to a cinematic past and our distance from it. With attentiveness, such details enrich our experience of a film's temporalization and may help us to understand it.

On the basis of these stylistic, narrative, and thematic elements, which comprise a film's temporal orchestration, it is not difficult to see how the work of analysis might expose us to a film's appeals again, if we let it. At its core, timeliness names a special attunement to temporality that happens in film viewing, as the chapters to follow will elucidate.

2

Biding Our Time

Rethinking the Familiar in Steven Soderbergh's *The Limey*

THIS BOOK OPENS SQUARELY ON the terrain of mainstream cinema, with an analysis of a film by Steven Soderbergh called *The Limey* (USA, 1999). Somewhat curiously, this is to begin with a director who has recently retired from theatrical filmmaking, and thus invites retrospective assessment.[1] For those familiar with his work, Soderbergh's extensive catalog evidences a preoccupation with what has gone before, whether in Hollywood or the European art cinema, and exhibits a certain playfulness toward established cinematic forms that insists on their continued resonance. Looking back at his career, we find a persistent refashioning of received cinematic materials: there are remakes like *The Underneath* (1995), *Solaris* (2002), and the *Ocean's Eleven* franchise (2001, 2004, 2007); and the vintage aesthetic of films like *The Good German* (2006) and *Eros* (2005).[2] Though the question of whether this approach has proved successful is apposite here, shaping our estimation of Soderbergh as a filmmaker, my interest in this chapter is more particular. I point to a film that invites us to consider Soderbergh's acts of appropriation as both a deliberate strategy and as a meaningful event for our critical practice. My claim is not so much that one film can help us make sense of the others—although it might—but that it opens up a space for thinking about our contact with filmic temporality and film history. For the purposes of the present study, *The Limey* warms us to the idea of timeliness, launching a thoughtful dialogue with its temporal forms that mobilizes our engagement as viewers.

An overview of Soderbergh's career invites us to see him as a skilled practitioner of genre: like Howard Hawks, he works in multiple modes, from the thriller to the biopic, the sci-fi narrative to the heist film, effecting a transparency of style that is responsive to each new situation. Over the years, popular and critical reception of Soderbergh's work has varied markedly from project to project. His début feature, *sex, lies, and videotape*, won the Palme d'Or at Cannes Film Festival, and subsequently became a surprise commercial hit. A noteworthy event for American independent cinema, Soderbergh's film demonstrated that a viable filmmaking practice was possible outside of Hollywood.[3] Soderbergh's second project, *Kafka* (1991), however, met with far less commercial success; similarly, the Depression-era *King of the Hill* (1993), and the revisionist film noir, *The Underneath* (1995) did not readily find audiences. Shifting gears, Soderbergh turned out two low-budget, filmic experiments: the first, *Gray's Anatomy* (1996), an adaptation of a monologue by the actor Spalding Gray, and the second, an anarchic comedy called *Schizopolis* (1997), starring Soderbergh himself. Next, a more conventional thriller, *Out of Sight* (1998), adapted Elmore Leonard's pulp novel for the screen. Only with *Erin Brockovich* and *Traffic* did Soderbergh finally secure a reputation within the mainstream; both films were released in 2000, and dominated the Academy Awards the following year.

But just prior to this turning point in Soderbergh's career, he made a smaller-scaled and significant film that is our subject here. Soderbergh's *The Limey* (1999) is in certain ways a familiar text: the film reworks conventional narrative tropes while gesturing self-consciously toward Hollywood's past. By "familiar," I refer to its premise as a revenge quest: apart from the recognition value of this narrative type, *The Limey* was frequently compared to John Boorman's thriller *Point Blank* (1967, USA) upon its release.[4] In interviews, Soderbergh foregrounds this link to cinema history, but locates *The Limey*'s influences elsewhere; most provocatively, he suggests that his film was conceived as a hybrid text, merging elements of the stylized British thriller with the diffuse narration of European art cinema—or, in his words, as "*Get Carter* as made by Alain Resnais."[5]

Relatedly, *The Limey* trades on the iconic status of its stars, Terence Stamp and Peter Fonda, and the intertextual associations they contribute to the project. Stamp's career spans British, Italian, French, and American cinemas from the 1960s to the present. His role as the eponymous hero in Peter Ustinov's adaptation of Melville's *Billy Budd* (1962) earned him immediate critical acclaim; soon after, he was named Best Actor at the Cannes Film Festival for his part in William Wyler's *The Collector* (1965). Throughout the decade, Stamp worked with a range of international directors, from Joseph Losey (*Modesty Blaise*, 1966), John Schlesinger (*Far From the Madding Crowd*, 1967), and Ken Loach (*Poor Cow*, 1968) to Pier Paolo Pasolini (*Teorema*, 1968) and Federico Fellini (*Tre Passi nel Delirio* or *Spirits of the Dead*, 1968). Subsequently, Stamp withdrew from the public eye for a time to live in India, resurfacing eventually in British films in the 1970s, and Hollywood films in the 1980s. On this basis, what Stamp brings to *The Limey* is quite complex: once one of the most recognizable faces of 1960s cinema, he comes to embody the hither side of sixties youth culture, marked by an accretion of experience and newly restored to visibility.

The Limey similarly exploits the laid-back persona of Peter Fonda; beyond his ties to a celebrated Hollywood family, Fonda is best known for his role in Dennis Hopper's emblematic biker film, *Easy Rider* (1969). *The Limey* also places notable players in supporting roles, importing a range of associations: Barry Newman, who appeared in another counter-cultural text of the period, Richard C. Sarafian's *Vanishing Point* (1971) appears alongside Fonda; additionally, Joe Dallesandro, star of numerous Andy Warhol films, such as *Trash* (1970) and *Heat* (1972) plays an aging, tag-along thug in *The Limey*. Finally, a piece of iconic casting intended for the film merits attention as well: a scene with Ann Margaret, in which she delivers an eight-minute monologue written for her specifically, was ultimately dropped from the final cut, but would have contributed yet another citation of 1960s cinema.[6]

Yet the film's references to, and reiteration of, a filmic past are something more than a stylized flourish or a limited nostalgic gesture.[7] When we engage the film's time structures, attending to the relation that develops between film and viewer, we find that *The Limey* challenges us to think about familiarity as a specifically temporal issue. It asks us to reflect on our capacity—or willingness—to recognize elements of the past both as aspects of our present situation and as determining features of the future. *The Limey* institutes such questions at the level of form, so that to cope with its shifting temporal parameters is also to participate in, and potentially confirm, a larger thematic agenda. In other words, the difference between "what is familiar" and "what is unfamiliar" is thematized by the film quite explicitly, and begins with our perceptual experience as viewers.

In what follows, I will propose a reading of *The Limey* that identifies within it two conjoined tendencies. First, *The Limey*'s initially confounding formal structure acts as a guide to its operations; by requiring us to make sense of a welter of rhymes and repetitions, the film actually teaches us how to be its viewer. Second, however, this perceptual training does not accrue to the viewer an unambiguous mastery of its systems. Rather, it furnishes us with a set of tools that proves inadequate; while these penetrate a surface logic, the film indicates that what has been at stake all along remains inaccessible. And it is this latter tendency that causes me to take up Soderbergh's film here, as an exemplary case: by acknowledging that *The Limey* rewards *and* resists our analytical efforts, we are brought closer to the principle of uncertainty that lies at its heart, and to a fuller appreciation of its richness as a text. Taken seriously, this thought will remind us that the task of reading a film does not always proceed in one direction, toward complete tractability; instead, *The Limey* performs a dialectical movement of old and new that finally questions the very idea of familiarity.

Finding Time: Temporal Structures and Defamiliarization

Given *The Limey*'s concern to unsettle what is familiar, it's helpful to think about the film's formal prerogatives is in terms of their capacity for *defamiliarization*. This technique, held by Russian formalists as essential to works of art, creates an ideal situation of perception that is characterized by an extreme awareness. As Victor Shklovsky writes in "Art as Technique":

> If we start to examine the general laws of perception, we see that as perception becomes habitual, it becomes automatic . . . Such habituation explains the principles by which, in ordinary speech, we leave phrases unfinished and words half expressed.[8]

Certainly habituation is part of our experience of film viewing. The formal language associated with classical narrative, for example, in its clarity and redundancy, does not insist that we continually notice it: thus, classical editing techniques, such as matches on action or limited temporal ellipses, can displace small pieces of time without sacrificing overall comprehensibility.[9] But what of films that strive to delay habituation, demanding greater vigilance from viewers? To this end, *The Limey* undermines familiar narrative mechanisms by exposing their limits, cleaving the continuous event into disparate fragments and reproducing the single instance in multiple manifestations. That these procedures frustrate our expectations of a legible temporal sequence is precisely their point: our awareness of time, and our confusion about it, are vital components of the film's formal objectives.

This is in line with Shklovsky's proposition that "the technique of art is to make objects 'unfamiliar,' to make forms difficult, to increase the difficulty and length of perception."[10] But if Soderbergh's film aims to defamiliarize time, this perceptual play is not just an aesthetic end, but also a guide to what the film means. Looking to *The Limey* in terms of the difficulties of its form, and with particular emphasis on its articulations of temporality, we find that it is deeply invested in the idea of temporal experience, both as it pertains to viewing practices (how do viewers make sense of narrative time?) and to broader, thematic preoccupations (how do we reconcile the past with the present?). This concern informs *The Limey*'s operations in crucial ways: both formally and thematically, the film relentlessly calls our attention to questions of temporal positioning.

The Limey's narrative centers on Wilson (Terence Stamp), a British career criminal released after nine years in prison. Having learned that his daughter Jenny died under suspicious circumstances in Los Angeles, he travels to America to find out who is responsible. With the assistance of an ex-con named Eduardo (Luis Guzman), and Jenny's friend, Elaine (Lesley Ann Warren), Wilson discovers that his daughter was involved with a man named Valentine (Peter Fonda), a middle-aged record producer capitalizing on 1960s nostalgia. In his search for truth and revenge, Wilson comes to see his relationship with Jenny with new clarity.

The opening sections of *The Limey* present a jumble of material that is not easily reconciled as a coherent narrative chain. Indeed, something of the film's prerogatives is signaled even within the opening shots: the first moments withhold the image entirely, instead offering a dramatic voiceover commentary ("Tell me. Tell me. Tell me about Jenny."), while the second shot commences as a blurred background, a faint relay of movements, that eventually snaps into focus. This initial displacement of the image, followed by an image that obscures its identificatory marks once again evokes Shklovsky's thinking. He writes:

> After we see an object many times, we begin to recognize it. The object is in front of us and we know about it, but we do not see it . . . [Conversely,] Tolstoy makes the familiar seem strange by not naming the familiar object.[11]

From the outset, *The Limey* plays with expectations of legibility by delaying the appearance of a conventional, establishing shot. Although Wilson is situated as a central narrative agent, emerging at the end of the second shot as an isolated figure, and positioned in the frame alongside the title credit as "the limey," the film produces this information with some reluctance, and in half-measures: the viewer is required first to look for him, within the frame, for twelve of fifteen seconds; further, the initial voiceover is not explicitly attributable to Wilson until he speaks, subsequently. (See fig. 2.1.) It is clear, in retrospect, that these shots would establish a great deal, were they laid out differently: the formal rift between words and speaker deflect the film's immediate assertion of a narrative object ("Tell me about Jenny.").

I privilege these details in particular because they indicate the degree to which *The Limey*'s opening moments initiate a different mode of viewing; more specifically, they signal the film's requirement of an unusually high level of attentiveness from its viewer.[12] While the manipulations of the shots in question are subtle, they are also instructive: the instance of information "projected" prior to its context (shot 1) and of a narrative landscape that is eventually clarified (shot 2) describe certain of the film's overarching strategies.

By examining the opening sequence, it is possible to obtain a sense of *The Limey*'s temporal manipulations as a whole. Running little over four minutes, yet consisting of thirty-nine shots, the film's first section compresses a wide array of spatial and temporal locations. Initially, the action moves from the public space of the Los Angeles airport to the

Figure 2.1. Opening title from *The Limey* (Steven Soderbergh, 1999).

more private space of Wilson's motel. We are presented with some of Wilson's personal effects, and specifically, with a newspaper clipping that reads, "Woman dies on Mulholland," and a return address printed on a worn envelope. (See fig. 2.2.) The shots that follow are discontinuous, depicting Wilson in a series of locales, repeatedly: on a doorstep, asking for the man named on the envelope ("Eduardo Roel"); on an airplane, surrounded by other passengers; in his motel room, lost in contemplation; in a moving car, holding up a photograph of a young woman to examine it in the sunlight; in a taxi, at night. These images are intercut with others, contributing further disorienting effects: a blue-filtered image of a young girl at the beach, smiling; a grainy, sepia-toned image of the same girl, gazing sadly through a doorframe; another blue-filtered image, where the young woman of the photograph appears as a passenger in a moving car. Finally, the sequence stabilizes, as Wilson's encounter with Roel is reprised and extended as a full conversation. Supplementing the image track are shifting layers of diegetic and nondiegetic sound: first, nondiegetic music and the sound of airplane engines are audible; the music ceases, replaced by the sound of running water; next, the sound of running water continues, accompanied by the faint tinkle of wind chimes; then, these sounds are replaced by the roar of the ocean, and eventually joined by a male voice (Wilson's), humming. Last, all sounds cease, save those clearly rooted in the diegesis.

Figure 2.2. Name on an envelope. From *The Limey* (Steven Soderbergh, 1999).

Obviously, a single viewing (or hearing) of the sequence does not yield many certainties; on closer examination, however, things do become clearer. In general, we can say that the film produces an ongoing "present" that is insistently ruptured by projections of future events. Within the sequence, these are frequently "near futures" that the present eventually overtakes; Wilson's first meeting with Eduardo, for example, is subsequently replayed as an event unfolding "now." On occasion these projections are of a greater scope, and are not contextualized until much later; the images of Wilson traveling by airplane can be understood as his flight home, by the film's conclusion. (See fig. 2.3.) In this respect, the projections into the future drive the narrative, once the viewer recognizes their method of functioning.

To complicate matters, the shifts between present and future are set alongside intrusions from the past. Once again, this temporal category is bifurcated, moving between events of the "recent past," and a more "distant past," produced as Wilson's memory. Significantly, these interventions not only signify a temporal difference, but also present certain problems of perspective. One of Wilson's "recollections," for example, corresponds with his time in prison, and is thus impossible as his literal viewpoint: the medium close-up of a young woman (Jenny), as a passenger in Eduardo's car, presents a view of the pair that cannot logically be Wilson's. While an acceptable context for this shot is offered

Figure 2.3. Wilson, coming and going. From *The Limey* (Steven Soderbergh, 1999).

subsequently, as an illustration of an anecdote that Eduardo tells later in the film, it does not actually convey Eduardo's point of view: the shot is of the car's exterior, and observes the pair objectively. Similarly, while flashes from the "distant past" can be attributed to Wilson, these are colored in a way that is enigmatic: if we take certain images to signify "distant past/Wilson" by the use of a blue filter, it is curious that the shot named above, conveying "recent past/Eduardo" is rendered likewise. Viewers of Soderbergh's other films will no doubt recognize this use of color filters as a characteristic gesture, but unlike the clearly demarcated chromatic zones of *Traffic* (2000), or the moody palette of his neo-noir, *The Underneath* (1995), the use of this device within *The Limey* does not always serve a clarifying function.[13]

Hence, the viewer is required to extract a linear story from a highly fragmented plot without recourse to reliable visual cues, such as an unproblematic color coding, or communicative transitions, such as dissolves indicating leaps in time. Viewer comprehension, therefore, relies on a system of familiarizing repetitions; while we cannot explain these flashbacks absolutely, we *can* discern a pattern of their appearance. Moreover, we come to accept the narrative pieces in an approximate relation to each other; within these terms, key formal differences signify a generalized "pastness," until the narrative places these details more specifically.

Additional formal effects convolute these arrangements even further. As with the use of color described previously, sound is deployed to form links between images and across temporal zones. In specific terms, only the nondiegetic music functions conventionally, ending abruptly before any temporal shifts occur. Elsewhere, the film constructs irregular sound bridges that tend to impede, rather than facilitate, narrative comprehensibility.

The sound of airplane engines, for example, is rooted in the "present" of the airport and the airport motel, as is the sound of running water; these sounds continue across images from various temporal zones. The sounds of wind chimes and of the ocean, however, are projections of future events: like the opening shot ("Tell me about Jenny."), these are aural references produced well before their context; both the wind chimes and the ocean's roar properly "occur" at the film's conclusion. Beyond the obvious spatial and temporal conflation that these effect, the film's use of sound describes a general, defamiliarizing strategy: what seems extraneous and nondiegetic is, more accurately, not *yet* diegetic, and will be familiarized by an emergent context. In this regard, the viewer learns to receive the film's sounds and images as partial revelations that will come to assume a more stable narrative positioning; concomitantly, the viewer's engagement must remain as dynamic as the film's manipulations.

Telling Time

On occasion, *The Limey*'s dialogue seems even to refer to this situation, as though delineating the viewer's dilemma for us. Consider, for instance, an anecdote that Wilson relates to a DEA agent about the things he has learned in prison; although his first impulse is to seek revenge on a prison guard when he meets him again on the outside, he soon reconsiders, as follows:

> What I thought I wanted wasn't what I wanted; what I thought I was thinking about was something else. I didn't give a toss. It didn't *matter*, see? This bloke on the bench wasn't worth my *time*. It meant sod all in the end. 'Cause you've got to make a choice: when to do something and when to let it go. When it *matters* and when it *don't*. Bide your time—that's what prison teaches you, if nothing else. Bide your time and everything becomes clear. And you can act accordingly.

This emphatic assertion, offered by Wilson midway through the film, actually tells us what we already know, as viewers: the film's earliest moments direct us to "bide our time" to ensure narrative comprehension.[14]

Relatedly, the film suggests another way of thinking about its formal structuring by foregrounding Wilson's use of Cockney rhyming slang: when Wilson says "china," for example, it's short for "china plate," a rhyme that stands in for "mate" (his actual meaning). Evidently, this vernacular points to Wilson's cultural difference, and situates him as a figure whose very manner of speaking seems out of place and time.[15] More compellingly, this riddle-like, abbreviated code resembles the film's operations, in important ways: we receive a term (i.e., the *sound* of the ocean), corresponding to a larger term (the ocean *itself*, as it appears in the diegesis), but actually indexing something else (the final confrontation between Wilson and Valentine, *at* the ocean). In this way, the film's formal arrangements may be seen as a self-conscious "roughening" of language that defamiliarizes conventional usages. As Shklovsky indicates:

> Every riddle pretends to show its subject either by words which specify or describe it but which, during the telling, do not seem applicable (the type: "black and white and 'red' read—all over) or by means of odd but imitative sounds (" 'Twas brillig, and the slithy toves / Did gyre and gimble in the wabe").[16]

As with the literary language cited above, *The Limey*'s defamiliarizing mode of articulation is initially confounding, but eventually penetrable;

once the viewer has witnessed one such riddle unfold, subsequent effects are more familiar, and increasingly legible.

Taking a Second Look

So if, on the one hand, we can say that the film's details are patterned in a way that assumes an eventual coherence, on the other, there remain certain elements that do not observe this logic. The film's use of sound again supplies a good example: Wilson's humming may occur in the "present" of his motel room, although this seems unlikely; otherwise, it is linked in a later sequence to a song Wilson sang in the past, and to his reflections, more generally. I raise this issue because it qualifies any simple assessment of the film's prerogatives: the humming not only resists a precise temporal location, it also presents a kind of experience that exceeds such designations. It seems apt to say that Wilson's humming somehow refers to *both* past and present, or to the hazy ground that lies in-between; in either case, moments such as these evoke a sense of time that is subjective and elastic and does not proceed logically as a series of consecutive instants.

Similarly, an episode occurs a little later in the film that asks us to rethink our preliminary understanding of its systems. Wilson persuades Eduardo to accompany him to Valentine's house, and on arriving, they find a large party in progress and decide to pass themselves off as Valentine's guests. Wilson first explores the house, and then stands with Eduardo, observing the gathering at a distance. The film presents Eduardo pointing out Valentine to Wilson, and then, quite suddenly, a flurry of images depicts Wilson shooting Valentine. This action is presented repeatedly, generating three versions of the shooting. While the film has suggested to this point that such projections are indicators of coming events, on this occasion, they are allied less reliably with Wilson's subjectivity, as a *wish* that is never fulfilled within the diegesis. The film introduces, then, a fresh set of defamiliarizing possibilities, describing subjective phenomena: memory, daydreams, and wishes exist alongside concrete events. What this effects is significant: although the film's fragmentary network of past, present and future becomes manageable, approximately, as "motivating events," "ongoing activities," and "events to come," the details associated with Wilson's psychology remain elusive. As I have intimated, these elements forward a kind of critique by their very presence because they point up the deficiency of our interpretive scheme. Though we have endeavored, as viewers, to "bide our time," this strategy uncovers only half the picture; there is, it seems, *another order* of experience to be reckoned with. So if we have learned, through familiarization, how to assess much of the profilmic material, *The Limey* poses questions that surpass these recuperative efforts, as well.

We might say that the film asks us not just to see things "out of their normal context," as Shklovsky would have it, but also to consider that sometimes the relation between a thing and its context is imprecise and mutable.[17] An additional example expresses this point quite lucidly: as I have indicated, the first meeting between Wilson and Eduardo is presented briefly, and then replicated by the film, so that the viewer receives the latter as a fleshed out repetition of the former. On closer scrutiny, however, the repetition is inexact, and instead offers a near identical, but different *version* of the same action. Specifically, a very slight camera movement is discernible in the first version, but not in the second; the angle differs slightly from one "take" to another; the actors' delivery of lines differs slightly, also. Thus, even at this early stage, *The Limey*'s articulations are more problematic than they appear.

In other words, *The Limey* generates two kinds of movement: a relay of defamiliarization/familiarization that promises an eventual clarity, and conversely, an assertion of problems of temporal experience that are less easily resolved. In so doing, the film indicates that its own explanatory map necessarily misses its mark: despite our efforts as viewers to place details within firm analytical categories, other factors persist that are potentially of greater significance.

Admittedly, this is awkward terrain to navigate, requiring us not just to account for the patterns spread across the film's surface but also for those details that seem not to form patterns at all. So might there be another way to think about *The Limey* that takes these points of resistance not as "negative space," but as potential sources of meaning? Put differently, can we offer a description of the temporal experience that the film produces that preserves (and cherishes) the unique quality of its cadence?

The Limey, Time and History

A possibility of this kind is opened up by Martin Heidegger's thinking, and specifically, by his analysis of the temporal character of existence in *Being and Time*. In that context, Heidegger's term *Dasein*, or literally, "there-being," is used to designate the entity, or being, that each of us is.[18] Of special relevance for this discussion, *Dasein* has its being in all three temporalities of past, present, and future. Time, therefore, is not experienced as a linear measure, but rather as a phenomenon that is more complex: it involves "throwness" (our negotiation of what comes down from the past), "fallenness" (our concern with particular "nows") as well as "projections" onto future possibility.[19] By this I do not mean to impose a Heideggerian reading squarely upon the film's machinations, but rather to suggest that it acknowledges a comparable situation. Expressed simply, *The Limey* asks us to consider time as a thing experienced "all at once," as a consequence of its formal fragmentation and its thematic interests. As Heidegger writes:

> Temporalizing does not signify . . . a 'succession.' The future is *not later* than having been, and having been is *not earlier* than the Present. Temporality temporalizes itself as a future which makes present in the process of having been.[20]

Within these terms, it's possible to think of *The Limey* as presenting a gathering of time that stresses our immersion in time as a whole. This notion is persuasive in two respects: first, with reference to the film's narrative loop, which presents an ending (Wilson's journey home) as a possible beginning (these images appear early in the film, as though depicting Wilson's arrival), and second, in regard to the film's conclusion, which answers Wilson's query ("Tell me about Jenny.") with recourse to Wilson's past.

In fact, the film's refusal of purely linear time is manifest at nearly every level: even the matter of Wilson's "otherness" as a character—as a "foreigner" on American soil, just released from London's Parkhurst prison—is cast as a specifically temporal issue, and one that emphasizes simultaneity over sequential ordering. For example, when asked how he learned of his daughter's death, Wilson describes this circumstance in terms of an uncanny foreknowledge that shatters his regimented prison routine:

> Oh, no—I knew. I knew *beforehand*. What time was it supposed to have happened? Eddie said, two in the morning. Well that's like, eight hours difference between here and London . . . that would have made it about, like, ten o'clock, my time. I was just going out in the yard. I was in the habit of saving my newspaper until then. You know—stretch me legs, breath of fresh air, bit of a read—stretch out the good part of the day, as it were. And I couldn't open the newspaper: it was like the pages was *glued* together, my hands were that weak. I thought I was having a heart attack! Course, I know I wasn't. Guy I knew, come up, "Here, Wilson," he said, "you're as white as sheet!" I said, "well fuck me, I've been in prison half my life, haven't I?" But he was dead on, because I'd felt all the blood drain out of my head. And I knew . . . I knew something must've happened to Jen.

Characteristically for *The Limey*, Wilson's recounting of this story is presented as a continuous recitation, but is dislocated by the accompanying images. The minute-long speech, as offered here, is impossibly stretched across three discrete settings: Wilson speaks from a chair in Elaine's apartment, from his seat at a restaurant table, and as the pair walks along the oceanfront. Thus, the anecdote extends beyond the details that the film presents, inviting us to read it as a forceful condensation: it is the course of an evening distilled to its memorable and affective content.

The story itself bears consideration, as well, for its explicit insistence on the simultaneity of experience across time zones. Though doubly removed from his daughter's life in Los Angeles (because incarcerated, and across the ocean), Wilson knows the fact of Jenny's death intuitively; that is to say, he knows it as something felt, as an authentically embodied experience. Not coincidentally, within Wilson's account, the more usual and objective source of knowledge—the daily newspaper—is quite useless to him, testifying only to his body's weakness. Thus the film's overarching pun—that Wilson has done time—is not to be taken lightly: the film suggests that this experience places Wilson in a privileged position that is unusually sensitive to lived temporality, in its multiple and encompassing orientations. Put another way, *doing* time is closer, and more basic to us, than all our rational ways of measuring it.

Introducing Heidegger's formulation of time into this context allows us to talk about *The Limey*'s temporal structure as a kind of holistic design in which the modalities of past, present, and future are closely imbricated. But more provocatively, the correspondence may move in the other direction, as well, to signal a further valence of Soderbergh's film: the thought occurs that *The Limey* may also be concerned with time in a deep sense, appealing to the continuous contact of memory and daydream, regret, and aspiration, within a tangled net of lived experience. In this sense, too, *The Limey*'s time can be called reflective and historical, because the film's telling of the present is not sufficient unto itself, but must always answer to the past and the future.

Borrowed Time: Ken Loach's *Poor Cow*

This raises the issue of *The Limey*'s own devising of film history, as evidenced by its use of footage from Ken Loach's *Poor Cow* (1967, UK). From the outset, Soderbergh and screenwriter Lem Dobbs had hoped, in casting Terence Stamp, to include material from one of the actor's prior films. Conceived as a narrative experiment, the inclusion of Loach's material was designed to exploit film-specific potentialities: by bringing together two discrete moments in Stamp's career within a single, motivated narrative context, *The Limey* would animate both past and present, allowing the viewer to obtain, via editing, a sense of the character's life experience as something accumulated, over time.[21] Obtaining legal permission for such an experiment was a lengthy process, involving not only Loach's film but also its source material—Nell Dunn's novel of the same title. Further, the scenes that Soderbergh most wished to use from *Poor Cow* featured the actress Carol White, who had died eight years earlier. Negotiations ensued for months and were not fully resolved until *The Limey* was in the editing stage. A final issue was the matter of obtaining Loach's permission, personally; though the inquiry had been settled legally, Soderbergh wished to have the director's creative consent. Fortunately, Loach approved the use of the material its newly conceived context.[22]

Loach's first theatrical feature was an ideal choice for use within *The Limey*, with several clear affinities in cast and characterization: *Poor Cow* presents a young Terence Stamp as a thief who becomes romantically involved with a working-class woman in London while her husband is in prison. Soderbergh lifts material from the earlier production and weaves it into his own, so that the extracts serve as a rich background that illustrates certain of Wilson's memories. Contextualized in *The Limey*, the grainy footage presents Wilson in happier times, among old friends, or with Jenny's mother before her death. (See fig. 2.4.) Soderbergh has

Figure 2.4. Terence Stamp in *Poor Cow* (Ken Loach, 1967). From *The Limey* (Steven Soderbergh, 1999).

made certain adjustments to Loach's material, sometimes reordering or cropping the images to accommodate their new context. Otherwise, *The Limey* emphasizes the discrepancy between old and new, insofar as the borrowed footage is presented as nearly monochromatic and often silent, effacing the more varied hues and sounds of Loach's original.

While this appropriation can be understood as a self-reflexive move, in keeping with *The Limey*'s reconfiguration of 1960s style and iconography, this explanation does not adequately address the resonance of the images themselves; not only is Wilson's character given range and depth through these details, but they contribute a powerful affective dimension, as well. In this respect, Soderbergh's indebtedness to Alain Resnais is relevant, when we consider that director's complex use of film-historical materials. For example, the invocation of French film history in *Mon oncle d'Amérique* (France, 1980) presents a series of black-and-white images—of Jean Gabin, Danielle Darrieux, and Jean Marais, respectively—breaking in on an otherwise color film, punctuating moments of acute emotional crisis. Thus, the images of the past are set in stark contrast to the activity of the present; at the same time, they are linked to this activity by a common movement or gesture, and correspond to each of Resnais's three protagonists. Most fundamentally, the images support and partially constitute the film's larger argument for the force of past as an indelible and formative influence.

Returning to *The Limey*, the silence and deliberately faded appearance of the older images in Soderbergh's film asserts such a "difference"—of time, location, and tone—as to seem almost of a different medium; their relative stillness and otherness evokes, in Roland Barthes's terms, the pastness of the photograph. As Barthes writes in *Camera Lucida*:

> The name of photography's noeme will therefore be: "That-has-been," or again: the Intractable. In Latin . . . this would doubtless be said: *interfuit*: what I see has been here, in this place which extends between infinity and the subject (*operator* or *spectator*); it has been here, and yet immediately separated; it has been absolutely, irrefutably present, and yet already deferred.[23]

It may seem odd to call these borrowed images "photographic," when they are neither a succession of stills, as in Chris Marker's *La Jetée* (1962), nor actual photographs produced as such within the diegesis, as in Antonioni's *Blowup* (1966). But this sense of their difference and distance as images is nonetheless palpable to us, as viewers. Rather than rendering this distinction as a hard contrast from black and white to color, Soderbergh's film presents the past as more contiguous with the present, but not identical with it. In other words, the past persists for us now, but registers as something wordless and somewhat *harder to see.*

Therefore, just as *The Limey* describes an experience of temporality that is of time "all at once," it also points to the discreteness of temporal spheres: while we swallow up the past, bring it into our daily concerns, and project it onto future possibility, the past also remains at one remove, in certain ways inaccessible and alien. Though we may wish to, we cannot own the past, as Valentine discovers, or stand over it objectively; in the last instance, it owns us, as Wilson's quest demonstrates. So, if Soderbergh's film is preoccupied with what has gone before, as its referentiality attests, it does not borrow images because they are familiar to us, or perfectly congruent with our present situation. By inserting pieces of the already complete, already contained narrative of *Poor Cow* within *The Limey*'s workings, Soderbergh creates a dialogue between old and new that brings the past into focus without fully overcoming its estrangement from the present. Notably, *The Limey* also extends this concern outward, configuring original footage as though it belonged to a nebulous "elsewhere": Soderbergh's image of Jenny as a young girl emulates the color and grain of Loach's material, and yet as a "new" image, remains distinct.[24] (See fig. 2.5.)

Figure 2.5. Soderbergh's image of a young Jenny. From *The Limey* (Steven Soderbergh, 1999).

Time and Time Again: Reframing Richard Lester's *Petulia*

Another key point of reference for *The Limey* concerns the work of filmmaker Richard Lester. Beginning in British television in the 1950s, Lester is best known for the Beatles films, *A Hard Day's Night* (1964) and *Help!* (1965). Also remarkable is the extent to which Lester's work tends, in the context of mainstream studio filmmaking, toward striking formal experimentation, as in his quintessential "swinging" comedy, *The Knack . . . and How to Get It* (1965).[25] An evident admirer of Lester's work, Soderbergh cowrote a book with the filmmaker in 1995. A hybrid and personal text, it transcribes a series of interviews with Lester, interspersed with Soderbergh's own journal entries over a yearlong period.[26]

Of special interest here is Lester's 1968 film, a relentlessly bleak reading of the late-sixties San Francisco scene, called *Petulia* (1968). The film depicts a recently divorced doctor who becomes involved with a young woman trapped in a desperately unhappy marriage. Though altogether different in its narrative premises, *Petulia* is an important background text for *The Limey* for its innovative construction of multiple and conflicting temporalities.[27] From the outset, the film features dramatic leaps in space and time, resulting in a narrative framework that is loosely articulated and elliptical. Strong contrasts in image and sound impart an array of disorienting effects: the opening images, for example, present a wide view of a colorless, industrial kitchen space, through which hotel staff push three older, formally dressed figures in successive wheelchairs. The compositions are cold, clinical, and nearly silent: the only audible sound is the clacking of wheels as the chairs pass. Though scarcely established narratively, the scene suddenly cuts away to a more intimate framing, in an entirely different location: here, brightly clad musicians (indeed, Janis Joplin herself) offer a raucous performance at a charity benefit. After several such juxtapositions, the two worlds are brought together: the procession of wheelchairs eventually arrives at the performance space and is awkwardly conducted through it. Crucially, this completes the scene's wry, unfolding "joke": the benefit, and live music for dancing—themed on a prominent sign as, Shake for Road Safety!—is actually *for* these accident victims, yet cruelly excludes them, as well. Class distinctions and an irreconcilable rift between youth and establishment culture are sharply delineated here; elsewhere, the film keenly observes divisions of gender, and the more diffuse oppositions of surface/depth, nature/technology, and feeling/indifference.

Like *The Limey*, *Petulia* proceeds via flashbacks and occasional flash-forwards in time. Most often, the past arises out of visual associations, motivated by elements briefly glimpsed in the diegesis: reflected light on a car recalls an earlier car accident; a lover's tender gesture evokes the prior movement of a surgeon's hand, tending to a wound. These are subjective links, forged within a single character's consciousness, although often the precise source of these recollections registers ambiguously.

Despite these stylistic affinities with *The Limey*, Lester's film finally proposes an essential difference from it: for *Petulia*, the formal fragmentation and scattered subjectivities endeavor to describe an experience of interiority, a deep-seated, psychic disturbance that responds to a situation that is broken and unlivable. In a world scarred by war and cruelly divided by class, where power is unevenly distributed along gender lines and its abuse is institutionalized, and where, in the name of "progress," the conditions of modernity have served only to evacuate human affect, the film's stylistic play inscribes and reiterates permanent effects of dispersal and disconnection. This is both a formal method and a worldview, and one that speaks strongly to the tensions of the Vietnam era.

Conversely, *The Limey* deploys something of these strategies, but seeks a revised application: by its formal rigor, Soderbergh's film sustains the possibility of a profound *connectedness* among its fragments, uncovering, in its circling movements, a continual mediation of past, present, and future that retains the ambiguities of lived perception. It is not so much that *The Limey*'s world is perfectly coherent, but that it understands its situation differently; rather than mourning some prior time that is lost to us now—a history blown to pieces, or otherwise over and done with—Soderbergh's film outlines a need in the present for renewed ways of seeing that history in terms of our place within it.

Lessons of Time

These considerations return us to our original query about defamiliarization and familiarity. *The Limey's* concluding movements once again evince a blurring of categories: although Wilson's quest has been to pierce the unknown (the circumstances of Jenny's death), he receives an explanation that is known to him, after all (Jenny's argument with Valentine restates her relationship with Wilson). This realization quietly curtails Wilson's confrontation with Valentine at the ocean's edge: it lights his face for a moment as gazes down at Valentine, before turning away. The film has offered pieces of this encounter before, repeatedly, so there is a satisfaction in seeing them click into place, unfolding in their narrative fullness.

Perhaps this final exchange reads as somewhat hyperbolic: here is Wilson raised above his long-held wish for vengeance; Valentine lies sprawled on the sand, his hands lifted in a gesture of supplication. But as is characteristic for this film, there is more to take in. Yes, we have seen these guilty hands before, but not just as a previous image; they are also the "slippery hands" of the DEA agent who passes Wilson information because his priorities are greater; more substantially, they are a version of Wilson's hands, as he has described them already—those sensing hands that recognized Jenny's death, across time zones, before it had coalesced as a fact of the present. Of course, hands are strongly associated with culpability, particularly of the kind that can't be washed away. But here they effect a kind of temporal transfer, spanning more years than the film presents. They show us that our responsibility to ourselves, and to others, is a sensation held by the body: it is as plainly marked there as an address on an envelope, if we just knew how to read it.[28]

By this, the film forwards two related propositions: that the past is inseparable from our present concerns, and more complexly, that the wisdom of hindsight is perhaps just the cold recognition that, despite our investment in the "here" and "now," we are also fundamentally engaged in a dialogue with "what has been." In this light, the film's play of defamiliarization/familiarization is not only an aesthetic end, but constitutes a wider, thematic project: the film suggests that we may not recognize what is most familiar to us, and by consequence, that what is most familiar may also be the most troubling.

This is an insight that *The Limey* possesses, and an important part of its persuasiveness lies in the film's decision to make our perceptual experience count toward this understanding. In our efforts to cope with *The Limey*'s refractory narrative system, we are able to glimpse the past as it informs an unfolding present, opening up to the future, but also as something that is never quite transparent to us, or fully exhaustible. By this, the film asks us to receive the idea that we may be indebted to the past in ways we do not realize; or, expressed another way, that our relation to the past is not one of mastery, where it is easily laid bare for present use. Rather, the film casts what has gone before as something that occurs *through* us, and perhaps without our consent; for *The Limey*, the past is that aspect of the present we so often fail to see.

If the significance of the past for the present is what Soderbergh's film aims to make explicit—and there are reasons to think this is the case—then we should note that its tasks of retrieval and reassessment are also basic ones for film history, though we may not at first perceive this resemblance. Contending with the various parts of *The Limey*, in acknowledgment of its inheritance of the old and its production of the new, its ambiguities and its commanding forms, and its primary insistence that the usual way of seeing things may not be enough to disclose what we are seeking, puts us in an excellent position to contemplate our own activity, as viewers. Because at a tangible level, *The Limey* reaches back into the past so as to give us certain pieces of it *now*, where such pieces—the fragments of *Poor Cow*, or the iconic presence of actors Stamp and Fonda—already bear significance and entail their own histories. In exchange, the film asks us to recognize the rapport of old and new, and to actively mediate the distance between them.

While Soderbergh's playful cinematic practice may seem a surprising setting for these reflections, they provide a credible background for both the film's formal arrangements and its own acts of appropriation. My initial assessment of *The Limey* was as a film of only apparent difficulty, which should, on closer investigation, open up as self-explicating text. But although the film does, in large part, explain its own functioning, it also presents details that are more recalcitrant in nature; indeed, these stray elements problematize any narrow view of the film's machinations. In this respect, *The Limey* shows us the heuristic value of timeliness, as it resists the certainties of method in crucial ways. By continually unsettling our sense of what is "familiar" and what is "unfamiliar," Soderbergh's text also underscores the terms of a shared film history, where appropriation is not merely repetition, but renewal, and the familiar is made strange once more by the force it gains from a new context.

3

Back and Forth

Reading Reverse Chronology in François Ozon's *5x2*

That's how it all began. Looking back on it,
I wonder now if it could have been on some day
Findable in an old calendar? But no,
It wasn't out of history, but inside it.

—John Ashbery, "Wooden Buildings"

We might assume that stories told in retrospect are usually clearer: with the benefit of hindsight, links between events become apparent, stray details assume sudden significance, and motivating factors emerge with new clarity. On this view, looking back at the past should improve our understanding of it because the patterns of our experience stand out more distinctly; relatedly, the dilemmas of the present may be clarified with recourse to the past because they find their roots there.

It's just this sort of thinking that is turned on its head by François Ozon's film, *5x2* (France, 2004). The film's description of a failed marriage is told backwards, starting with the signing of divorce papers and concluding with the couple's first encounter. And yet this retrospective telling, from ends to beginnings, does not provide full disclosure or arrive at transparency: instead, the film persistently foregrounds the ambiguous nature of human interaction, emphasizing occasions of silence, separation, and opacity. In what follows, I will trace the formal and thematic contours of *5x2*, to show how the film's quality of open-endedness is, in fact, a considered feature of its temporal design: as we shall see, a calculated use of temporal ellipses, which creates noticeable gaps in time, effects a deformation of the film's overarching formal structure that deepens the film's meaning. This is the peculiar timeliness of *5x2*: it uses reverse chronology in unfamiliar ways, to uncover a complex picture of temporality and the nature of our engagement with it.

In the last two decades, François Ozon has made sixteen feature-length films, as well as numerous shorts, to considerable critical acclaim. At the outset of his career, he was situated by critics, alongside filmmakers like Catherine Breillat, Claire Denis, Gaspar Noé, and others, as part of the "New French Extremity" or in other words, as contributing to a cycle of contemporary French films featuring extreme and graphic representations of sexuality and violence, as an evident provocation to viewers.[1] But this initial designation must be qualified, or withdrawn entirely, in the face of the films that followed: at least since his enigmatic feature, *Sous le sable* (*Under the Sand*, France, 2000), Ozon's films exhibit a certain quirkiness, cultivating strategies of ambiguity rather than straight-ahead shock tactics. So the longer view of his filmmaking practice has served to clarify some of its prerogatives. But scholars have so far been reluctant to take on the formal rigor of Ozon's work: while acknowledging that he is something of a stylist, the extent to which the aesthetic design of the films might mobilize their meaning has received little sustained attention. As a result, auteurist assessments of Ozon's cinema do not discern all of its continuities—and more pressingly, the deep structure of its temporal articulations.[2] Fortunately, these difficulties dissolve when we begin to notice the way the films do time.

A survey of Ozon's cinema suggests that issues of time and temporal mediation are signature concerns for the director, developed in formal and thematic variation across his films. Ozon's first feature, *Sitcom* (1998), deliberately foregrounds its temporal markers by offering slightly confounding, and strongly Bunuelian intertitles (such as "Four months earlier" and "Four months later"). Further, the critically acclaimed *Sous le Sable* (*Under the Sand*, 2000) traces a kind of doubled temporality that, like its widowed protagonist, distinguishes between fantasies of the past and realities of the present only reluctantly. Ozon's *8 Femmes* (*8 Women*, 2002) recalls the cinematic past by affectionately reprising Douglas Sirk's melodramatic aesthetics.[3] Finally, *Le temps qui reste* (*Time to Leave*, 2005) proposes a certain temporal play by its very title: while the original French marks "the time that remains," the English title produces a different, and more active, emphasis. This wordplay is a considered detail, rather than an instance of faulty translation: the film's closing images entertain both significations.

But let's return to the film that is the focus of this chapter. At first glance, one might expect *5x2* to be an entirely legible work because it actually announces the terms of its own structure. As the title indicates, the film is comprised of five distinct episodes about two people—specifically, the Parisian couple, Marion and Gilles. These episodes present significant events in the couple's relationship, charting a period of about five years: the film begins with their divorce, and then looks back at a dinner party at their home, the birth of their child, their wedding, and concludes with their first romantic encounter. Transitions between episodes are plainly marked: brief fades separate each section to indicate, by convention, temporal ellipses; further, extra-diegetic music caps each episode, signaling a shift in orientation to the viewer. These are fairly predictable parameters, especially given the prominence of complex chronologies in recent narrative cinema.[4] But there is more to take in here: Ozon's film introduces an element of disturbance into these operations, calling into question the fact of their legibility.

Although we may already know something about the narrative of Ozon's film—that it recounts the story of a marriage, for example, or that it does so via reverse chronology—we cannot say at the outset how exactly its narration will proceed. So, it is useful to examine the film's opening movements in some detail, to see how the ground is prepared for this narrative experiment. In particular, we need to attend to the way the film establishes its narrative terrain, to discover at what point, and by what means, this terrain discernibly mediates temporal issues. This preliminary analysis will illuminate key formal principles while clarifying the way the film directs our engagement with time, as viewers.

5x2 opens in a magistrate's office, with the reading of an official divorce decree. An initial medium-long shot frames a group of people seated around the magistrate's desk: at left is the divorce lawyer, at center is Gilles, and at right is Marion, her face visible in profile. In the background, a man works at his desk: clearly, these proceedings are an everyday transaction, a standard routine of this office. The next shot is a reversed perspective that analyzes the space more specifically: a medium shot of Marion and Gilles, sitting side by side, offers a more direct view of their responses to this event while registering the awkward space between them. (See fig. 3.1.) Once again, slight movements are perceptible in the background of the frame, as people walk back and forth in an

Figure 3.1. Lawyer's office. From *5x2* (François Ozon, 2004).

adjoining office; as previously, this detail effects a subtle contrast between the particularity of Marion and Gilles's situation, which is tense and emotionally fraught, and the brisk, ongoing activity of the world around them. As the magistrate continues to read, new framings emphasize the distance between the couple even more strongly by presenting Marion, and then Gilles, in separate and successive medium close-ups. Finally, the meeting concludes with the couple's agreement to the terms and the signing of the document.

But the next narrative turn is jarring. Cutting to a different location and to an event already in progress, an odd, emphatic framing, tilted sharply downward, presents two pairs of feet walking up a hallway. The angle gradually adjusts to reveal Marion and Gilles, side by side, proceeding along a hotel corridor. What is striking about this transition from one space to another is that it commences *in medias res*: the new mobile framing, simultaneously tilting and tracking, conveys a strong sense of forward movement and purposive activity. At the same time, the somewhat unorthodox camera angle, which settles into a conventional framing only gradually, is slightly disorienting, and draws attention to the transition itself as a minor rupture.

If there is a deliberate awkwardness about these formal maneuvers that asks us to take note of them, the scene that follows certainly confirms the sense that somewhere between the magistrate's office and the hotel, a piece of time and a significant section of the exposition has been elided. As the scene unfolds, it becomes clear that Marion and Gilles have arrived at the hotel for a sexual encounter—a notion that hardly follows from the divorce proceedings, shown previously. This development is unexpected because it runs counter to the aim of those proceedings—the official dissolution of Marion and Gilles's relationship—but more curiously, it fully belies the attitude and comportment of the couple throughout that sequence, which was remarkable for its perfect impassivity.

Our first impulse in interpreting a scene like this might be to construe it as a prior moment in time, as a dalliance occurring well before the couple's separation and divorce. This is to situate the scene within a logical progression, aligning its content within a more conventional set of expectations. But the film refuses to be read in this way, and insists, somewhat perversely, that the two scenes are successive. In fact, the dialogue is responsive to this dilemma and explicitly confirms the scene's relative temporal placement for us. When Marion emerges from the bathroom undressed, but wrapped in a towel, this exchange ensues:

> GILLES: Have you put on weight?
>
> MARION: No.
>
> GILLES: Why the towel? Because we're not married now?
>
> MARION: I don't know.

Once we accept that this scene follows directly from the last, it becomes necessary to assess its parameters differently. This is not a step backward in time, but rather a refusal of convention; the usual order of things is simply not observed here. Evidently, it would be easier to make sense of the scene if the film were more forthcoming in its detail: with respect to narrative presentation, there has been no departure from the magistrate's office, no discussion between the couple, no checking in at the hotel's front desk. Instead, the film effects a temporal ellipses, passing over these events to depict Marion and Gilles carrying out a decision whose origins remain obscure: given the idiosyncratic nature of this choice, the factors that motivate it are conspicuously displaced. Significantly, then, what we may initially read as a temporal reversal is actually a progression whose terms are so loosely articulated as to resist immediate chronological placement.

Indeed, the question of what has motivated this tryst, and the extent to which it was agreed on consensually, proves critical in what follows. Although Marion initiates their lovemaking, she soon breaks away from Gilles, first calling the idea "ridiculous" ("This is ridiculous. I should never have come here. It doesn't make sense."), and then, when Gilles persists, screaming for him to stop. What has led to, or would explain, this scene becomes an urgent matter as the encounter escalates into sexual violence: whether determined by a spontaneous decision, or as a deliberate act of irreverence, things have gone completely and terribly wrong.

Crucially, we need to reckon with the difficulty of this scene, or with the degree to which both its presentation and content are radically disquieting. By presenting this episode so early in the narrative, virtually unsupported by contextualizing detail, the film makes it into something that demands interpretation: Whose idea was this? Why did Marion agree to it in the first place? Yet *5x2* does not equivocate about the brutality of the scene, or reduce its implications: repeated, close framings of Marion's face, disconnected and tearful, plainly convey her suffering. Thus, the film effects an uneasy conflation of terms that puts pressure on the task of interpretation itself and on the temporal background—the unstated past—that makes this present possible. At the same time, it raises questions that run in the opposite direction, but remain integral to our experience: how could any background, or knowledge of the past, make this act explicable, or offer an adequate justification?

If the point being made here is yet too oblique, the film restages it, in variation, within the narrative itself. Toward the end of the scene, Marion reemerges from the bathroom to find the hotel window wide open and Gilles nowhere in sight. She assumes the worst, rushing forward to look for his body on the street below. After a moment, Gilles's voice is heard to remark acidly, "You think I'd kill myself over you?" and a quick reverse shot reveals him standing near the door, coolly observing Marion's movements. Like the temporal shuffle presented previously, the film constructs another situation that strongly calls for interpretation—and in this case, where a seemingly empty room and an open window are the most salient elements. But it should be noted that *5x2* fundamentally complicates this assessment: first, the film suggests, by Gilles's ruse, that our best guess about a situation is susceptible to deception, and to the unthinkable; second, it also shows us, by Marion's actions, that interpretation is a kind of presumption, a claim to know something in advance, that inevitably limits the possibilities of its object and for this reason may fall into error about it. By the spareness of its materials, *5x2* relates such considerations to matters of temporality; leaving so much open to question, the film gestures toward a past that might explain these events, but stops short of making complete assurances.

It's a not a coincidence that *5x2* should begin this way, conflating notions of reversal and regression, and exposing an uncomfortable interface between intimacy and violence. As a film that operates by reverse chronology, and which intends this device as more than an empty formal gesture, the opening section shares in this overarching design, setting the agenda for what follows. At a basic level, this material heightens our awareness of time, as viewers, by presenting us with interpretive problems that make questions of temporal ordering a locus of their meaning. As I will detail in the discussion to follow, these scenes correspond to the larger structures of the film, which deploy reverse chronology to similar ends. But more emphatically, the real achievement of this opening section is that it shakes us out of our indifference about time, preempting the possibility that we might take up the remainder of the narrative unmindful of the events we have just witnessed. In this sense, *5x2* begins to show us, however disconcertingly, how temporal experience matters to us, by offering up its contradictions, its uncertainties, and dangers as ineluctable aspects of our engagement. In other words, questions of time are not merely a feature of the film's content, or a limited issue that may be extrapolated from the narrative only retrospectively; rather, *5x2* sets these questions directly to work on us, as viewers, so that our experience of the narrative is enframed and inflected by temporal considerations.

Examining Reverse Chronology

Thus far I have discussed only the opening section of *5x2*, analyzing two successive scenes that occur before the film's initial movement backward in time. Before turning to the film's next chapter, however, and thus to its first foray into the past, it is useful to briefly consider the nature of reverse chronology itself, looking specifically at the workings of this device.

As a point of departure, we might observe the way reverse chronology relates to film's earliest days and to the unique capacities of the medium. From cinema's inception, exhibitors exploited the trick of *reverse motion* to the delight of audiences: historical accounts of the early Lumières short, *The Demolition of a Wall* (1895), for example, suggest that projectionists might first screen the film conventionally and then replay it in reverse, feeding the filmstrip back through the hand-cranked mechanisms of the Cinématographe. Thus the film's visual interest and novelty, documenting the process by which a wall is toppled by workmen, is effectively redoubled: shown in reverse, the wall seems to rise out of the dust, as though "magically" reconstructed for viewers. Evidently reverse chronology differs from this, involving not the perceptual "trick" of backward motion but rather an encompassing narrative design that presents story events in the opposite order of their occurrence. But in both cases, an effect of defamiliarization is achieved by cinematic means: if the replayed Lumières film utilizes cinematic technology to show us the magic inherent in an ordinary action, films of reverse chronology set the forward flow of film in tension with a backward-reaching narrative, finding unexpected relations between past and present by altering their usual temporal articulation.[5]

Or, we might think of reverse chronology as a modification of classical precepts. Where classical narrative is organized as a forward-moving, goal-directed unity that begins by establishing an initial situation or "cause" (the Apaches are coming; it's time to get out of town) and then goes on to elaborate "effects" (the passengers of the stagecoach encounter many difficulties, including an Apache assault, but are eventually restored to safety), a film like *5x2* runs the opposite course, retreating from an "effect" in the present (a couple's divorce) to its "causes" in the past (a series of formative events in their relationship). On this basis, we should note that each kind of narrative encourages a distinct mode of viewing: if the classical film engages us with matters of "What comes next?" or "Will *x* achieve *y*?," the narrative of reverse chronology poses things somewhat differently, motivating questions like, "Is this why she acted this way?," or "Is this how circumstance *x* came to be?"

This is not to say that conventional chronologies avoid such questions, or conversely, that stories told in reverse are necessarily more complex. At issue here is the way the very structure of reverse chronology organizes our viewing experience, bringing certain lines of questioning to the forefront and thereby accentuating particular planes of viewing activity. On the one hand, reversed narratives immediately confront us with the particularity of their form and with the requirement that they be read differently: by the simple fact of their backward movement, they draw attention to the way formal structures activate narrative material, shaping and delimiting our experience of it. On the other hand, by making narrative engagement a retrospective project that directs us not to a future narrative outcome but to an undefined point of origin in the past, reversed narratives circumscribe the temporal range under consideration to dwell on the rich terrain connecting "past" and "present." This narrowed focus tends to highlight the active interpretive work we do as viewers—that we read a scene in light of information already attained, or discern a film's patterns and repeated elements as they unfold over time.

We can compare this viewing scenario to that of the classical detective film, for instance, which also delves into the past to resolve a dilemma in the present: in such films, a narrative agent directs the investigation and may take credit for resolving it successfully. With reverse chronology, however, the narration itself assumes a retrospective form, leaving the viewer to make connections between its parts and to arrive at appropriate conclusions. This differs again from the temporal mechanism of the flashback, which involves a reflection on the past that is generated by a character's consciousness: though the subjective nature of this device certainly invites ambiguities, it differs from reverse chronology in its orientation so far as it is usually mediated by a governing subjectivity. Thus, the tasks involved in watching any film—such as the comparisons we make between one sequence and another, the linking of character motivation to action, or more generally, the way we continually assess filmic material to situate it in time—are delineated by films of reverse chronology with special lucidity. For these narratives, the forward drive of narrative undergoes an inversion, deflecting narrative agency onto an actively interpreting viewer.

Of course, formal difficulty exists for these narratives (as for all others), as a matter of degree. In the context of experimental cinema, a fascinating case is Anne McGuire's *Strain Andromeda The* (USA, 1992), which reverses, cut for cut, Robert Wise's tale of an invasive alien virus, *The Andromeda Strain* (USA, 1971). This transposition strongly heightens qualities already present in Wise's film, exposing its temporal discontinuities and bristling tensions more plainly; it also unhinges the film's causal logics, disrupting narrative progress and the coherence of shot relations. These effects are unsettling: answers now precede their questions, and causes follow effects, creating the uncomfortable sense that such queries are perpetually unresolved. More broadly, McGuire's film unravels the (already unsteady) reassurances of *The Andromeda Strain*'s closure, generating a narrative arc that leads inexorably back to the crisis, rather than emerging from it.

But McGuire's project is canny in other respects, particularly for the extent to which it manages to sustain a kind of narrative tension. Though the momentum of the original plot no longer serves, the reversed tale remains compelling, forging new and provocative juxtapositions. In part this relates to the tendencies of the source material: Wise's film often relies on images of people looking, and is in some sense about technologies of visualization, as evidenced by the multiplied views offered in matte shots, and by a continual privileging of computer screens, microscopic slide imagery, binocular views, pages of test data, and other visual discoveries. Thus the original film is so much saturated with these visual exchanges, continually shifting between a character and what she or he sees, that a reversal of these procedures somehow retains their narrative energy.[6] In McGuire's retelling, the connections that arise from shot to shot are made illogical and false, and thus undermine the premises of scientific rationality in powerful ways.

Within narrative cinema, however, only a small number of films use reverse chronology as a framing structure, and deployed to less radical ends.[7] A well-known example such as *Betrayal*, for instance (David Jones, UK, 1983) carefully suppresses any confusion that the device might generate. A cinematic adaptation of Harold Pinter's play, Jones's film seeks primarily to preserve the integrity of its source material, emphasizing verbal exchange over formal complexity; indeed, the film's clear structures foreground the long conversational passages of Pinter's screenplay but do not generate particular aesthetic tension.

Betrayal's narrative spans a period of nine years, conveyed in seven separate episodes. Like *5x2*, the film traces a romantic relationship back to its beginnings, but here the narration is highly communicative: each episode begins with an intertitle that positions the segment temporally and in relation to the last ("A year earlier"; "Two years earlier," etc.). Another consistent feature of Jones's film is a single musical theme that recurs between episodes: these brief interludes clearly mark the narrative's chronological divisions and, like an *entracte*, point to the film's theatrical origins. Otherwise, the film reestablishes its players and its settings unambiguously at every turn: by its exclusive focus on three principal characters as they circulate within identifiable locales (a London flat, a favorite pub), *Betrayal* sustains a sameness across its episodes that reduces difference to the single variable of time. This format supports the film's overarching thematics and the content of its dialogue, which evidence a concern with the way repetition discloses a subtle transformation of relationships over time.

Looking to contemporary French cinema, Gaspar Noé's *Irréversible* (2002) is an obvious comparator for *5x2*. An exceptionally graphic tale of violent sexual assault and revenge, Noé's film intensifies the disorienting effects of reverse chronology while capitalizing on the shock value that this revelatory structure may induce. In contrast to Ozon's way of doing time, whose provocations derive from a play of ellipses, *Irréversible* unfolds unblinkingly in extended takes, exploiting the dilation of time rather than its obscurity. The formal contrast between the films tells us much about their underlying interests: as the title suggests, *Irréversible* does not seek to raise questions about time but to insist on its terrible certainties. Unlike Ozon's project, Noé's film eliminates ambiguity rather than sustaining it, electing to make everything horrifyingly explicit.

As these examples indicate, reverse chronology does not necessarily entail interpretive difficulty and may, in fact, function as legibly as chronological ordering. In such cases, it is like classical narrative propelled in the opposite direction, but where this reversal has notable consequences. Because even within a context of coherence, the device induces a distinctive mode of viewing: we might say that narratives of reverse chronology are inherently compelling, quite apart from the stories they tell.

A key factor in the dynamic of reversed chronology may be the films' promise to disclose an originary condition, appealing to a desire to get down to the root of things, to discover the foundations of a situation by our own careful discernment. The effort to locate a cause in the past that might illuminate the present would seem psychoanalytic in its premises, as though the very structure of the films were primed to perform a kind of auto-analysis. But for these films, the suggestion is not that root causes have been hidden or repressed, as such, but that the way they belong to the present is obscured because they are held apart from us, in time.

Temporality and Transition

Returning to Ozon's film, on the basis of its opening sections we can expect *5x2* to approach temporal questions with a kind of reticence that favors ambiguities. To this end, the film's first transition in time is unaccompanied by explanatory cues or intertitles: Marion leaves Gilles in the hotel room and gets on the elevator; there is a brief, intervening fade; a new scene opens, presenting Gilles at home, feeding dinner to their son Nicolas. Extra-diegetic music marks this transition, but does not really facilitate our understanding of it: on the soundtrack, an Italian pop song swells as Marion makes her departure, its exuberance entirely at odds with her attitude of silent resignation. At the same time, the song is an unlikely bridge for the tender domestic scene that follows.[8]

Without an explicit time frame, it becomes necessary to gauge the temporal relation of one scene to the other ourselves, filling in the informational gap that an intertitle might supply. Thus, the fact that Gilles and Marion share a domestic space in the new scene situates it as prior to their divorce; the presence of their child, however, indicates that this must be a fairly recent past. Additionally, that Gilles seems slightly younger-looking, because without a beard, supports this assessment. These arrangements have other consequences, as well: comparing the two scenes, in an effort to place the second chapter in relation to the first, causes us to remark more diffuse relations between them. The new scene forges a sharp contrast at the level of content and form. Gilles's cruelty and selfishness, foregrounded previously, is here replaced by his evident tenderness and patience as a parent. And at the level of the image, where the previous chapter closed with a shot of an elevator door, focusing on its cool metal exterior, the new chapter opens with a close framing of young Nicolas's face, delicately colored and suffused with warmth. Transitional moments like these are invaluable to our analysis because they reflect the film's temporal character most keenly. Surveyed across the film as a whole, such transitions consistently produce visual contrasts and semantic contradictions: put simply, things look different and *mean differently*, from one temporal phase to another.

The shift from the second chapter to the third, for example, effects something comparable: an intimate framing, awash in blue evening light, presents Gilles and his son as they sleep. After an intervening fade, the new scene opens with a long shot of a yellow-lit, hospital corridor; Marion eventually appears, a small figure within the wide frame, evidently pregnant and alone. This transition features pronounced contrasts in lighting, framing and in the kind of space depicted, giving over from private to public spheres; but more substantively, as the new scene proceeds it becomes clear that the real contrast is between Gilles's presence as a devoted parent and his conspicuous absence in this context. So, an already ambivalent characterization is compounded by new information and complicated over time: abandoning Marion during the birth of their child, Gilles is shown to be both responsive and remote, deeply attached and yet oddly disconnected. In this way, each chapter of the film expands on the last by seeming to partially disconfirm it, unfurling a past whose dimensions are discordant and uneasily arranged into a stable picture. In this way, *5x2* asks its viewer to take a nuanced view of its characters and narrative events that is open to their capacity for contradiction, encoding their essential ambiguity as a temporal issue.

A look at the remaining transitions confirms this assessment. The third chapter of the film concludes with Gilles phoning Marion to apologize for his absence: he does not offer an explanation for his actions, simply saying, "It's complicated." The accompanying images are dark and rain-swept, underlining Gilles's remoteness as he telephones from his car: indeed, what emerges most strongly from this scene is a sense of the physical and emotional distance between the couple, reflected by the constrained and separate spaces they inhabit and in the desultory quality of their conversation. (See fig. 3.2.)

This bleak episode, emphasizing silence and separation, opens out in the next chapter to the occasion of Marion and Gilles's wedding—or otherwise, into an episode that opposes the last in key respects because it presents the formation of a union, rather than evidence of its precariousness, and frames this event as a kind of halcyon moment. Notably, what might be rendered in a lesser film as a contrast so artificial as to be unaffecting here transcends these terms by the sheer appeal of its arrangement: the images of Marion and Gilles as they stand before the minister, surrounded by family and friends, are golden-hued and wel-

Figure 3.2. Separation. From *5x2* (François Ozon, 2004).

coming—as though a sun-warmed space had suddenly opened up for us, as viewers. The scene conveys a sense of immediacy, or "presentness," that derives from a felicitous combination of natural light and freshness of mise en-scène: the open, communal quality of the space, bathed in morning sunlight and filled with people, contrasts markedly with Gilles's isolation in the last chapter, and infuses a kind of sensuous detail into these proceedings. (See fig. 3.3.) That this episode serves persuasively

Figure 3.3. A hopeful picture. From *5x2* (François Ozon, 2004).

as a temporal background for the last rests on its sensuous qualities, or the degree to which it produces not just a straightforward account of the marriage ceremony but a strongly affective description of it, to render narrative circumstances as a palpable, unfolding event. In fact, the scene's particular quality of presentness contributes another layer to the film's temporal design, so as to subtly evoke multiple temporalities. First, the sense of a tangible present developed here coexists with our more basic understanding of the scene as belonging to the past. Yet, in important ways the scene is futural, as well: the wedding ceremony, in its warmth and optimism, opens up like a promise, projecting toward the future in all its luminous possibility. At the same time, however, this idealized view of things is qualified by an event we have witnessed already—namely, the reading of the divorce papers in the film's first chapter. Thus, the retrospective framework of *5x2* allows us to see an unfolding present as it reaches for the future—but with the knowledge that this moment and its attendant aspirations are already past. Significantly, while this latter consideration severely limits the former, it does not really reduce its affective power: if anything, our knowledge of the narrative outcome tends to heighten, rather than diminish, the force of this hopeful picture.[9]

As will become clear, Ozon's film specializes in such curious configurations, using the terms of temporal reversal to show us a thing and its counterpoint as they sustain and re-inflect each other. As I have indicated, this tendency encourages a considered assessment of the film's characters and events that acknowledges their divergent shadings. But more pertinently, what demands acknowledgment here is the way one facet of a phenomenon may appear salient in a given context, yet recedes from view over time; correspondingly, what serves as mere background in the present may assume new prominence in the future. This might remind us that the task of interpretation is temporally constituted and therefore always in progress: it is an effort to read the past through the conditions of the present, where this effort is necessarily partial and incomplete because open to future revision. The film's complex treatment of temporality reflects this protean aspect of interpretive experience by forming a close association between the opacity of a situation—its resistance to elucidation—and matters of temporal positioning. In other words, temporal flow is bound to a parallel movement toward understanding, where the viewer is the center and active mediator of these trajectories.

These ideas help us with the film's final transition, which follows from a further—and entirely unanticipated—reversal. To this point, *5x2* has emphasized the inconsistency of Gilles's character, making him an unlikely object of sympathy: an emotional and sexual bully, yet also a caring parent, Gilles's relationship with Marion has seemed somewhat one-sided so far as narrative events have tended to display his bad conduct. Correspondingly, Marion's character is equally ambiguous, but expresses itself differently: she exhibits a kind of quiet strength that is difficult to fathom, and that is easily mistaken for passivity. Yet in this case, the transition extends from a scene that thoroughly complicates this picture. After a joyful wedding celebration, Marion and Gilles retreat to their hotel room, where drunkenly, and comically, Gilles falls asleep before Marion is undressed. Finding her new husband thus indisposed, Marion looks upon him smilingly and leaves to stroll about the hotel grounds. She observes, from a distance, two other couples still at the wedding reception: her parents are on the dance floor; Gilles's brother also remains, chatting with a young waiter who is clearing tables. But here things take an abrupt turn: Marion walks away to a secluded section of the grounds where she encounters another guest in the hotel—an American actor spending his last evening in France. With little fanfare, Marion and the American have sex; after a brief temporal ellipsis, Marion is seen racing back to the hotel room, fearful of discovery. She finds Gilles there, still sleeping peacefully.

What is interesting about this narrative development, beyond its surprising aspect, is the way it causes us to reflect upon the film's narrational strategies to gauge their reliability. First, there is the fact of the scene's implausibility: Marion's actions appear unmotivated because are inexplicable by narrative evidence. Further, the film seems deliberately to frame this encounter on the order of a cliché, complete with artificial staging: initially, the scene is verdant and moonlit, too perfectly composed for credibility; subsequently, Marion's hasty return to the hotel room occurs in the early light of dawn, as though enacting the terms of a familiar fable. Given these details—that the episode clearly departs from our understanding of the film's characters so far, and seems even to observe an incongruous set of aesthetic procedures—the thought occurs that perhaps this episode did not "really happen" at all, but rather is produced by a character's consciousness. Is this merely a fantasy that Marion imagines, or a fragment of Gilles's dream?

This interpretation is hard to justify in light of the film's obtaining operations. Far from encouraging this sort of subjectively inflected episode, *5x2* has consistently refused such revelations, remaining reserved on the question of character psychology while dwelling, observationally, on the surface: recall, for instance, the open hotel window in the film's first chapter, and the suicidal impulse that it alludes to but never corroborates. And if *5x2* sometimes offers privileged views to its viewer, such as glimpses of Marion's expression unseen by those in the diegesis, those instances do not qualitatively differ from the construction of shots elsewhere. So if the encounter between Marion and the American is not an utter fabrication, yet seems to pull away from an otherwise objective narrative fabric, we need to make sense of it by other means—and specifically, by returning once more to the film's propensity for contradiction, its way of holding apparent oppositions in tension to reveal their coexistence and interplay.

Scrutinizing the terms of the transition itself provides some insight: the shots in question involve a close framing of Marion, having returned to the hotel room, embracing Gilles and telling him she loves him; after a short fade, the new chapter opens with a wide exterior shot of a beach, initially unoccupied. A figure moves into the frame, and is then joined by Gilles. This is a woman who is not Marion; evidently the film's movement into a deeper past finds Gilles in a previous relationship. It's not difficult to perceive the "match" between these chapters, even though they represent distinct temporal phases: if Marion substitutes another man—a stranger, in fact—for Gilles on their wedding night, here her place in the narrative is taken by a woman we do not recognize, observing a related substitutional logic. This comparison does not make Marion's behavior more legible, or directly equate the two situations: while Marion's actions were unsanctioned in the last chapter, the woman who appears here is, in fact, Gilles's girlfriend. But attending to the shadings of the transition allows us to see these details as part of a broader pattern that enlarges itself over time: we know that Marion will eventually replace Gilles's girlfriend, and that another woman, named in the film's first chapter, will ultimately replace Marion.

Similarly, the remarkable reversal that Marion's actions manifest—fundamentally revising our understanding of her relationship with Gilles and the balance of power between them—does not produce a contradiction but rather a more comprehensive picture. Paradoxically, Gilles's distance from Marion and his closeness to their child somehow sustain each other; likewise, Marion's silence and her suffering are held in place by an astonishing capacity for willful action. Notably, the film does not develop these events so as to make their consequences explicit: there is no suggestion that Gilles ever discovers Marion's infidelity; instead, this remains as an unacknowledged, and oddly suspended, episode. Reflecting back on the dreamlike quality of Marion's encounter with the American, we can make better sense of its appearance by observing that it possesses the fugitive quality of memory: hovering uncertainly between fact and fiction, it may be that the encounter looks the way it does because, despite its significance, its reality has been suppressed within Gilles and Marion's marriage. Thus, the film's temporal course comes to include situations that are not strictly bound by objective time, but are more loosely located by the affective experience that they generate. Taken as an event that occurred, but which receives little objective confirmation (no one witnesses it, or learns of it subsequently), Marion's encounter with the American belongs to a succession of narrative events, and yet cannot be placed unproblematically as the "cause" or "effect" of any particular instance.

From this vantage point, we can discern the deep imbrication of the film's temporal and hermeneutical coordinates: on the one hand, *5x2* demands an attitude of openness from its viewer that asks us to revise our interpretation of things over time; on the other hand, its textual organization encourages a holistic conception of time itself that comprises both objective and subjective registers. So if *5x2* suggests that interpretation is temporal, and concomitantly, that temporal experience is subject to multiple interpretations, there remains to examine the rich and variegated descriptions of temporality that the film offers elsewhere. Having attended to the way time is articulated across the film's chapters, and hence across discrete temporal phases, I want to look closely at three representative episodes, each of which the film presents as temporally continuous.

In-Between: Reading the Temporal Interval

The first episode involves a dinner party at Marion and Gilles's home, where Gilles's brother, Christophe, and his new boyfriend, Mathieu, are their guests. A dinner-table discussion about relationships and fidelity turns sour when Gilles relates a story from the past: his anecdote concerns an occasion over a year ago, where, in the aftermath of a friend's wedding, he participated in an orgy while Marion watched from the sidelines. Conspicuous in Gilles's recitation is the extent to which the story is directed at Marion, who knows it already: the shots, alternating between the pair, work to emphasize her reaction; further, Gilles often frames his remarks as though she were the only listener ("You wanted to sit there and watch, just watch.") In its retelling, the story effectively, and painfully, revives a past dynamic in the present, once more situating Gilles in an active role while Marion passively observes. And for viewers, of course, Gilles's anecdote acquires special resonance as the film proceeds, when the terms of Marion's own infidelity are later presented for consideration.

The section that follows is even more striking in its evocation of temporality, unfolding as a protracted and wordless interlude that is overlaid by music. A wide framing initially presents Gilles and Mathieu, seated at frame left, while Marion and Christophe dance, at frame right.

Though Gilles and Mathieu are talking animatedly, their conversation is dropped out; instead, nondiegetic music (it might also plausibly arise from the diegesis) dominates the scene, seeming to motivate both camera and figure movement. These arrangements produce the sense that things have been slowed down to permit detailed observation: the steady camera moves continuously, passing leisurely from one pair of people to the other; along the way, it notes slight gestures and shadings of facial expression, as though pursuing a study of the small exchanges that comprise human interaction. Eventually, Mathieu rises from his chair to join Marion and Christophe as they dance. This detail would not attract particular notice, except that it pointedly recalls, and revises, the terms of Gilles's story at the dinner table: here Marion dances with two men, while Gilles observes. Thus, the status of the anecdote, as a recollection of the past, is quietly called into question: it is not a matter of the story being true or false, as such, but that it might be an account of Marion's sexual experimentation rather than Gilles's. Characteristically, the film does not privilege one interpretation over the other, but instead preserves a productive ambiguity: the past remains as a suggestive middle ground, sustaining divergent possibilities.

Interestingly, the kind of description effected within this scene attends to the details of a temporal interval rather than to any particular event: sound and image combine to convey an experience of an evening as it winds down, the indeterminate phase after dinner but before the end, the pleasure in lingering over a last drink, before leaving. This is to dwell on a kind of time that is more usually elided, an in-between phase where "nothing happens" but that nonetheless distills the mood of an evening. We might call this a deliberate saturation of time that seeks to reveal its affective texture; by paring away the scene's narrative content (such as verbal exchange) to emphasize its basis in feeling (subtle relations between characters), Ozon's film yields an experience of time that is supple and immersive and whose descriptive force is palpable to viewers.

The second episode is one that we have touched on already, and concerns Gilles's absence during the birth of his son. This circumstance is delineated through a series of shot alternations, presenting Gilles at his office, at a restaurant, and finally in his car, while Marion endures at the hospital. It is worth attending closely to the film's articulations for their complex treatment of temporal experience. Initially, Gilles receives a call from Marion: he assures her that he will leave his office and join her at the hospital ("Don't worry; I'll be there soon."). But any sense of a predictable progression—or of Gilles's personal reliability—is ruptured by the succession of shots that follow. An image of Marion being wheeled into the delivery room cuts rapidly to an incongruous shot of a restaurant table; here, the camera focuses on a pair of hands cutting into a plate of steak, a half-finished glass of wine at left. After a moment, the camera tips up to identify the diner as Gilles: he eats with energy and appetite, and appears in no particular hurry.

The next framing is more distant and implies a brief, temporal ellipsis: now the camera observes Gilles through the restaurant window, his meal consumed and glass empty, as he smokes a cigarette and lingers over coffee. The camera tracks in slowly, bringing Gilles's face into closer proximity, but crucially, the new, shifting composition fails to make his expression or attitude more comprehensible. Instead, it actually emphasizes the fact of his enclosure and separation: as the camera rolls forward, we begin to notice the intervening surface of the windowpane, reflecting the activity of passersby on the street. Similarly, the diegetic sound that accompanies these images is rooted *outside* the space Gilles occupies, relaying the clamor of city traffic. Though Gilles's face is eventually framed in close-up, his glance is averted—and correspondingly, just as the mobile camera comes to rest, the image cuts back to the hospital and to Marion, as she lies on the delivery table. In a comparable way, subsequent shots of Gilles as he sits in his car place him as a remote figure: pictured through the car's windshield and partially obscured from view by the lashing rain, Gilles is set at a remove, and cannot be brought into legibility.

Taken together, these stylistic maneuvers effect a deliberate movement toward an object that is finally frustrated, pursuing a more concentrated viewpoint that is ultimately refracted and dispersed. By this, the film's formal details show us how the very process of seeking engenders its own difficulties, to find itself turned away from its object, distracted or excluded from it. Yet this section has more to show us, again aligning matters of interpretive difficulty with those of temporal experience. To this end, this sequence conveys more than a simple alternation between spaces over an unfolding time span: specifically, it demarcates a rift between two sides of a shared situation, producing descriptions of two very different experiences of time as they occur simultaneously. On the one hand, there is the impending or *inevitable time* that Marion experiences before the birth of her child—a kind of time that cannot be rationalized or parceled out, but must be lived or suffered through, as duration. On the other hand, there is the time that Gilles is killing, or using up, while he dines at the restaurant, unwilling or unable to meet his commitments. We might observe that this latter sort of time seems less authentic, or more artificial, because as presented here it seems to function parasitically, in avoidance of something rather than for itself.

Significantly, however, this may come closer to the way we think of temporal experience, in everyday terms: preoccupied with what is most immediately at hand, we focus on the "time until" a given event, or with having "time enough" for a particular activity.

But the more pressing point would be that Ozon's film offers up two options, one cleaved from the other, though constructed as happening at once: time as we *live* it, experienced by the body rather than abstracted from it, set against its indifferent usage—that is, time as we merely spend it or lose it, pass it idly, or hold ourselves apart from it. In a certain sense, what is reprehensible in Gilles's conduct, beyond what is obvious, is here expressed as a temporal relation; though we may sympathize with Gilles's dilemma, it is harder to condone it—because in his detachment, he chooses a kind of stalled, solitary time over its more authentic expression. On this view, it is little wonder that the answering image of Marion, which serves as a counterpoint, should resonate so differently: the intimate framing of her face in profile is remarkable in its purity; unobstructed and diffusely lit, the image seems to enclose the very heart of Marion's experience.

Finally, however, there remains the film's persistent tendency to qualify such oppositions, refusing any unalloyed contrast. To this end, Marion's experience opposes Gilles only in a relative way, because it is not strictly "natural," either: the narrative explicitly establishes that Marion must undergo an induced labor, as is necessary for the baby's safety. By the inclusion of this detail, *5x2* foregrounds another instance—in this case, at the level of content rather than form—of *temporal intervention*: like the film's larger narrational pattern, which sets the forward flow of time against itself, and the various temporal "riddles" within the narrative, which bring us into contact with time's refractory nature, Ozon's film seeks to disclose the nature of temporal experience by submitting it to manipulation, to show us the way such experience is always mediated, transformed, and altered by conditioning contexts.

Off into the Sunset: Renewing a Timeless Image

The last episode brings us to the closing moments of the film. Given the reversed narrative structure of *5x2*, the ending actually marks a relationship's beginnings: the concluding scene presents the "youngest" versions of Gilles and Marion as they meet at an Italian seaside resort. This section clearly establishes certain tensions that exist between Gilles and his (present) girlfriend, Valerie: in the context of this relationship, Gilles appears carefree and unself-conscious, evidently more compatible with the adventurous Marion—who is vacationing alone—than with his pessimistic partner. By this, the film contributes additional shadings to its complex logic of characterization: in this prior incarnation—that is, within a different relationship and at an earlier moment in time—Gilles seems nearly unrecognizable, so far as the situation discloses a different valence of his personality. Yet the film's overriding structure—moving inexorably from "now" to "then" and continually amending its picture of the present with recourse to the past—maintains that this version of Gilles, in its spontaneity and optimism, belongs to the Gilles we have encountered already. In fact, *5x2* challenges us to consider that these very qualities, which seem to contradict our understanding, actually indicate the limits of our assessment: the film's temporal framework asks us to conceive of Gilles's youth and exuberance, not as something that is strictly over and done with, contained and circumscribed as "who Gilles was then," but as more flexible features that obliquely inform the present, constituting "who Gilles is now."

The film's final section begins with an image of Gilles, clambering down a hill on his way to the beach, towel in hand. There he meets Marion, who is also alone. Marion inquires about his plans for the morning, asking why he has not accompanied his girlfriend on a hike as scheduled. Gilles makes a slight reply, and one that suppresses the argument that has ensued the night before: "Valerie went alone. I wasn't up to it. I felt like sleeping in and getting a tan." Notably, the weight of prior knowledge, that is, of conversations and events depicted previously, here resonates most strongly: the spare terms of Gilles and Marion's conversation are inevitably augmented by what we know already. This effect partially accounts for, and is activated by, the long pauses that characterize their exchange:

> MARION: Have you and Valerie been together long?
>
> GILLES: Four years.
>
> MARION: Are you married?
>
> GILLES: Why do you ask?
>
> MARION: I don't know. No reason.
>
> GILLES: No (*pause*). We're thinking about it *(a long pause: 15 seconds)*.
>
> MARION: Shall we take a swim?

This interaction is framed as a continuous two-shot, presenting the pair sitting side by side. (See fig. 3.4.) Gilles's last response, however ("We're thinking about it."), motivates new framings: in the obtrusive silence that follows his answer, the scene cuts to a closer view of Marion, and then of Gilles, before returning to Marion. These shots invite speculation, but do not decisively reward it: if our awareness of what will come to pass between Gilles and Marion pervades this material, lending it significance, the relay of glances itself remains suggestive, rather than specific.

The subsequent shift in perspective is arresting, and once more relates matters of temporality to a range of interpretive issues. Cutting to a reversed angle that frames the couple in long shot, the new vantage point yields a composition that, in its familiarity and perfection as an image, reads as a supreme cliché. Gilles and Marion are pictured against the broad stretch of waterfront, a distant cliff and sailboat just discernible behind them: framed in this way, they literalize the idea of *walking off into the sunset*. The shot is at once so familiar, and so artificial, as to assume the generic contours of a postcard or advertisement: extra-diegetic music enhances this effect, featuring a restrained arrangement of strings and flute that differs qualitatively from the Italian ballads featured elsewhere. (See fig. 3.5.) Indeed, this final and idealized image seems out of place within *5x2*, as though culled from another film with an altogether different sensibility; most clearly, it forms an extremely unlikely point of closure for the narrative that precedes it. One wonders, in the face of this closing image, how exactly to receive it: has the film suddenly swerved

Figure 3.4. Early encounter. From *5x2* (François Ozon, 2004).

Figure 3.5. An enframed cliché. From *5x2* (François Ozon, 2004).

into a conventional, romantic mode—or might it ask us to negotiate the difference between such a mode and its own narrative predilections?

Attending closely to the film's details yields a compelling answer, and one that testifies to the scene's particular self-consciousness. Evidenced here is not just a familiar image that sits uneasily alongside the film's cynical machinations, but a creative conceit, an ironic effect that arises from a deliberate and impossible compression of time. The foregoing sequence of Gilles and Marion at the beach, which leads to this conclusion seamlessly, as temporally continuous, is set in the early afternoon sun.[10] But here Ozon's film presents a temporal event that should logically occur much later, surging forward from the unfolding time of its fiction to capture, however improbably, the precise moment of the sun's setting.

There is in this a joke about closure, a commentary on the arbitrariness of narrative endings that Ozon's film effects by (re-)producing an image that is, in a strict sense, patently false.[11] But this move is important in two other ways. First, as I have suggested, it brings us up against a stock, romantic image, highlighting the gap between the associations that it carries and the tenor of the film overall. The sunset, which usually designates an open-ended and essentially optimistic outcome, here stands as woefully incongruous, because our specific knowledge of the future—that is, all that the narrative has relayed to this point—deforms its usual connotative range. This is not to say that the closing image is unevocative, or that its placement in the narrative fully deprives it of sensuous and semantic force; rather, it achieves an unsettling, compound effect that is the film's signature feature. The sunset imparts not just a conventional meaning, nor one that uniformly opposes it; instead, it lights up a space of hopeful possibility that is unclaimed by the narrative but that nonetheless resonates for it. Put another way, although the overwhelming optimism of the image reads as excessive, and invites us to acknowledge its absurdity, this does not mean that it is unaffecting: in the context of Ozon's film, the sunset registers a doubled idea of romantic aspiration *and* its failure that attains surprising poignancy.

Second, the sunset stands as a monolithic or *timeless image* that the film's rigorous formal terms cannot readily assimilate. To this point, we have reckoned with a filmic structure whose backward movement insists that we actively attend to shifting temporal relations, continually synthesizing past and present. The film has held our engagement in time by presenting its narrative content not just as a chain of consecutive elements, but as events that are temporally mediated, that come together and gather significance over time. In this context, the final image appears as an aberration, producing a picture of time that is nowhere else in evidence; it adheres to an impulse to still or suspend time as a perfect moment, abstracted from flux and flow. Properly speaking, this is more an idea of time than an experience of it; enframed and infinite, detached from the details of the past or their consequences for the future, this is what time looks like conceived as a romantic, waning present. Thus, the sunset here produces a strong contradiction because, as a fixed, generic image, it operates by assumptions that are quite alien to the film's workings.

But we should recall that *5x2* has sometimes appropriated clichéd imagery so as to undermine our expectations of it: consider, for instance, the fanciful quality of Marion's tryst with the American and the way it seems to observe an incompatible story-telling logic. Similarly, on this occasion a conventional term is deployed, but does not play out predictably: we might say that the closing sunset is made timely by its integration into the film's formal design, where it signals "the end" of a story that is also its beginning. Thus, its status as a generalized image set outside of time is sharply modified, because it is put to work again by the film's encompassing structures. As the final image of Ozon's film, the sunset elicits a complex temporality, mediating a future told already, experienced as past, but offered up for contemplation now, within an unfolding present.[12]

The film's conflation of "beginning" and "end" is not just a formal flourish, but a meaningful configuration for the narrative itself. Specifically, it invites us to regard Marion and Gilles's relationship as one that has always borne the seeds of its own destruction—because in its retrospective survey, the film has located patterns of interaction and transgression, discernible over time, which relate plausibly to the relationship's failure. But for viewers, it's hard to say that *5x2* really resolves these premises, or indeed, that this kind of clarification has ever been the film's project. Although the events depicted by the narrative are recognizable rites of passage—the couple's first meeting, their wedding, the birth of their child, and so on—and might therefore be considered "representative," these incidents are oddly incomplete and yield few certainties. In fact, this material unfailingly foregrounds the narrative's limits, or what it does not show us, by alluding to more extensive circumstances that lie outside of reach.[13]

So if the film's backward structure sheds new light on things, uncovering the richness and permeability of temporal experience, it does not pretend to show us all there is, or to finally disclose "the big picture." If anything, *5x2* strongly counters this idea by leaving so much unsaid and unseen. By showing us how one moment in time may extend and reprise another, and how apparent contradictions prove, on reflection, to sustain a common situation, Ozon's film formulates an argument against the linear logic of cause and effect, loosening the hold of assumptions made on this basis.

Because time is not merely a residual issue for *5x2*, but an encompassing mode of articulation, we need to think about the idea of temporality that the film offers, as well as its wider implications. The film's reversed narrative structure affords an experience of time that is, intuitively speaking, other than usual: by the simple strategy of chronological reordering, *5x2* effectively defamiliarizes time, wrenching it from its conventional place in the narrative background where it often facilitates coherence. For viewers, this structural shift causes us to notice time—which means noticing our engagement with it. The backward form of Ozon's film does not simply "tell" time, in a secondary way, but makes it the engine of narrative investment: it shows us the work of time—the way narrative situations are mobilized and transformed by it—and also the way time *works on us*, as viewers, to motivate and reward our engagement. This returns us to the idea, named at the outset, that narratives of reverse chronology in certain ways mimic the mechanisms of hindsight, to reveal the origins or root causes of things with unprecedented clarity. This is to expect such narratives to put a defamiliarizing framework to familiarizing ends; ultimately, their upending of conventional temporal coordinates arrives at greater coherence, delivering a satisfying solution for an obtaining narrative problem. But *5x2* is clearly motivated otherwise than this, and takes up the device with unusual self-consciousness. Indeed, Ozon's film seems to have borrowed the strict symmetries of reverse chronology so as to disclose compelling alternatives: as we have seen, the film's affective temporal descriptions frequently overflow their chronological contexts, or do not matter to them; similarly, in its backward movement, *5x2* actually pursues an ambiguous temporality, revealing the silent force of the past in the present, and the way it shows up, looking unfamiliar, as the future.

4

Enduring Time

Temporal Duration in Tsai Ming-liang's *What Time Is It There?*

> What then is time? Provided that no one asks me, I know.
> If I want explain it to an inquirer, I do not know.
>
> —Augustine, *Confessions*

It is not unusual, in a public place, to ask someone the time: stopping a stranger to make this sort of request is a familiar practice, and one that ensures, by its sheer neutrality, a certain range of response. At a minimum, one will actually learn the time, or whether the stranger is able to report it; more promisingly, however, the question may lead to a fuller discourse between two people, serving as a prelude to greater intimacy. It is in this sense that asking about the time functions as a device, or a transparent excuse, that is not an end in itself so much as a means to closeness and contact with others. Asking the time is a public act that may lead to more personal communication; it safely facilitates new social relations by cloaking these in objective questioning.

This thought brings out a subtle correspondence between temporality and human proximity—marking the way that an inquiry about time may also mask an unspoken desire for contact with others. Specifically, this configuration will help us to consider a further case study whose very title formulates a temporal question: Taiwanese director Tsai Ming-liang's eighth feature, *Ni neibian jidian*, or *What Time Is It There?* (2001). This concern with time and proximity not only furnishes much of the film's subject matter, appearing legibly along its surface, but, as I will argue, their correspondence is built into the film's very design, conspicuous and consequential for our viewing experience.

The Experience of Time as Duration

In the preceding chapters we have examined cinematic temporality as an effect of chronological structures, analyzing in particular the dramatic leaps in time produced by narrative flashbacks and flash-forwards, as well as the effects of reversed narration and temporal ellipses. In what follows, I will look at a different set of stylistic procedures tied to the recently designated category of "slow cinema," and strongly associated with the aesthetics of contemporary Taiwanese film practice, analyzing the combined formal effects of static framing, deep space, and the long take.[1] In place of an intricate play of time sequences, what matters for this kind of cinema is the experience of temporal duration, or the unfolding of time enframed within a single, layered space. This is to shift in emphasis from the primacy of editing structures—time dynamically articulated across images, mobilizing temporal nodes of "before" and "after"—to an unhurried evocation of time, attaining less to narrative order than to sustained temporal description. Such films linger on the interval between "before" and "after," observing the rich and approximate terrain of "meanwhile" rather than a more conventional temporal scheme. Where mainstream film style endeavors to manage time, paring away what is extraneous to narrative progression because "nothing happens," and correlatively to manage space, clarifying pertinent detail via selective framings, our encounter here is with a deliberately protracted form that imposes new demands on viewers.

Beyond the explicit temporal question posed by its title, *What Time Is It There?* asks us to be mindful of time in other ways: the film's calculated formal design demands a particular kind of engagement from us, calling attention to the texture and tenor of our temporal experience. This effort to induce a heightened awareness of time, or to reflect the experience of it differently, also forges a quiet commentary on conventional storytelling procedures: as we shall see, Tsai's film unsettles the workings of familiar temporal markers to expand their usual semantic range.

Intransigent Time: Engaging the Film's Opening Movement

What Time Is It There? is a triadic narrative featuring three players: a young watch-seller (Hsiao-Kang) who works on the esplanade above downtown Taipei; his mother, widowed in the film's opening scenes; and a girl (Shiang-chyi) who purchases a watch before leaving for Paris.[2] As the film drifts from one character to the next, it traces subtle correspondences across these lives that relate, in different ways, to time. But more substantially, Tsai's film pursues a productive tension between its fixed framings and the leisurely temporal unfolding that they enclose. By this, it outlines a way of coping with temporal ambiguity, locating a deep coherence between the limitations of our perspective on the world and the way that we abide, with others, within it.

Our analysis begins with a consideration of the film's opening sections, attending to the way that *What Time Is It There?* initiates its contact with viewers. To this end, the first shot institutes both the compositional strategies and the kind of pacing that will characterize the film overall. The film opens with a static framing of a deep space, divided into three distinct spatial zones. The composition strongly favors shades of green: the walls and objects are similarly tinted, as though the space were infused with a verdant stillness. Closest to the camera, in the foreground, a small table stands at right; in the middle ground, at left, is a small cooking area from which a man emerges with a dish of hot food. In the farthest background, again set to the right, a doorway is visible that may lead outside. The man carries his dish to the table and sits, leaving his meal untouched. He lights a cigarette and remains there smoking for some moments. Eventually he returns to the kitchen to call someone's name (his son, "Hsiao Kang"); when no one answers, he resumes his seat at the table. (See fig. 4.1.) Finally, the man walks to the back of the space and steps outside, still visible through the outer doorframe. He moves a potted plant and stands smoking, his face in profile.

This single shot lasts three minutes and thirty-nine seconds, depicting very little. It presents two ordinary actions that apparently amount to nothing: a meal is served, but not eaten; a name is called, but without response. What is highlighted, then, is the passage of time unchecked by consequential happenings: this seems a blank, uneventful time, an experience of sheer duration. In contrast to the formal economies of classical narration, where time is compressed or pared away in the service of dynamic narrative activity, here the unfolding of time assumes greater prominence, to become the subject of the scene. Indeed, this sense is reiterated most clearly by the trivial act of smoking a cigarette: here is

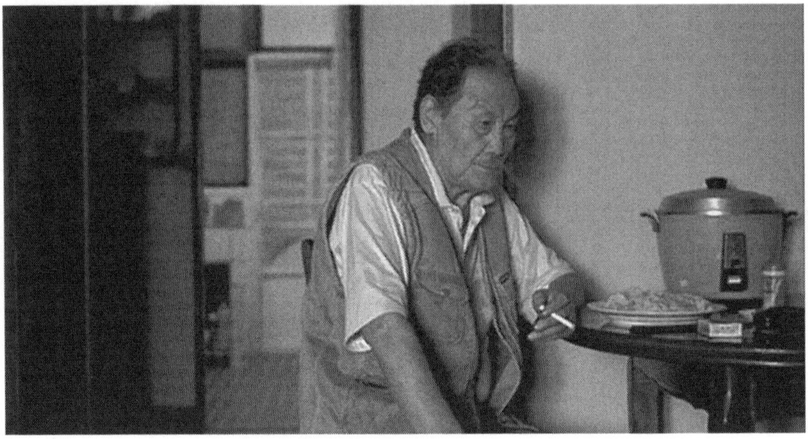

Figure 4.1. Opening scene from *What Time Is It There?* (Tsai Ming-liang, 2001).

another "nonevent" that lasts nearly the length of the shot, marking time wasted or spent for itself.

As a study of particular circumstances, the shot dwells on the surface of things rather than seeking penetrating insights. On the one hand, the image is carefully composed to observe the man's pathway through the space, and in this way makes him its focal point; yet on the other hand, his presence seems nearly incidental to the composition because it receives so little emphasis. The framing does not shift to accommodate his movements or to bring them into focus; at the same time, the camera does not grow inattentive, or drift away, to locate a "true" narrative object. Instead, the framing offers an unwavering observation of the space, pictured in its everyday usage: this is what life looks like unpunctuated, free from dramatic embellishment.

If the longevity of the shot encourages us to interpret it, this task is certainly not a transparent one. Although the man is clearly lost in thought, it is hard to gauge his silence, to place it as meaningful or arbitrary. As depicted here, the man is but one element of a multilayered composition: his face is not open to examination; his glance is often averted and unreadable. Whether we understand these aesthetic arrangements as an effort to preserve ambiguity by the restraint and distance that they impose, or conversely, as a flattening out of ambiguity, as though to eclipse it by ordinariness, our engagement with the image can only respond to its formal terms in ways that tend to deflect our usual modes of questioning. Faced with an image that promises little in the way of conflict or action, that remains indeterminate, refusing full articulation—and yet that obstinately *persists* onscreen, demanding our attention—it becomes difficult to uphold expectations of narrative agency or outcome in the usual sense. Instead, we need to respond to the particular viewing situation that the image sets up, suspending the wish for a precise narrative object to assume a slightly different stance that *shares in* the kind of temporal experience that the image describes. Provisionally, we might call this an attitude of patience, or even endurance, where our relation to the image, as viewers, is held open to the stretched-out, tarrying time that we find there. By consequence, the guiding question with respect to the image may be something like, "What should I take from this situation?" rather than, "What exactly is the man doing or thinking?" This interpretive shift has an important counterpart: we begin to regard each shot as its own temporal complex; like a theatrical act, or the distinct movements of a musical composition, each shot offers a unique working through of time, yet also serves the larger narrative project. These static framings, by their formal rigor, exert a kind of hybrid energy, opening up a wide interpretive space while self-consciously containing it. In any case, to remain with the image in this way, bound to its steadiness and silence, requires an unusual receptiveness to the terms of its unfolding that does not foreclose its possibilities.

The second shot answers the first, challenging us to grasp the relationship between them. This is a medium shot of a young man, seated alone in the back of a moving vehicle: he holds a container wrapped in brightly colored cloth on his lap and a pair of long reeds in his left hand. The composition is orange-hued, as though taking its light from the vivid object that he carries. As the shot proceeds, the status of this object is clarified for us: evidently, the young man bears the ornaments of a funeral, including a canister of ashes that he addresses directly ("Dad, we're going through the tunnel. You have to follow us, okay?"). In contrast to the first shot, this image is charged with energy and mobility: the roar of traffic pours in through the open window; a stream of oncoming cars, approaching and rushing past, appears through the windshield. But more pressingly, what is unresolved in the first image is now oddly inverted: this is the young man named in the first shot, but not seen; he has emerged out of absence to become the subject of the image. Correspondingly, the older man featured in the first shot has suddenly been displaced, or perhaps better—*contained*: he, too, is "present" in this second shot, though now as a collection of ashes.

In this respect, the relationship between the first image and the second—between father and son, or past and present—comes to concern the inherence of one in the other: in fact, the second image seems lit up by the past, suffused by the orange glow of the funerary ashes. Yet this is not quite our first impression of these details, as viewers: initially, we must reckon with the dramatic rupture between the images, the abruptness with which the unfolding present of the first shot is swallowed up by the second, suddenly set at a significant remove in time without warning or explanation. In general, the dilemma presented here is a commonplace routine of editing—a consequence of time elided, or dropped out, of the narrative exposition. But as will become clear, the film aligns this sort of temporal break with issues of presence and absence, and with the particular matter of the accessibility of the past in the present. This pertains to the visibility of the past *and* our capacity to recognize it under new conditions: to read these shots, and to make sense of their compound meaning, involves the tacit acceptance of temporal relations that may elude our grasp, because they are subject to unexpected transformation.

The third shot develops this point quite lucidly. Like the first image, this is a complex composition, but here the action is set at a considerable distance from the camera, narrowly framed at center between two tall rows of cabinets (for storing funeral ashes). The players appear in the farthest plane of this tight, vertical space: a man wearing a bright ceremonial gown is visible; the young man from the previous shot stands on a stool, reaching up to set his container of ashes into the uppermost section of the cabinet. As he steps down, a third figure (a woman, his mother) becomes discernible behind them. A brief ceremony is conducted, still observed from this remote vantage point; finally, the participants bow as the service moves toward its conclusion.

Even at this preliminary stage, the film articulates a subtle point about the remains of the past and their mode of occurrence in the present; the funeral ceremony that this last shot presents seems to concede to the past's obdurate character, its way of remaining just out of reach. Given the richness of this material, it is useful to recapitulate the three temporal modes that the film has described already, as three successive shots: first, there is the steady, "thickness" of time in its unbroken unfolding; second, the sudden transformation of past into present, and the traces of one carried forward to the other; and, third, there is the strong suggestion that the formal observance of the past in the present is not an overcoming of distance, but an event that shows us the finitude of our perspective. On the face of it, such observations may seem discrepant because they gesture in several directions at once: How should we understand time as obdurate but somehow transmutable? Or think of the past as *part of* the present and yet always at a distance? These shadings assume greater congruence, however, when we consider the kind of experience that they generate for viewers. What these three shots have in common is their special unwieldiness; each presents a conception of time that is, for one reason or another, a little opaque. Despite their persistence onscreen, and thus the lengthy period we are given to observe their arrangement, each shot refuses full legibility; while we can easily enumerate the various details that the shots present, their point or purpose remains obscure. Thus, the film's opening images raise to perception the essential elusiveness of temporal experience by the interpretive difficulty that they pose; even when offered up for prolonged inspection, time does not lend itself to unproblematic assessment.

A small, but perceptible, disturbance on the image track renders this point forcefully. As outlined above, the third shot depicts a funeral ceremony, pictured at some distance. But significantly, this event is not quite concluded within the duration of the shot; instead, the scene unexpectedly terminates, suspending the players midbow, and replacing the bright image with a sudden blackness or blankness. This transition is unconventionally abrupt, curtailing onscreen action prematurely; moreover, the film does not immediately produce a new image, but rather persists in darkness, effecting a lingering pause that endures for a full seven seconds. Gradually, the blackness opens up—in increments—as a new shot: initially, only a sliver of light bisects the frame, then, the edges of a doorframe can be discerned, as the door opens. Finally, spatial relations are illuminated for us: the camera is positioned at the threshold of one room, looking out into the adjoining space; a single, silhouetted figure hesitates and then passes through the frame, moving from the darkness into a half-lit hallway. This figure is recognizable as Hsaio-Kang, presented in shots two and three. Although it is the middle of the night, he is wakeful; he emerges from his bedroom and heads toward the kitchen.

Rather than moving directly to the narrative import of these details, we need to address the impact of the disruption itself, the way it wrenches us out of the flow of narrative activity to foreground a kind of pause or interval. We might recall a prior film that deploys a similar long take style, but conjoins its filmic segments very differently—namely, Alfred Hitchcock's celebrated experiment in narrative form, *Rope* (1948). In an effort to present the illusion of continuous time, Hitchcock finds a way to mask the (perceptible) transitions from one film reel to the next. To do so, he elects to have the camera drift away from the action at such junctures to focus on a dark object within the frame, such as the back of a dinner jacket. Consequently, the reel changes are smoothed over: the "breaks" in the filmstrip appear naturalized within the diegesis, affording the impression of seamless narrative progression.[3] Clearly, this situation contrasts markedly with Tsai's film, where the rupture in continuity is something that we are expressly asked to notice; yet the comparison remains an instructive one, so far as it sharpens our sense of the latter film's strategies.

Because Tsai's film leaves us in the dark for some moments, it is difficult to define the precise status of this pause in the film's machinations. It's tempting to read the break between shots three and four in terms of familiar narrative structures—that is, to emphasize its resemblance to a long fade, or something like it, differing only in the suddenness of its arrival (it does not "fade" so much as snap into blackness) and its duration onscreen (the pause it effects is elongated; it calls attention to itself). In standard usage, a fade-in is an optical effect that gradually illuminates a new scene out of blackness; conversely, the gradual dimming of a scene as it concludes is called a fade-out. In either case, the device is thoroughly conventionalized within narrative film practice to indicate a break in continuity: as viewers, we recognize that such transitions signal a distinct break in time, often accompanied by a change in location. Considered this way, the enveloping blackness that follows from shot three does look like an abrupt fade-out, marking time passed or elided. And pursuing this line, the drawn-out transition to shot four in certain ways resembles a fade-in, so far as the scene is illuminated little by little by the movement of the door, slowly opening like an aperture.

Yet the more plausible assessment of this break is not as a temporal cue or marker but as a straight cut, followed by an indeterminate temporal phase that belongs to the narrative itself. In other words, this is not a legible temporal indicator, marking a certain lapse in time—although the resemblance is suggestive. Rather, this is a representation of time that is shrouded in inscrutability: this is what time looks like, in its unfolding, before we define or recognize it. Thus, the film opens up a productive rift between "time elided" and "time unfolding": our confusion about the status of these moments responds to their brief conflation, as one version of time gives the appearance of the other. On this view, Tsai's film performs an intriguing inversion of Hitchcock's formal strategies, effecting a different sort of experiment: where *Rope* endeavors to stretch narrative time across a filmic rupture, so as to conceal it, *What Time Is It There?* here presents unfolding time as though it were a temporal gap, or a patch of emptiness on the filmstrip.

Central to this dynamic is its palpable difference from conventional storytelling procedures. Time presented and experienced *for itself* is precisely what disappears from classical narrative exposition; as viewers, we are more accustomed to conventional signposts of time (fades, dissolves, etc.) than to the task of reckoning with it more directly. Thus, the film's initial project is to strip us of familiar assumptions about time so as to challenge our habitual ways of seeing it; in this sense, our doubt and confusion about time—we might say, our need to ask about it—is a preliminary condition that the film sets up, engaging us in a new kind of work, as viewers.

This point invites us to reflect once more on the terms of Bazin's aesthetics, holding their specificities against the details of Tsai's film. On the basis of what we have examined thus far, it is clear that *What Time Is It There?* seeks to preserve, by its long take structures, the sensuous fullness of events in their autonomous unfolding. But as the "rupture" detailed above would indicate, the film also points to the formal margins that enclose such representations, refusing the communicative transitions that conjoin one temporal event to another unproblematically. So this is not unfettered duration, but one that highlights the forms that cultivate it: stylistically, it is more on the side of Welles than De Sica, where the ambiguities of reality sometimes emerge from a tricked perception.

Here Tsai calls attention to the mechanisms of filmic construction and their contractual limits: the film raises the possibility that such mechanisms might suddenly cease or fail, displacing us, if temporarily, from the flow of storytelling into a breach or "hole" beyond the claims of narrative coherence.[4] It's not a coincidence that this formal rift should occur when it does, abruptly curtailing a scene that depicts a funeral ceremony. The film here evokes, at the level of form, what the narrative has sought to describe already: like the sudden blankness that overtakes the scene, blotting out the action, death is the ultimate displacement from time, an intrusive and unforeseen event that raises the edges or limits of temporal experience to new visibility.

That a certain confusion should result from this, concerning the difference between "time elided" and "time unfolding" is not accidental, either: this blurring of terms is finally productive because it tacitly proposes two ways of conceiving the finite and temporal nature of existence. On the one hand, death may be conceived as a radical break or dropping off point; on this view, it is an elision of time, in the old, etymological sense of that word—time "crushed out" or "dashed." Conversely, a very different conception of mortality sees it as intrinsically tied to temporal flow: though appearing as a break or endpoint, death is always ongoing; it is the condition toward which existence tends. *What Time Is It There?* does not aim at once to resolve this contradiction, or to designate a single path of reading: instead, the film insists that we tolerate this dilemma for a while, without presuming mastery; only the experience of time itself, as mediated by the film's particular unfolding, will show us how to respond to it.

These details evoke the kind of ambiguity that preoccupies Merleau-Ponty, and in a related way, Bazin, played out here as a profound temporal uncertainty. Like the fixed viewpoint imposed by the film's static framings, the movement between narrative segments is similarly constrained, effecting a perceptibly impaired or stalled temporal articulation. Thus, for Tsai's film, the question of how pieces of time relate or *belong* to each other, to become mutually constitutive of meaning, is a fundamental one. This issue, conveyed most keenly in moments where language and logic would seem to fail, is continually adumbrated by the film's formal structuring.

Fixing Time: Temporality and Duality

If the opening sections of *What Time Is It There?* work to induce a state of vulnerability or "openness" to time, in viewers, these strategies also prepare the ground for the more overt commentaries on temporal experience that follow. Most clearly, references to time and time-keeping devices recur throughout the narrative, suggesting a deep preoccupation with temporality that afflicts each of the players. This pervasive concern is shown to relate, in different ways, to the experience of loss or isolation: the idea of "fixing" time here assumes a doubled sense, involving both the impulse to control or master time by stilling it *and* the expectation that time might undergo remedy or repair—that somehow, holding it fast might restore displaced conditions of proximity, or intimacy, with others.

As I have noted, the film's protagonist, Hsiao-Kang, works as a street vendor in downtown Taipei, selling watches to passersby. The first view of this busy, urban space presents Hsiao-Kang facing a prospective customer (Shiang-chyi)—a young woman looking for a dual-time watch for her trip abroad. Unsatisfied with the goods on display, she admires only the timepiece the boy is wearing; he refuses to sell it, saying that it would be bad luck because he's in mourning. The girl is unmoved by this explanation ("It doesn't matter . . . I'm a Christian") and persists in her inquiry; finally, Hsiao-Kang agrees to find another watch like it, or to part with his own.

This is the first of three brief conversations between Hsiao-Kang and Shiang-chyi and although these are routine encounters, initiating and completing a retail transaction, they prove formative for the narrative that ensues. For this reason, it makes sense to consider the object that ostensibly motivates this exchange: Hsiao-Kang's conspicuous and desirable dual-time watch. Obviously, the watch itself offers a doubled picture of temporality; it is a measure of time in two places that registers the difference and distance between them. This duality is compounded further by new terms of exchange, as the timepiece is transferred from Hsiao-Kang to Shiang-chyi; unable to find a replacement piece, Hsiao-

Kang sells his own watch, although with some reservation. Now the watch can be said to relate two different time zones (Taipei, where the watch is purchased, and Paris, where the girl will travel) and two separate lives (Hsiao-Kang's life, and his recent loss; Shiang-chyi's travel plans) *and also* a range of assumptions, or world-conceptions that are often received as oppositions (East and West; Buddhism and Christianity). We have seen something of this tension already in the conflation of "time unfolding" and "time elided"—but here the dichotomy relates spatial coordinates as well, and extends to global systems of meaning.

It is worth noting that the film suggests a connection between these characters even before the watch is exchanged: an earlier image of Hsiao-Kang, standing in the hallway of his home, is subtly echoed by a subsequent shot of Shiang-chyi, contacting him by telephone. In both cases, strong, triadic compositions are favored, placing the human figure at center, a stable area to the left, and a bright zone with perceptible movement at frame right. Alongside these similarities, there are evident differences; comparing the two images, we can see that from one to the other the boy is replaced by the girl, the timeframe shifts from night to day, and the location changes from interior to exterior space. Thus, by its compositional prerogatives, *What Time Is It There?* invites us to observe sensuous correspondences across its images, despite their polarized appearance. As will become clear, this dialectic of sameness and difference is a productive one for the film's operations that eventually discloses broader registers of meaning.

Returning to the more particular question of time-keeping, the film has more to say about these matters, as suggested by two salient scenes that follow. In the first of these, Hsaio-Kang appears in a brightly lit store interior, examining new merchandise for his business. The aesthetics of the space are remarkable for their colorful excess: presented in a wide framing, the store overflows with every kind of time-keeping device; further, this crowded composition distractingly registers several distinct clock-movements simultaneously. Most prominent within the frame are the enormous clock faces that hang from the ceiling, set to different times; below, the store's tall shelves are packed with merchandise, while smaller clocks and watches spill over onto every available surface. (See fig. 4.2.) The teeming quality of the composition invites us to think of it as literalizing the idea of space pervaded by time—an emphasis that would certainly seem to cohere with the film's thematic interests. Yet a closer look at the specific terms of the image—the way its overabundance seems calculated and even comical, delivering a perfect welter of visual information—qualifies this impression, suggesting that the image does not reflect "time," as such, but rather an excessive desire to measure it. Put another way, the shot speaks an obsessive relation to temporality, where clocks and watches, in their innumerable forms, assume a fetishized status; that is, the image testifies to the basic unwieldiness of temporality by picturing, within a single setting, so many efforts to contain it. Evidently, there is something sharply compensatory in this, as though the profusion of devices strove to offset the elusiveness of temporality by endless permutation. But this "overregulation" of time, performed by countless timepieces, does not actually capture or consolidate it; rather, the image tends, by its very excess, to diminish reliable formulations such as "standard time" because it presents temporality as dispersed and refracted through multiple iterations.

This thought gains credence from the interaction that follows. Hsiao-Kang brings several items to the counter for purchase and the clerk recommends a new style of watch that claims to be "unbreakable." The appeal of such a watch, one would assume, is its ability to withstand careless treatment: whether knocked or dropped, it will continue to function. The boy examines the timepiece and strikes it across the counter, testing its sturdiness. He pauses to light a cigarette, and then throws the watch to the ground energetically. A small tinkling sound indicates that he has managed to break the watch, or certain of its parts; under extreme conditions, the watch is about as fragile as any other. The clerk retrieves the broken pieces, telling Hsiao-Kang, "Don't go overboard!" And as this exchange suggests, an important aspect of the excess, described above,

Figure 4.2. Time-keeping. From *What Time Is It There?* (Tsai Ming-liang, 2001).

would seem to extend or emanate from Hsiao-Kang himself: a lack of care about time-keeping is clearly not the problem here; instead, *too much* care—an overinvestment in the possibility of holding time, or keeping it—infuses all of the boy's actions, playing out in this scene as the sparest kind of comedy.

The shot that ensues presents Hsiao-Kang once more selling watches in the city square. He appears in the close foreground, standing in half-profile; he leans against a metal railing, striking one of the "unbreakable" watches against the post. The image endures for over twenty seconds, with little variation: at the edge of the wide frame, a stream of people proceed up a flight of stairs, and then cross the square on their way to work; in the far distance, a monk is visible, wearing a flame-colored robe. Apart from this, there is only Hsiao-Kang's impassive stare and the repetitive and pointless (no one approaches him) action of his arm. By this, the shot conveys the quotidian alienation of urban life, presenting Hsiao-Kang as an isolated figure set within a teeming public space. But more precisely, his detached stance and automatized movement betray an unusual accord with the merchandise that he sells: put simply, Hsiao-Kang embodies the regulated rhythms of public time-keeping, as evinced by his fixed gaze and the pendulum-like oscillation of his arm.

A question naturally arises concerning the relation between this shot and the last: how do we reconcile Hsiao-Kang's indifferent stance here with his excessive, overinvestment in temporality, identified previously? I want to suggest that these contrasting attitudes be considered as reciprocally constitutive modes; this dynamic helps us to assess this scene and the overarching tensions of the film as a whole. Whether we conceive of Hsiao-Kang's (pre)occupation as watch-seller as the public expression of his private obsession with temporality—or perhaps as the objective face of a subjective dilemma about time—*What Time Is It There?* asks us to remark the coexistence of private/public, subjective/objective, and to contemplate the correspondence between these divergent modes. However we specify these terms, it is clear that the film emphatically relates acts of affectless, temporal regulation to powerful undercurrents of feeling; like the supersaturated retail space described above, Tsai's film shows us that temporal experience is not reducible to the ways we measure it, or to the devices that hold it in check. Instead, our primary experience of time is that it always gets away from us—despite our best efforts, we cannot say in advance how time will move us because we do not know our share of it.

The shot forges other connections, as well, to propose a perceptible, if still inchoate, alliance between the film's characters. Specifically, the dull clang of the watch, striking against the metal rail, is revised in the next shot, and freshly contextualized: Hsiao-Kang's mother appears at frame left, standing before a food vendor; here the slow, metallic clanging produced by the watch becomes a rapid, purposeful chopping, as the vendor prepares some cooked duck. Although Hsiao-Kang and his mother are pictured in separate spaces, and engaged in distinct activities, there remains this wordless linkage between them: it is as though the sad circumstances that they share—the death and mourning of Hsiao-Kang's father—are manifest in such oblique details, encoded as visual patterns or sonic similarities that resist linguistic expression.

So an attentive viewer will discern a basic structuring principle that sustains these episodes, serving both as an organizational framework for the narrative material and as a locus of its meaning. Effectively, this principle entails two kinds of movement. First and most apparently, the film delineates in successive scenes poignant experiences of isolation faced by each of the characters. Although the players do encounter each other more directly—as when Hsiao-Kang sells his watch to Shiang-chyi, or shares a meal at home with his mother—such interactions are depicted as either failed or fleeting, always falling short of mutual understanding. But *What Time Is It There?* also produces an insistent countermovement, facilitated at the level of form, which discovers small echoes and alliances across shots, such as those specified above. In a comparable way, the film offers up larger rhymes and resemblances across whole narrative strands—as when Hsiao-Kang's sleepless nights in Taipei are reiterated by Shiang-chyi's wakefulness in Paris, or when his sudden Francophilia (manifest by a new admiration for French film and French wine) is paralleled and inverted by Shiang-chyi's persistent homesickness.

What is important about these points of connection is that while they are unremarked by the film's characters, they are readily observable to viewers. In other words, *What Time Is It There?* foregrounds these details by filmic means; it is the film's particular arrangement of material—the way one shot calls forth another, or a common element is highlighted within different contexts—that raises these relations to visibility. Consider, for example, the way two consecutive shots, though in some respects opposed, are forcefully conjoined by formal means. In the first, Shiang-chyi explores an empty hotel corridor. The composition is nearly monochromatic in its grayness, and surveys a blank space; the girl stands before a door, listening; then, she moves to the foreground, opens a window at right, and leans outside. While a more conventional narrative would likely offer a reverse-shot at this point, showing what Shiang-chyi sees, Tsai's film exploits this expectation to produce an "answering" image that signifies differently. Rather than looking out into the external world, the second shot pictures its refusal: here, Hsiao-Kang's mother sits before a glass aquarium in her home, her anguished face outlined by its silvery illumination. The tank holds a large, white fish, which she believes incarnates her husband's spirit; she reaches out to stroke the glass, asking, "Is that you coming back to me? . . . Do you miss me?" Although these shots clearly differ perspectivally, contrasting Shiang-chyi's outward-looking stance with the extreme introversion of Hsiao-Kang's mother, they do create an affective continuity: the pallid tones of the Parisian hotel seem reflected, and concentrated, by the form of the luminous white fish; more substantially, the pair of images suggests a quiet accord from one to the other, likening Shiang-chyi's solitary status in Paris to a condition of intense bereavement. By this the film develops a certain intimacy between the players without naming its exact nature: instead, the graphic match shows us obverse situations, binding the loneliness of "leave-taking" to the abjection of "being left behind."

Thus, the experiences of isolation that the film describes—the way Hsiao-Kang and his mother live together, yet seem estranged, or the way Shiang-chyi's trip to Paris is a painfully solitary one—are presented both as radically separate, lonesome episodes and as belonging together in ways that cannot quite be grasped. The film's project, then, is to show us how such experiences mediate each other and accrue significance, *over time*; in this sense, our experience of the film is a kind of temporal attunement, in which our viewing stance comes to accommodate the deliberative pace of the narrative's unfolding while absorbing the subtle correlations that this pace permits.

We might even suggest that the film's patient observation of detail, activated by our sustained engagement as viewers, brings such correlations into being; were it not for the film's considered formal structuring, and the forbearing attitude it demands by its long, descriptive sequences, these nuances would surely be passed over. Indeed, this thought inspires a still more provocative one that opens the film's procedures to a kind of metaphysics: Under different conditions, would these correspondences exist at all? As we shall see, *What Time Is It There?* comes to reward the idea that human isolation, or exclusion, might be countered by new ways of seeing. That is to say, Tsai's film offers itself as a model for a renewed receptivity: by its meditative framings, the film shows us what it is to really notice the world, and the surprising points of contact it sustains.

These issues are clarified further when we examine the larger-scale rhymes that the film develops, arising from Hsiao-Kang's particular obsession with time-keeping. After selling his watch to Shiang-chyi and learning of her impending trip to France, the film presents Hsiao-Kang in a range of spaces, resetting every watch that he owns, and every clock that he sees, to Paris time. No clear explanation is offered for this fervid activity; rather, it is an all-consuming passion, sparked by a very brief encounter, which comes to dominate Hsiao-Kang's life and energies. It is hard to say whether his wish to control time, or to "share" Paris time with Shiang-chyi, really concerns the girl herself: it might equally reveal his attachment to the object she has taken from him—the dual-time watch, and its linkage to loss and conditions of mourning.

In parallel scenes, Hsiao-Kang's mother is presented at home, consumed by her own private rituals: as per Buddhist tradition, she checks the water level ("yin-yang water") in a teacup, looking for signs of her late husband's presence; she continues to prepare his favorite meals, as though he might join her; she guards even the insects in their home, lest one of them should house her husband's reincarnated spirit. Eventually, her behavior grows more erratic, recalling Hsiao-Kang's own compulsive routines: she sits alone, folding lotus flowers out of paper, until the room is laden with them; later, she drapes the windows in heavy cloth, cloaking her home in perpetual darkness. In these excessive instances, the idea of keeping time assumes a strong, protective sense that involves the desire to "preserve" or "retain" it: it is not just the issue of temporal difference that matters here—as when Hsiao-Kang resets clocks to Parisian time—so much as a wish to stem the flow of time itself, clinging to that temporal phase (nighttime) in which the past is felt most keenly, and permeates the present.

These rituals necessarily collide with her son's, and to tragicomic effect: when Hsiao-Kang resets the family clock, his mother mistakenly interprets this shift as the work of her husband's spirit, signaling his presence. This episode offers another instance of "dual time," now split between Paris—and more abstractly—a further realm, beyond human perception. That clock-time is able to sustain these conflicting terms tells us much about our use of it: it is an objective frame for our subjective desires, and never more than this; it metes out the hours and minutes on which our hopes and sympathies are fastened, and is hollow without them.

Meanwhile, Shiang-chyi's time in Paris seems a cruel displacement, inducing in her a longing for the familiar rhythms of Taipei. She appears alone in a range of public spaces, her solitariness underscored by the strangers who surround her. In cafés and restaurants, she is unable to read the menu, or to communicate with others, because she does not speak the language; in the evenings, she lies awake in her hotel room, disturbed by sounds that are perhaps produced on the floor above. In this, she shares with Hsiao-Kang and his mother an uncanny nightly vigil: each character, though independently, is sleepless in the evening, whether listening for the return of a departed relative, or, in Shiang-chyi's case, kept awake by another kind of phantom presence. As we have noted already, the characters are bound to each other in ways they do not realize; and as viewers, we are privy to the experiences that hold them in common, and cannot help but discern the way their isolation is qualified by surprising imbrications of feeling.

Taken as a comprehensive formal system, these maneuvers tend to complicate conventional expectations of temporal sequence and simultaneity. Phrased in the familiar language of film analysis, what we have here is a species of crosscutting that seeks to establish *more* than the fact of temporal coincidence across spatial zones. The force of these structures will seem descriptive by nature, rather than goal-oriented: this is not a paralleling of episodes designed to propel narrative action, as such, or to relate causes to effects. Nonetheless, the narrative structures outlined above—namely, the slow shift from one character to the next, marking both their solitary status, and eventually, the way this remoteness is oddly *shared*—are finally productive, although what emerges is closer to an equivalence of times ("this situation is comparable to the other, although its exact temporal location is unspecified") than to a precise mapping of concurrent activities. The alternation of sequences thus invites us to consider the qualitative dimension of time, over its quantitative measure; the experience of time, acutely felt in circumstances of sleeplessness, boredom, and waiting, is in this way held open for contemplation.

Mediating Cinematic Times: Film as Reflection and Reference

In interviews, Tsai has expressed a strong interest in Chinese philosophical traditions, and in Buddhism, specifically. This would account for the ritualized practices and iconography represented in *What Time Is It There?*, as well as the critical attention that this aspect of the film's content has generated.[5] By extension, it is not difficult to discern a certain consonance between Buddhist thought and the film's contemplative aesthetic: Tsai's intricate filmic design reveals a rich connectedness among things, and across situations, which seems to transcend ordinary (worldly) perception. As this relates to temporality, the film offers an alternative conception of time that is experiential in nature: as we have seen, this kind of time is highlighted by the film's drawn-out, static sequences and by the affective temporal descriptions that they enclose. Further, this sort of time is shown to be uncontainable by the "objective" logic of clocks and watches, or by standard parameters of filmic construction: instead, it gives the appearance of excess and approximation, showing up in unexpected emotional affinities and in overlapping coordinates of past, present, and future.

But I want to suggest that the film's particular claim merges such ideas with an unmistakable reflexivity about the medium: *What Time Is It There?* proposes that film is uniquely able to show us these patterns of interconnectedness, raising what is otherwise undisclosed to sudden visibility. What's more, there is the suggestion that the global picture of things that film facilitates may even offset the vicissitudes of modern experience: by so often, and so steadily, framing scenarios of shattering alienation, Tsai's film invites us to reckon with such conditions, and to see see them as shared with others, *in time*. These are weighty considerations that *What Time Is It There?* has not fully articulated to this point. In what follows, I will trace a series of episodes that elucidate the film's alignment of film and temporality more explicitly, steering us toward the narrative's ambiguous conclusion.

Here is an initial scene to consider: Hsiao-Kang appears at a kiosk on the street, inquiring about French films, or films about Paris, from a vendor. He is told that they "specialize in classics" and have both *Hiroshima, mon amour* (Resnais, 1959) and *The 400 Blows* (Truffaut, 1959)—as it happens, two founding films of the French New Wave.[6] An abrupt cut brings us to the next shot: this is the boy's bedroom, in darkness. At frame right, a small television plays a scene from Truffaut's film. At frame left, the boys sits, cradling a pillow; he watches the film, smoking. For those familiar with the narrative of *The 400 Blows*, the film's appearance here is apt: Truffaut's protagonist, Antoine Doinel (Jean-Pierre Léaud), has also lost his father, and is on tentative ground at home; he attends school as rarely as possible, finding solace in the movies and other entertainments.

Our first assessment of this shot will note the tension expressed by its principal parts: on one side, the boy sits in perfect stillness and silence; on the other side, the television screen produces a lively, kinetic image and the joyful sounds that accompany it. (See fig. 4.3.) The film-within-the-film plainly serves as a compositional counterpoint, emphasizing Hsiao-Kang's desolation by its own palpable exuberance. Beyond this evident disparity in energy and tone, however, there is more to say about the functioning of the older footage in this context. Specifically, the scene depicts Truffaut's young protagonist, Antoine, skipping school to go to the fairground with a schoolmate. Looking closely at the image, we find that it presents a familiar attraction that is usually called a "Rotor." The Rotor is a large drum or barrel placed on end: inside it, the riders stand a little apart from each other along the periphery. As the drum rotates, and attains full speed, the floor drops out beneath the riders' feet, leaving them pleasurably suspended by the centrifugal force generated in rotation.

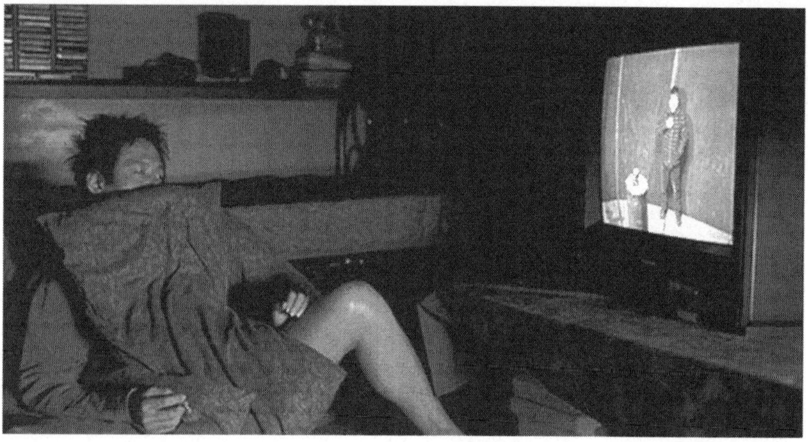

Figure 4.3. Watching Truffaut. From *What Time Is It There?* (Tsai Ming-liang, 2001).

Concerning these details, I want to draw attention to the way Truffaut's scenario aligns with Tsai's own preoccupations, although in subtle ways. Notice the specific conditions of the Rotor itself: each rider stands alone, in evenly spaced sections, pinned in place for the duration of the cycle. While the riders are separated from each other spatially, this is a group activity: all the participants share in a common, thrilling sensation. Indeed, their collective experience provides a secondary order of entertainment, witnessed by those who stand on the observation deck above the ride. These moments from *The 400 Blows* are not just notable for the contrast or difference that they provide. Rather, they concentrate Tsai's premises, offering up a dialectic of "separation" and "connection" that is figured by the mechanisms of the Rotor itself. Admittedly, *What Time Is It There?* pursues this dialectic in a measured fashion, as something that unfolds across successive scenes. Yet it seems right to identify an important accord between the two films, despite the years that separate them, and their aesthetic differences. As will become clear, this scene from *The 400 Blows* models the dynamics of Tsai's film, though in an intensified form: it presents a scenario in which an artificially induced isolation is qualified, or overcome, by waves of common feeling.

If a distinctive play of separation and connection arises here that is meaningful for both films, is this the extent of the scene's resonance? This dynamic signifies in other directions, as well, relating to older contexts of film viewing. For example, we can read these moments as another occasion of "dual-time" in which old and new filmic experience are brought together within a single image. On this view, Tsai's citation of *The 400 Blows* not only invokes a particular piece of film history, but also an entire mode of cinema-going: on the one hand, it evokes a traditional scenario of film viewing in which the separateness of each viewer is mediated by a collective, theatrical context; while everyone responds uniquely to this situation, the conditions of film viewing, and the film itself, are shared terms, experienced together. On the other hand, the reference also speaks to the historical phenomenon of the French New Wave and the unusual confluence of film viewing, film criticism, and filmmaking that distinguished it: in that context, cinephilia found its place within a collaborative community that served to refresh it, merging individual sensibility and achievement with collective enthusiasm.

Taken further, this tension between separation and connection is grounded in the basic material of the medium: although comprised of numerous discrete units, the filmstrip, when projected, effects the illusion of motion by their dynamic correlation and interplay. Like each rider of the Rotor, the individual frame participates in a larger, mobile structure: stasis and solitariness are transformed via movement and recombination, generating new experience, and potentially, certain kinds of pleasure.[7] Significantly, the emergent patterns in *What Time Is It There?* perform a slow articulation this process, transforming separation into connection as a prolonged temporal event that is constituted by filmic form and experienced, or *endured*, by viewers.

In this account, only the gradual unfolding of Tsai's narrative will make this dynamic more explicit. At this stage, Truffaut's film appears within *What Time Is It There?* as something self-conscious and a little separate, reduced to a small portion of the frame, and replicated by a TV screen. Thus, the play of separation and connection that the borrowed image invokes as yet remains contained: it is an inscription of cinema's past that gestures toward older cinematic traditions—or otherwise, an emblem for a lost form of film-going, or film community, that Hsaio-Kang just glimpses. That Truffaut's film resurfaces elsewhere in the narrative, however, testifies to its deepening semantic force: a further excerpt follows from, and intensifies, a rare, close framing of Hsiao-Kang's face as he lies awake at night, weeping. Here the scene from *The 400 Blows*—in which the young protagonist steals, and then furtively drinks, a bottle of milk—entirely fills the frame. Once again, the excerpt contrasts with the manifest details of Tsai's narrative, but enlarges its affective potency: Hsiao-Kang's tears seem to answer to Antoine's greedy drinking, as though the emotional outpouring of the first image were reflected and replenished by the second.

Later still, the surprising appearance of Truffaut's iconic actor, Jean-Pierre Léaud (as himself), extends these premises to comic effect: Hsiao-Kang's viewing of *The 400 Blows* is subsequently "matched" by Shiang-chyi's encounter with the actor at the Montparnasse cemetery. As the pair converse, Shiang-chyi rummages through her handbag, looking for a telephone number that is ostensibly Hsiao-Kang's; Léaud offers *his* number instead, which she accepts, but never uses. Thus, Truffaut's film, as an exemplar from the past that reappears, in various forms, in the present, again serves as a sensitive interface: it mediates an unspoken relation between Hsaio-Kang and Shiang-chyi that is borne across time and place. If the significance of this exchange is muted—after all, Shiang-chyi does not recognize Léaud, but receives him as a stranger—this deflection is part of its point. The episode's comic shading proposes that this sort of blindness is, in fact, inevitable: as Shiang-chyi's interaction evinces, the film not only dwells on complex patterns of connectedness among its players but also their persistent failure to apprehend them.

Therefore to read these filmic citations merely as a self-conscious play of reference—or to reduce them to the particular contexts that Truffaut's film invokes—is to glean only half their value. These details facilitate new work in their revised context by reflecting the past as that which "shows up" in the present, if unrecognized and unexpectedly. We might say that Tsai's film seeks to describe the way the past is actively sustained in the present—not merely as an artifact or dead trace—but as something animate that participates in the present's continual unfolding. Clearly this way of thinking about temporality differs from the objective mechanisms of the dual-time watch, which displays competing times in two locations. Nor does it resemble a stubborn clinging to the past by shutting out the present, as practiced, in different ways, by each of the film's characters. Instead, this is a conception of temporality that recommends an openness to time, rather than a willful movement to impede it; it is an invitation to wait for time to show itself as a meaningful coalescence of "then" and "now." In other words, *What Time Is It There?* directs us toward an authentic temporality that derives from our experience of it, on the specific understanding that film, as a temporal medium, is uniquely qualified to disclose such profound intersections.

Let's turn to a further scene that outlines this idea more specifically. An extreme long-shot takes in the Taipei cityscape: the camera's perspective is elevated and slightly tilted, observing the tops of buildings from above and at some distance. Urban noise is conspicuous here: the roar of traffic and busy jackhammers rises from the street. For the first fifteen seconds, the only movement in the frame is that of passing cars, reflected on a building's glass exterior; as yet, the shot seems to lack a discernible subject or focal point. Yet this impression eventually gives way when, at the center of the frame, our attention is drawn to a moving figure on the rooftop; the figure is barely perceptible, a mere speck against the wide urban space. At this range, the image must be carefully observed just to say what it depicts: the figure stands at the rooftop's edge, holding a long pole that is tied off with a scrap of red cloth; leaning over the guardrail, and stretching downward, he directs the pole toward the public clock on the building's face. And by this, the details of the scene suddenly light up for us as viewers, clarifying the terms of a meticulously staged joke: this is Hsaio-Kang, of course, still resetting Taipei clocks to Paris time, but here this ambition is raised to surprising new heights. As he works to complete his task, passing cars and cyclists are still reflected in the glass, contrasting Hsaio-Kang's single-mindedness with the indifferent rhythms of the street below.

We have witnessed this sort of activity already, as the eccentric focus of Hsiao-Kang's daily routines. But in this case, the scenario is more freestanding, and modulates our engagement in particular ways. There is the way the scene evokes comedic associations from the history of cinema: in its emphasis on the public clock, the shot strongly recalls an iconic image of Harold Lloyd, from *Safety Last!* (1923). More pertinently, the shot's arrangement and mode of unfolding will remind us of the sly staging of Jacques Tati—and particularly, the deep space and long take structures deployed to scintillating effect in Tati's *Playtime* (1967).[8] The now-familiar tendency of Tsai's film to ally Hsiao-Kang with older film traditions is here extended, situating Hsaio-Kang not just "alongside" or "in relation" to a cinematic past, but very much *within* it, enframed by, and mobilizing, such associations.

But it is worth pausing to consider the particular contribution of Tati's work at greater length. First, we should note the extent to which *What Time Is It There?* seems indebted to *Playtime*: at the level of content, both films concern the idea of travel, and specifically, travel to Paris; formally, each production features an intricate design that choreographs multiple unfolding actions and reflections across a complex mise-en-scène. By consequence, each film demands a special attentiveness from viewers and a willingness to accept their considered filmic pace. Beyond these details, the strongest affinity between the two films concerns their picturing of urban experience: indeed, *What Time Is It There?* has appropriated, and reconfigured, Tati's central premise—that the experience of modernity can be conceived as a variegated, mobile pattern that we share in, and help to constitute, but rarely see.

Tsai's film does not simply lift this premise so as to hastily transplant it, however: his use of this idea, and the calculated forms that facilitate it, profoundly alters its original affective register. For *What Time Is It There?*, with its twinned emphasis on time and isolation, Tati's ironic travelogue darkens and grows melancholic. The "joke" of failing to see our place in the world is necessarily transfigured when posed as a temporal question: it assumes a more serious character as it bears on the corresponding issue of mortality—or the way we are inevitably, and painfully, displaced from others in time. Thus, the optimistic closing of *Playtime*, in which the tourist's view of Paris is transformed as a sudden, luminous patterning, is exchanged in Tsai's film for something like acceptance. In this context, the tension between the fixed frame (which delimits our perspective) and the experience of temporal duration (the unbounded unfolding of time) are terms that—like the perpetual play of separation and connection analyzed above—must finally be *lived through*. While the narrative of *What Time Is It There?* moves toward a conclusion that is both clarifying and restorative, its basic claim is this: film does not release us from time, or afford us mastery over it; rather, it shows us the conditions of our temporal experience more clearly, so that we can begin to cope with them.

Time Rewarded: Making Peace with the Present

I have suggested that *What Time Is It There?* institutes, in its final sections, a reconciliation of terms that approximates a process of healing. By this I mean to identify a thematic and formal shift that occurs in the film's latter stages: with characteristic subtlety, this turn brings about a revised orientation among the players that creates new affective proximities. Specifically, the film presents a triangulated series of scenes that moves from Hsaio-Kang to Shiang-chyi to Hsiao-Kang's mother, successively: this series amplifies the film's previous procedures insofar as relations between the narrative strands are more plainly marked, effecting a stronger sense of simultaneity.

Having reset the public clock, Hsiao-Kang is pictured on the rooftop, and then in his car, drinking a bottle of (French) wine; Shiang-chyi becomes ill in a café, but is assisted by another girl from Taiwan, who invites Shiang-chyi to stay with her; Hsiao-Kang's mother appears at home dressing herself formally, as though preparing for a romantic evening with her husband. With passing time, each narrative strand is resumed and undergoes small developments: Hsaio-Kang now sits in his car, drinking into the evening; Shiang-chyi appears in the girl's apartment, waiting as her new acquaintance prepares for bed. Hsaio-Kang's mother sits at the family dining table, a red flower behind her ear; she serves the meal and raises a glass to her phantom guest. Eventually, each character reaches out to make contact with what is in their midst:

Hsaio-Kang has sex with a prostitute who approaches him; Shiang-chyi turns to her new friend, as though to a lover; Hsiao-Kang's mother masturbates, alongside a prominent framed photograph of her late husband.

Critics have consistently emphasized the bleakness of these encounters, pointing to the way that each character fails to achieve meaningful contact with others.[9] And indeed, there is something to this impression: Shiang-chyi is rebuffed by the girl, and departs awkwardly in the morning; Hsaio-Kang awakens to discover that the prostitute has already left, and taken his case of watches with her; Hsiao-Kang's mother remains as alone in her life as before. But whereas these episodes operate by a substitutive logic that would seem to diminish their basis in authentic feeling, when we read them more particularly as a matter of temporality, and in terms of the film's encompassing temporal scheme, they signify quite differently. More precisely, these moments—despite their evident imperfection or "failure"—accelerate the film's argumentation, proposing a new order and a refreshed sense of possibility: for the first time in the narrative, the characters avail themselves of what is immediately available, seeking out, and engaging in, *present-tense experience*. That in each case this experience is sensual enriches this point: it forwards the idea that only our immersion in the immediate sensations of the present—whether shared with "meaningful" others, or with their surrogates—can shake our attachment to the past, cleaving us from that time we can no longer see; only the gratifications of this moment will restore us to ourselves, freed from the tasks of clock-watching (and setting), comparisons of "then" and "now," and endless works of mourning. Losing ourselves in the present, rather than lamenting the past or keeping it, will set us right again, once more open to the future in its infinite possibility. And crucially, it is not the present itself, taken as an objectified instant, that performs this conversion, but rather the act of losing ourselves in it, letting go of time as something monitored or measured, so as to reckon with it authentically.[10] My emphasis on the temporal character of these episodes—remarking the way they are frankly substitutive, but also present a type of authentic experience that cannot be dismissed—illuminates another dimension of Tsai's project that we have touched on already: film affords this kind of experience, too, serving also as a reflection or surrogate. As a temporal medium, film shows us the necessary transformation of the past into the unfolding present, directed toward the future.

Perhaps it seems slightly improbable to read these scenes this way, asking them to sustain, despite first appearances, a substantial turn in the narrative's premises. But when we examine the concluding moments of *What Time Is It There?*, attending closely to the way they unfold for us as viewers, it is clear that something significant has shifted in the film's logic that answers to the temporal patterns the film has disclosed to this point while rewarding our receptivity as viewers.

A final scene that presents Hsaio-Kang and his mother begins as a long, narrow framing circumscribed in shadow. The shot's arrangement recalls, in a quiet way, a striking composition that appeared early in the narrative, depicting the funeral ceremony for Hsaio-Kang's father. The camera perspective looks down the hallway of their home, to a distant doorframe that leads outside: a figure is visible, engaged in activity, but remains slightly indistinct. Eventually, Hsiao-Kang can be made out clearly, carrying a large bundle of fabric: he has dismantled the window coverings that his mother installed, so that daylight once more reaches their home. He passes through the frame, and to the left, while the camera remains stationary; for a few moments we are left with this vacant composition, observing only the layered planes of the image, before Hsaio-Kang reappears to stand at frame right.

The next shot recalls a prior composition as well, but one that is more recent: reiterating an earlier image of his mother, Hsaio-Kang sits at frame right, looking toward the framed photograph of his father, at left. Arranged in this way, the precisely balanced terms of the composition, and the unusual intensity of the photograph itself, make for a odd, resonant "two-shot": while Hsaio-Kang gazes at the photograph sadly, his father's face seems to look out at *us* in a way that is arresting. The division of the frame between "father/son," "past/present," and "absence/presence" coheres with the film's established themes, which have continually dwelt on such dualities. But now the lingering image facilitates a slow revelation that transforms all that it enframes. As the moments pass (the shot endures for over a minute), Hsaio-Kang's attention turns from the photograph to the space beside him—and our attention, shifts, as well. Though at first unnoticeable, there is a third person in the frame: Hsaio-Kang's mother lies sleeping just behind him; we recognize her bright, formal dress. Hsaio-Kang removes his jacket, and places it over her gently, in a tender gesture that is unmatched by anything the film has presented thus far. Thus, the recognition that we experience as viewers, in our delayed perception of *all* the image presents, here accords with a deeper awareness that Hsaio-Kang registers; he, too, sees his mother as though for the first time, in a sudden perception of her loss as it keenly reflects of his own. The shot concludes in silence, as he lies down beside her, sharing the space that she occupies, and perhaps finding comfort in it.

Leaving Hsiao-Kang and his mother in this way, the film turns to Shiang-chyi, in Paris. The first shot offers an unusually close view of her face: she looks tired and terribly sad; her mouth trembles and her face is streaked with tears. At this range, we cannot say where she is, but only that she sits outside, wearing her coat. A second, wider perspective places the girl in an identifiable setting; she dozes in a chair at the edge of an ornamental lake. As is characteristic for Tsai's film, the planes of the image contrast distinct layers of activity; as Shiang-chyi sleeps in the foreground, children play in the far background. Eventually, a single piece of action solicits our attention; at the edge of the frame, in the distance, a pair of kids can be seen pulling a large case across the park. Of course, this is Shiang-chyi's suitcase, removed surreptitiously; the children's excitement at this prank registers clearly on the soundtrack by their exclamations. This small event conjoins the scene to one we have seen before; it is a clear rhyme for the prostitute's theft of Hsaio-Kang's case of watches, but now recast in Paris. A third shot produces another view of the girl, pictured from above; as she sleeps, the drama of her valise continues to play out—and to comic effect. Now the composition is diagonally bisected: in the lower half of the frame, Shiang-chyi is motionless, unseeing; in the upper half, however, her suitcase reappears, slowly drifting past in the pool. (See fig. 4.4.) The suitcase eventually passes out of the frame, but the camera remains here, waiting: it leaves us to observe—for a further twenty-three seconds—the faint outline of a Ferris wheel reflected in the water, and eventually, a pigeon's energetic march along the pool's edge.

These details are assembled to offer a particular description of time, combining slight temporal ellipses between shots, as Shiang-chyi sleeps,

Figure 4.4. Drifting time. From *What Time Is It There?* (Tsai Ming-liang, 2001).

and a kind of continuous, drifting time that is reflected in the pool's mobile surface. We might observe in this combination a slight shift in formal prerogatives: by offering the varied perspectives of Shiang-chyi, each a little different from the other, the film reminds us of the resources of montage, locating them in ambiguity. In fact, these shots constitute the film's most emphatic effort to picture time as something whose passage is unseen. If Shiang-chyi's sleeplessness throughout the narrative—like the obsessive nighttime rituals of Hsaio-Kang and his mother—amounted to a sort of clock-watching, a monitoring of time rather than yielding to it, this tendency is here overturned. The film now presents temporal experience as something that, in a certain sense, watches *over us*, and not the reverse: our faith in time, or our willingness to give ourselves over to it, is finally restorative; though we may be stripped of our "baggage" in the process, we are also refreshed.

The concluding images of *What Time Is It There?* delineate this proposition most clearly. A final perspective of Shiang-chyi reverses its original positioning: now she appears in the most distant plane of the image, still sleeping, while a man in the foreground can be seen to retrieve her case from the pool with his umbrella. He sets it on the pavement, and then steps forward so that his face is visible: it seems that Hsaio-Kang's father—or his ghostly surrogate—here makes an extraordinary, last-minute appearance. The camera again lingers, quite literally unmoved by this astonishing development; finally, this framing gives way to an extreme long shot that brings the narrative proceedings to a close.

The calculated symmetries of this last composition feature an enormous, rotating Ferris wheel (visible in reflection, previously) centered in the distance; two tall street lanterns appear in the middle ground, set at either edge of the frame.[11] The man who may be Hsaio-Kang's father stands in the foreground, and slightly to the right: the scale of the shot sets him at some distance from us, and thus refuses perfect legibility. He casually lights a cigarette, and looks back toward the camera—or perhaps toward the girl, or her case—and then walks away, toward the great revolving wheel in the distance. (See fig. 4.5.) As he disappears from view, the shot cuts to black. The scene's diegetic sound persists, however, carrying the faint noises of the park beyond the terms of the image track. The film concludes in this curious zone of in-between, with this dedication: "To my father, and Lee Kang-Sheng's father."[12]

What should we make of these ambiguous details, as a culmination of the film's overarching premises? And more specifically, what picture or conception of temporality does *What Time Is It There?* finally produce? To approach these questions, we need to attend closely to the dialectic of "seeing" and "unseeing" that the film's closing moments trace. As I

Figure 4.5. Final shot from *What Time Is It There?* (Tsai Ming-liang, 2001).

have noted, the episode involving Shiang-chyi's suitcase foregrounds the unseen dimension of temporal experience; here temporal flow occurs apart from direct observation, as an event whose autonomous unfolding does not require that anyone notice it. But this scene also emphasizes that time is accessible to us in other ways: while not an object for perception, temporal movement is disclosed in its reflections—like the delicate trajectory of the case as it drifts across the pool's surface, or more concretely, as a filmic event through which temporal experience is dynamically mediated.

Yet there are additional details here that compel examination. First, there is Hsaio-Kang's father, whose sudden reappearance calls into question the integrity of what we see, or have seen; further, there is the way the film concludes not with an image, but with a stream of sounds that surpass it, suggesting the persistence of things beyond what the eye legislates. On the face of it, this material might be read in light of issues external to film's workings—that is, as a playful version of Buddhist aesthetics. Like the great Ferris wheel that dominates the frame, these details potentially evoke the eternal cycle of death and rebirth, and the impermanence of all things.

But I want to address these elements as they belong to the film itself, in their particular figuration of temporality. To this end, this question of what we can and cannot see has been a determining aspect of the film's formal prerogatives throughout: Tsai's scrupulously designed, static framings consistently draw attention to the visual limitations they impose.

Correspondingly, however, their long duration invites us to understand these limits as temporally inflected—or in other words, as a fixed perspective that we do not choose, but learn to accommodate over time. The rewards of waiting, or enduring, such framings are intimated by the film's concluding images: their justification surely lies in the unexpected connections they disclose, in the grief that is finally shared by Hsaio-Kang and his mother, finding them closer to each other than before, and in the unusual poetry of small events in their unfolding, typically unobserved.

These considerations offer some rationale for the film's title, as well, which asks not about the time "here," but "*there*"—over there, where you are, *where I cannot see*. Thus, the locales of Taipei and Paris, and their various overlapping coordinates, are not the endpoints of this exchange but rather a rich specification. Beyond the significant cultural dialogue that Tsai's film opens up, reflecting the way his own film practice actively mediates the past, and in particular, the French film traditions that he cherishes, *What Time Is It There?* finally forwards a wider, existential claim.[13] As I have endeavored to demonstrate, the film addresses the way our perspective is fundamentally limited: despite our efforts to keep or fix it, we only see the scrap of time that our lives entail, and this but indistinctly. This situation leaves us to wonder, or to ask about, other times, and other places. But it may, under special conditions—such as those that cinema creates—allow us to glimpse the patterns of our experience in the present, and to welcome the versions of the past that are enfolded in it.

5

Deep Time

Methods of Montage in Terrence Malick's *The Tree of Life*

[N]o less a miracle now, this present hour, than it was in the beginning.

—Terrence Malick, Screenplay, *The Tree of Life*[1]

IN THE FOREGOING CHAPTERS WE have examined a range of temporal modalities across contemporary cinema, each affording a distinctive experience of cinematic time. Following from the defamiliarizing repetitions of *The Limey*, the reversed time scales of *5x2*, and the elongated and enduring temporal structures of *What Time Is It There?*, we now turn to a final filmic case study that complements these discoveries in important ways. This chapter analyzes a title whose timeliness once more arises from fragmented editing structures, orchestrating filmic time through discrete shots whose combinatory logic does not proceed predictably.

Our exemplar for these purposes comes from American filmmaker Terrence Malick, with his recent film, *The Tree of Life* (2011). As we shall see, Malick's film generates a distinctive temporal mode that is encompassing and immersive, yet markedly discontinuous. Like *The Limey*, *The Tree of Life* gives us fragmented time—but uniquely. If Soderbergh's film structures time as a riddle, or a puzzle, that is historically inflected, *The Tree of Life* claims its viewer more fervently, mobilizing a temporal constellation that moves (us) like a song, or a prayer.

Spanning nearly four decades, Terrence Malick's career now comprises seven distinguished feature films. This limited output reflects the careful consideration that informs the director's work, as well as his reluctant relation to the imperatives of a commercial industry. A twenty-year hiatus from filmmaking, and a nearly career-long refusal of press interviews has not diminished the critical interest in Malick's films, which have earned multiple nominations for American and international film prizes.[2] Despite these attractions, however, scholars have not yet produced a study of Malick's cinema that can be called comprehensive, and which assesses the films' aesthetic and intellectual dimensions in equal measure. If anything, the literature on Malick reveals a marked tendency to hold these valences separate, suppressing the cinematic technique of the work so as to privilege a generalized, thematic content. Thus Malick's films are frequently characterized as "philosophical," yet are rarely interrogated as dynamic experiences of cinema.[3] Given the formal range and complexity of the films, this situation is surprising and demands a refocusing of scholarly attention. My critical objective in these pages is to produce a fuller picture of *The Tree of Life* that squarely addresses its intricacies of form and feeling, while clarifying the broader terms of the director's work. Such insights emerge from our engagement with the timeliness of Malick's film, bound up in its unfolding as an exhilarating temporal orchestration.

The task of reading *The Tree of Life* is certainly daunting; the film does not lend itself readily to compact critical analyses. Recipient of the Palme d'Or at the Cannes Film Festival, Malick's film was also nominated for three Oscars. It was named "Movie of the Year" by the American Film Institute; received top honors for technical achievement from American, Australian, and British Institutes of Cinematography; and claimed a spot on *Sight & Sound*'s prestigious Greatest Films List (2012). With these accolades, the film also garnered surprising vitriol, loosely aimed at both style and theme. I want to suggest that the film's basis in montage rather than long take structures is a relevant factor in this critical reception as well as a meaningful feature of its overarching aesthetic, encapsulating in important respects the film's challenge to received interpretive frameworks. *The Tree of Life* departs from the preferred aesthetic of the contemporary festival film, which in recent years has favored a slowed cinema of the long take. Within this study, the attenuated temporal design of Tsai's *What Time Is It There?* exemplifies such priorities perfectly by its formal spareness and contemplative pacing.[4] As we shall see, Malick's film is constructed on very different premises.

Further, *The Tree of Life* stands as a transformation of the recognizable stylistics of Malick's earlier work, revising in key respects its characteristic blend of wide compositions and mobile camera. As I will demonstrate below, the film pursues a cadence that is newly accelerated, speeding and splintering the filmic features that we have come to associate with Malick's work to recast their significance within a recalibrated temporal system. So even beyond the thematic content of *The Tree of Life*—which undeniably presents its own challenges—there is something uncustomary about its formal textures, generating an elusive sense of time for viewers.

Given these resistant qualities, it makes sense to approach *The Tree of Life* in terms of the idea of interpretation. However one feels about Malick's film, the singularity of its achievement—its epic scale, ambition, and for mainstream cinema, its relative opacity—is something to be reckoned with. For critics, particularly after the premiere at Cannes, the task of interpreting the film must have seemed overwhelming, as evidenced by certain shell-shocked assessments. The divided responses that the film inspired speak to its idiosyncratic appearance and interpretive richness: for many critics, Malick's project possessed admirable qualities, but remained basically unwieldy or excessive as a cinematic object. We might say that the film proffered "an embarrassment of riches" to viewers so as to account for the tone of discomfiture even mild mortification—that surfaces across several prominent reviews. To this end, three commentaries are salient for my purposes here. The first is from *Variety* critic Robert Koehler, who writes,

> Malick wants to convey love's force, and, as he deems it, "grace," but he can't find cinematic correlatives for it . . . A detectable pattern emerges: Ideas are stated, and then not explored in cinematic terms. Worse: the ideas contradict one another.[5]

For Koehler, the creative failure of *The Tree of Life* stems from a fundamental breach between its style and substance: he finds the film lacking on both counts, and wholly unable to bring its divergent strands into mutual coherence. Indeed, the only pattern Koehler detects within the film is really an outline of his own frustrations with it, as the film continually piques and then overturns expectations. Something similar is expressed by J. Hoberman, formerly of the *Village Voice*, who likens *The Tree of Life* to the experimental work of Stan Brakhage—but with a difference. He writes:

> More than any other Hollywood filmmaker, Malick has a capacity for the sort of off-center compositions, small camera moves and sudden blurs or shifts in light one might associate with Stan Brakhage Unlike Brakhage, Malick is not a man to keep his sense of perspective or his big ideas to himself. The word "cosmic"is insufficient to characterize his notion of the O'Brien family or describe the movie's audiovisual bombast . . . Malick's craftsmanship may be everywhere evident but, however flashy and intermittently beautiful, his filmmaking can be shockingly banal. Inspired scenes (a toddler relating to a baby) or shots (a mega close-up of a can kicked out of the frame) arrive as morsels floating in the movie's primeval soup . . . The movie disengages the mind, even as it dulls the senses.[6]

Like Koehler, Hoberman does not discern much connective tissue in Malick's film, binding its form to content; by consequence, it registers for him as a kind of broken signal whose intermittent "flashes" are too scant, or widely spaced, to plausibly produce meaning. On this view, *The Tree of Life* can be dismissed as something empty and immodest: writ so large, who could fail to discern the film's aesthetic significance, if there were any? A final variation on this critique comes from Amy Taubin, who puts the problem as follows:

> It's a pity that . . . Malick didn't trust the expressiveness of his images. Instead he loads the soundtrack with voice-over, couched between prayerful and preachy, and an overabundance of music—most of it with funereal or religious overtones—that makes the film seem like kitsch, beginning to end.[7]

Taubin also posits a disconnect between the film's form and its ideas, but on her account it is a problem of *too much*, rather than too little: if only *The Tree of Life* showed more rhetorical restraint, perhaps offering its images in silence, or at least with greater self-consciousness, it might appear less embarrassingly earnest to critics.

My point here is not simply to quarrel with these assessments but rather to highlight a common theme. Across these reviews we find a tendency to separate the film's content from its filmic procedures—and even to suggest, as Koehler does, that the film is doing nothing cinematically, or at least not anything that can be reconciled with a familiar conceptual scheme (beyond a passing resemblance to other films). In this respect, the film's critical reception reprises a problem of the academic scholarship on Malick: even where critics are attentive to matters of technique, which is rare enough, they fail to discern the mechanisms by which such details catalyze meaning.

Likewise, it is striking that prominent critics—and here Jonathan Rosenbaum can be added to the group, as well—characterize *The Tree of Life* as *kitsch*, rather than art: the film is somehow both obscure and excessively obvious, owing to a perceived lack of formal rigor and a failure to articulate its intellectual substance at the level of style. Notably, this designation serves to set the critic above the work, and thus relieves her of its claim: after all, kitsch is what we call art when it should know better (because *we* do).[8] Another way to put this is to say that critics have tended to withdraw from the film's timeliness, absenting themselves from its dynamic temporal claim. While there is no denying the film's intensities, one wonders if they might be read more sensitively—for instance, as measured components of a deliberate design, rather than as uncharacteristic lapses in directorial judgment.

This extended preamble highlights the difficulties of grasping a film, especially an inordinately ambitious one, on the basis of an initial screening; it also underscores the evident fact that subjective preference and dominant frames of reference will inevitably color any critical assessment. But the issue here is not so much about correcting a false impression as it is redirecting its line of critique to make it productive again. I propose that critics' impatience with Malick's film—and specifically, with the quality of ambivalence that they ascribe to it, its way of uncomfortably pulling in two directions—is, in fact, a profound descriptor for *The Tree of Life* that reaches deeply to its fundamental filmic procedures. The film does not simply compel divided responses, but rather is built on a principle of ambivalence that informs its aesthetic patterning and systems of meaning. Its timeliness derives from this principle, organized as a filmic matrix of continual deflection and redoubling. But in order to appreciate this idea, we need to situate it concretely in terms of the film's complex orchestration of images and sounds.

Engaging the Opening Sequence

The Tree of Life begins with a pair of elements that demand careful consideration—first, to say something about their identity and then to sketch the formal terrain that they establish for subsequent procedures. The initial image is a quotation from the book of Job, presented as the film's epigraph; the second is an abstract image that endures onscreen for about forty seconds (to reappear later, as a transition between the film's early sections and as its closing image). Below, I will examine these elements separately, although their impact derives from their overlapping placement.

Let's begin with the epigraph. It reads: "Where were you when I laid the foundations of the earth? . . . When the morning stars sang together, and all the sons of God shouted for joy?" These lines are drawn from God's speech out of the whirlwind in the book of Job, a text that will resurface more than once to articulate dilemmas of suspicion and faith for Malick's film. So to begin with the book of Job is obviously to foreground matters of faith at the outset—but it is also a way of pointing to a text of unusual hermeneutical depth, and more precisely, to a moment within that text that encapsulates both the fact of Job's suffering and the difficulty of God's reply. It is, after all, a moment of pushback, asserting a forceful, if playful, challenge: the lines immediately preceding those of the epigraph read as follows: "Who is this that darkens counsel by words without knowledge? Gird up your loins like a man, I will question you, and you shall declare to me."[9] Contextualized in this way, we can discern a fuller rhetorical emphasis: the lines ask impossibly, with quiet irony, whether Job can account for events that necessarily exceed his understanding because they predate his very existence. The only way to hear such a question, much less respond to it, is to acknowledge one's epistemological and temporal finitude. So what we're confronted with here, at the very beginning of *The Tree of Life*, is a problem of understanding that is inflected by time, phrased as a series of questions that are unanswerable and whose manner of framing the narrative is complex.[10]

The next element to consider is the abstract image. Following on the epigraph, there are several seconds of darkness; eventually, a sinuous coil of orange light appears, flickering warmly at center frame. This flame-like form is accompanied by the sound of crashing waves and the faint call of sea birds, although their relation to the image remains indeterminate. An additional sound element is introduced by whispered voiceover, when a male voice speaks ("Brother. Mother. It was they who led me to your door."). These spare and disconnected details once more advance a dilemma that relates insistently to time: with the initial, establishing queries that these elements raise (What am I seeing? What am I hearing?) comes another thought that is temporal (*When* are these elements occurring?), and which complicates straightforward notions of simultaneity. Thus, the film quietly demands that we cope with multiple temporalities here—to receive, without equating, several strands of unmarked time suggested by the image and soundtrack.

Nonnarrative film, and experimental works in particular, routinely deploy such strategies of fragmentation, rejecting the thoroughgoing logics of narrative integration. But for all its strangeness, the opening section of Malick's film eventually moves *toward* a narrative rather than away from it, and therefore initiates a rift that is not so much a repudiation of storytelling principles as it is a preemptive blow to claims of narrative mastery. It asks us to receive sound and image as imbricated elements whose occurrence and significance cannot be reduced to a single chronological point; instead, these elements assume, and begin to generate, an alternate temporality that is loosened and generous, and which dissolves standard structures of "then" and "now" to privilege a continuous fluctuation. We might once more recall *The Limey*, which also begins with an eruption of sound in advance of its establishing procedures. But for *The Tree of Life*, such prefatory elements function more cryptically. They do not just ask us to wait for an eventual clarification of premises but to accept the unspoken terms of their obfuscation—to believe, in some sense, that the absence of narrative structure holds a purpose that is redemptive and not merely arbitrary.[11]

Returning to the flame-like image, there is still more to say. It is a filmed version of a work by the light artist Thomas Wilfred called *Opus 161* (1965–66), a composition of light, color, and form that continually transforms in time. Wilfred called such works lumia, first developing devices for his light installations in the 1920s, a number of which came to be held at the Museum of Modern Art and other venues. Though the artist did not permit his works to be filmed during his lifetime, citing insufficient results of such experiments, Malick obtained permission to include the work through the collectors Eugene and Carol Epstein, recording the lumia at the Los Angeles County Museum of Art and at Epstein's home, in Los Angeles. As originally conceived, the piece's running time is said to be one year, three hundred and fifteen days, and twelve hours. The filmed excerpt set within the opening section of *The Tree of Life* lasts only forty seconds, presenting a tiny portion of the original work's duration and wide-ranging color spectrum.[12] Like the film's opening epigraph, the lumia is a fragment, a shard of a larger work with its own (massive) hermeneutical claim.

Andrew Johnston makes the case, in a recent essay on Wilfred's work, for thinking about lumia in relation to the technologies and creative inclinations of cinema, particularly as these facilitate new perceptual experience.[13] Thus the recorded snippet of Wilfred's lumia, appearing by special permission in Malick's film, is a considered detail that immediately demands—even for those unfamiliar with the source of the image or its theoretical underpinnings—a certain patience and receptivity from viewers, encouraging us to experience time as something independent and intractable.

Figure 5.1. Light. From *The Tree of Life* (Terrence Malick, 2011).

The lumia also initiates a delicate exchange of light and shadow that is elaborated throughout Malick's film, though this pattern may register but fleetingly for viewers. It shines forth first as a small blue candle lit in memory, (See fig. 5.1.) and in the glow of lanterns and flashlights; it recurs as sunlight pouring through a small, squared window, projecting radiating lines on the ceiling. Correspondingly, there is the camera's way of dwelling on shadow as its path traces the elongated shapes of children at play, arms akimbo or weirdly outstretched in shadow puppets (see fig. 5.2)—and also its pause to observe, momentarily but with deliberation,

Figure 5.2. Shadow. From *The Tree of Life* (Terrence Malick, 2011).

the shadow cast by the Father, extended before him as he surveys his life, and hanging over his head like a darkened cloud.

For the film that follows, such images will work to reiterate an opposition of light and darkness that draws familiarly on the Christian theological tradition. But eventually, we will see that these details also pose, in their semantic accumulation, a more acute perceptual question, marking what we can never see of ourselves—we might say, the imprint of our way through life, the way we continually reflect a light and also cast a darkness. To be clear, this is not the rational optics of Plato's Cave; rather, there is something in Malick's images that is always more permissive, diffuse, and Dionysian. In any case, it is the first point in a lesson that *The Tree of Life* will patiently carry out, inviting us to think of our lives not as something that yields to the structure of our expectations, but as the condition of their possibility.[14] Last, that light and darkness are also temporal markers naturally formulates a pertinent question: How should we reconcile ourselves to the grayed temporality between them? As we shall see, this is a binding question for the film as a whole, etched in light across its aesthetic components, drawing together disparate spaces and times.

To better grasp the functioning of the film's opening section, we might think of the way biblical narrative serves Kierkegaard's purposes, in *Fear and Trembling*, and in particular, the conditioning effects of that text's opening sections, its Preface or "Exordium." Here the story of Abraham and Isaac is told four times, in ruminative variation, to bring about a particular attitude in the reader—an openness or attunement toward the text(s) that accepts its quality of arbitrariness and absurdity, its essentially refractory relationship to understanding. My point here is to say that Malick's film pursues a related kind of attunement for its viewer though the successive procedures of its opening sequence, beginning not just with a reference to Job's suffering, but to the overwhelming task of making sense of it, before giving way to the fluctuating and recalcitrant temporality of the lumia. As points of entry to *The Tree of Life*, the epigraph and the lumia in this way shape a preparatory situation for the viewer. These elements are not just thematically suitable, but formally necessary: they begin to mediate the film's terms of engagement.

Now to consider the remaining details of the film's opening sequence. First, a female voice speaks: it belongs to the young girl who is pictured, and to the mother she will become. She introduces a pair of terms, naming the counterconcepts of Nature and Grace. Elucidated as "two ways through life"—moving in self-interest and openness, respectively—this conceptual pairing alludes to the writings of theologian Thomas à Kempis.[15] The terms are presented here with remarkable efficiency, performing a swift distillation of rich concepts. The narration grants a spare, but sufficient explanation of each, lending greater legibility to the accompanying images, which would seem quite disparate without this device. The combined effect of the images and voiceover is to approximately align each term with the film's main characters: images of the mother, first as a child and then as an adult, are paired with the discussion of Grace; correlatively, the father is prominently framed at the family table as the narration delineates "the way of Nature." These coincidences of sound and image are satisfying because they provide viewers with a way of dealing with the abstract ideas more concretely. At the same time, these linkages are not so tightly wrought as to extinguish their suggestiveness.

But we should look more closely at the film's formal textures, attending particularly to shot relations and the compositional features of the image. Taken as a whole, the opening sequence runs approximately five minutes and is comprised of thirty shots. This unfolds as a fairly brisk montage: before the final shot of the sequence, shot lengths alternate between three and seven seconds. The first images frame a young girl (the mother, pictured as a child), leaning forward to gaze out a low window; as her eyes take in the green space before her, the camera wavers slightly, restating the drifting movement of the window frame in the breeze. The "naturalness" of this camera movement, as if generated by the wind itself, is set in contrast to a quick cut: the image of the girl is split as two successive views, generating a sudden experience of duality and pressing a sharp awareness of time on the viewer.

In the succeeding shots, a compact system of repetitions opens up, formulating what I will designate as *compositional reversals*. By this, elements are pictured on one side of the frame, and then the other, contrasting and completing each other from shot to shot: first, yellow sunflowers appear clustered at frame left, and then at frame right, in two consecutive camera perspectives. (See figs. 5.3 and 5.4.) This effect is elaborated by alternations of camera angle, framing things from above, and then from below: here, the camera's gentle movement observes the young girl's hands as they grip the wooden window frame; there, its vantage point is tilted upward to the sky, capturing streaming rays of sunlight.

Each of these images also features a deliberately cropped composition. A lovely though unsettled shot presents the young girl standing at center, clutching the soft body of a baby goat. While her positioning in the frame is legible, her face is largely averted; at the same time, the frame level is set lower than is conventional, displacing the uppermost

Figure 5.3. Sunflower 1. From *The Tree of Life* (Terrence Malick, 2011).

third of the composition. (See fig. 5.5.) As a result, one feels as though the frame is dropped or weighted down, creating an image that appears slightly odd, and slightly tense, severing the composition at the eyeline in a way that violates classical principles. A similar sensation is evoked when the camera drifts away from its subject intermittently, first drawing close to the girl and her father, tilted upward, and then receding, glancing

Figure 5.4. Sunflower 2. From *The Tree of Life* (Terrence Malick, 2011).

Figure 5.5. Cropped composition. From *The Tree of Life* (Terrence Malick, 2011).

toward the grassy space at their side. This is another "natural," breezy movement by the camera, unmotivated by action or firm correlations. On the one hand, the gesture seems characteristic of Malick's cinema, insofar as the camera's movement is descriptive rather than action oriented. But here it also contributes a distinctive tension: there is a feeling of duality about the camera's stance, as though it could not help but conjoin absence to presence, or indifference to attentiveness. The film here invites us to mediate two modes of possibility, tacitly emphasizing with every shift in attention that there is always *more* beyond what we see.

So the sequence offers a way of engaging the dialectical movement of Nature and Grace—or, thinking of the film's repeated references to the book of Job, of faith and suffering—and asks us to actively synthesize these terms, as viewers. This assessment of the opening section answers to its details persuasively. But we should pause here with the matter of how these observations square with the familiar contours of Malick's cinema. The question is, what should we make of Malick's montage?

Malick's Montage System

In certain respects, *The Tree of Life* is stylistically consistent with the director's older work. Across the films, Malick's aesthetic has tended toward spare images, as though deliberately emptied out, lengthy descriptions of the natural environment, and compositions in which the human figure appears diminished in scale against an expansive context. Think of the glorious compositions of *Days of Heaven* (1978), for instance, with their wide articulations of figure to ground. Characters and character motivation are typically reduced in importance against a contemplative background; voiceover narration complements long passages of visual description. Likewise, Malick's direction of cinematography has tended to favor camera movement that is aligned with natural phenomena more so than human action. Memorably, this includes the camera perspectives in *The Thin Red Line* (1999) that might be called "tidal," because they rise and fall like waves—or alternately, that race through fields of tall grass, creating an effect that is tactile and windswept. Such practices persist in *The Tree of Life*, too, though in variation. Where the earlier films might feature a camera movement that shifts in the breeze, as though in mute accordance with it, in *The Tree of Life* such affinities are formed near-continuously. The film's description of childhood is caught up in its lively rhythms, actively outlining something playful, or ludic—as when the camera pursues the pleasurable flight of a swing, or moves in sympathy with the spontaneous tempo of boys at play.

But what is new here, and noticeable, is a greater commitment to *montage*. While this has always figured to some degree in Malick's cinema—he is not particularly a director of long takes—its self-consciousness in *The Tree of Life* is striking, and signals a shift in the temporal logics of his cinema. Malick's earlier work, from *Badlands* forward, deploys a mode of editing that might be termed deflective, tending to turn from the obvious action rather than interrogating it. In his review of *Days of Heaven*, Gilberto Perez points to an analogous phenomenon that he refers to as an "interruptive principle." For Perez, the film is marked by perceptible discontinuities that serve to complicate and enrich narrative motivation and meaning.[16] To my mind, the deflective tendency of Malick's editing grows more pointed with *The New World* (2005), where the transition from one shot to another begins to generate autonomous effects by an enhanced abruptness.[17]

With *The Tree of Life*, however, we engage a new montage system. The film's emphatic cutting inaugurates a peculiar tension between and across its images, tracing an observable play of their interconnection and rupture as they oppose and constitute each other. Hence the sunflower appears not in a single, authoritative perspective but as twinned possibilities; correspondingly, the camera's frame selects a view, and concentrates it, but also alludes to the expansive world that it cannot contain.[18] By splintering the scene into successive views, the temporal resources of montage are subtly reconfigured, forging a kind of time that is additive (this *and* that) rather than progressive ("this *and then* that"). Time does not advance more efficiently here, despite its evident abridgement, nor is it transformed into anything narratively productive. Instead, it supplies a framework that is both incisive and yielding. Even in montage, *The Tree of Life* models a special kind of attentiveness, compelling its viewer to look again, and to look differently, while accepting its swift accretion of images and sounds. As I have suggested, the film by this departs from the long take aesthetics of contemporary cinema, generating a dynamic montage that somehow retains the contemplative quality of duration.

Then there are the racing, reckless shots that deliver the news of the youngest son's death. With the voiceover's promise ("They taught us that no one who loves the way of grace / ever comes to a bad end."), the camera tracks behind a young, blond boy, who briefly turns to show his face. Here the shot cuts abruptly, replacing the boy with an image of rushing blue water, peering down precipitously into a bottomless gorge. The shot endures for six seconds—a wordless picture of a "bad end"—before the camera descends, edging closer to the water's white foam. The shot that follows performs a sharp reversal, shifting from the violent torrent to the skyward stretch of tree branches and sun. With the camera's upward surge, the voiceover extends the initial promise with another ("I will be true to you / Whatever comes."). Next is a low-leveled perspective, looking down a pathway to the family door. An upturned tilt and a forward track show the arrival of a messenger, who seems to move with the speed of rushing water. The next shots show his message received, keenly conveyed in three searing jump-cuts. In the first shot, the Mother moves from the darkened doorway to the bright kitchen, tearing the envelope; next, she continues to read the telegram and throws it down; finally, the camera circles high above her as she comprehends the news, reeling as her body does, and then cutting away with her sudden sob. This human sound is curtailed by the rising noise of the next shot, flattened by the roar of an airplane's engine.

The effect of these shots is wrenching: camera positioning and movement are closely aligned with the body, implicated through the cutting in a kind of spectacular, staggering time that projects an experience of pain and unexpected loss. The early exchange of shots, between the young boy and the rushing water, fashions a terrible magician's trick, showing us R.L.'s death as a kind of spontaneous disappearance that asserts itself, as though hypothetically, years in advance of its implied narrative placement. Hence, the rationale for these shots is the true temporality of lived experience as it falsifies standard measures of time keeping: the Mother's grief occurs here because it is encompassing, belonging even to the years that precede it. I will return to this important point in what follows.

For now, two associations suggest themselves as ways of conceptualizing these formal strategies more lucidly. First, we might think back to *Badlands*, and Holly's fascination with optical toys. The reversals that I identify in *The Tree of Life* effect something similar, though it's not just an optical trick: like the stereopticon, the eye is made to compare two slightly different perspectives on the same image, while also merging these to apprehend, if not "depth," then perhaps an eventual wholeness. So Malick's early work shows a similar concern with transformations of perception and highlights their basis in visual technologies. A further association, surprisingly enough, is to the theory and practice of Sergei Eisenstein. As remote as Soviet montage may seem from the aesthetics of Malick's cinema, both modes of film practice work on us in ways that are intellectually stimulating and boldly visceral, constructing complex shot relations to compel the synthetic activity of viewers. More specifically, it's valuable to think of Malick's reversals in relation to Eisenstein's concept of formal flux, in which a compositional element may be transformed into its opposite while retaining its identity. This association invariably alters received ideas about Malick's cinema by pointing to its exacting formal character.[19]

Another section of the film, occurring much later, shows us these formal prerogatives extended. This sequence runs for about three and a half minutes, and is largely driven by montage. The first image is a wide framing of the street; in the distance, an industrial building is visible, as a lone figure walks past. The structural core of the sequence is the father's voiceover ("I wanted to be loved because I was great. / A big man"), naming his regrets and failings. Against the stable flow of spoken narration, Malick's images once more produce a series of quiet reversals, but in this context the shots are slightly longer, chiefly between four and nine seconds, and therefore permit a little more unfolding within them.

The initial, distant framing of the factory gives way to a pair of perspectives of the father, first angled from the front, and then from the back. In both cases, the camera perspective is initially skewed, and then makes an adjustment, as though struggling to find its true orientation. The next shots look upward at the factory ceiling, and then squarely at the father as he crosses a bridge, before sweeping downward to glance vertiginously at the ground below. In these gestures, aspiration and defeat are brought close to each other, joined centrally by the father's conflicted blend of faith and purpose. The shots also call forth the urban space that Jack will occupy as an adult by their graphic similarity, disclosing their affective connection across time and space.

Perhaps the most acute series to consider is a fine play of shot/reverse shot that presents the boys' mother walking through town. A doubled-perspective of her movement—framing her smiling approach, and then her back, as she moves on—facilitates a small revelation: the wordless parade of lifted hats that she inspires, raised in chivalrous greeting, as she comes and goes. That the father's ongoing voiceover here asks us to behold "trees" and "birds . . ." as possible sources of glory, rather than Mrs. O'Brien herself, is a meaningful detail that competes with the image, but does not contradict it. Rather, it shows us that even in setting ourselves the task of authentic seeing and listening, our efforts are imperfect; we are bound to miss what is right before us, to find the experience that we are immersed in willfully eclipsed. But these moments, like so many in Malick's work, also suggest that cinema might help us to retrieve this awareness. These systematic reversals, both sweeping and subtle, are not simply formal flourishes but affective turns that actively engage us as viewers. They are the chief mechanism in the film's invitation to see things differently, letting go of a monolithic understanding of our lives so as to glean the other side of things.

Cinematic Structures and "Deep Time"

This fine-grained analysis of the opening sequence allows us to apprehend the film's overarching design more richly. The formal structure of *The Tree of Life* is clarified when we envision it as six filmic segments that relate, both specifically and very distantly, to the life of the O'Brien family, residing in Waco, Texas. The film's first movement is introductory, extending from the epigraph and the lumia. As I have discussed already, this section initiates key formal and thematic parameters, and is framed in terms of the family's grief at the loss of the youngest son (R.L.). Second is a shorter sequence that introduces the eldest son (Jack) as an adult, situated within an alienated, urban setting. The third section is a startling break from the previous, contemplating the formation of the universe and its various life forms (including, most famously, the interplay of dinosaurs); these events appear to relate, if abstractly, to the fluctuating energies of the lumia. Returning to the O'Briens in the fourth section, the film's narration grows sprightly, charting the birth of the children and the boys' early days. Next is a protracted series of sequences that may be conceived, for the sake of clarity, as a single expansive unit, focused in alternate strands around Jack and his father. Comprising more than half of the film's total running time, this fifth section shifts in stretches between father and son, conveying their mutual affection and antagonism, as one reflects the other. Interspersed with these strands, and complicating them, are scenes establishing the mother's influence, lending a clement counterpoint to the father's discipline. Finally, the film makes another surprising shift to the whitened shores of an imagined afterlife, where family members are astonishingly reunited, coinciding with and completing versions of themselves. From this, the film concludes as it began, restoring Jack to his contemporary setting, and then returning to the enigmatic lumia and the sounds of birds and the sea. While the reiteration of these details lends symmetry to the film's framework, it does not diminish their mystery.

Admittedly, this broad segmentation is somewhat provisional: one could easily propose alternate ways of construing the film's material to read it differently. But the pressing point for this study is to conceptualize *The Tree of Life* in terms of temporality, to give a rich description of the experience of time that it generates. Held against this mapping of segments we see most plainly that the film's temporal frames are approximate and impossibly wide-ranging, as though extrapolating the temporal vagaries of the epigraph and the lumia. As I have argued, the opening moments raise questions about time without positing a particular temporal orientation. The sections presenting Jack's childhood unfold through the 1950s, though the film conveys this information indirectly; conversely, the film's first section, depicting the family's loss, actually occurs nineteen years later, at the time of R.L.'s death. We have remarked this chronological rupture already at the level of the shot. But how is it justified within the larger temporal structure?

It's tempting to say that what matters for Malick's film is the emotional impact of these narrative strands rather than their relative temporal placement; that is to say, the gradations of the past are inverted to remind us that "remembered time" differs from clock time in vital ways, particularly as the heart grieves. While I would accept this reading, we need to put pressure on it to appreciate the thoroughgoing precision of Malick's design, grasping the way these details are calculated and not merely chaotic. Here, they advance the ontological claim that the possibility of loss precedes all having, and thus gives rise to it, to deliberately reverse more expectant modes of thinking. So the scrambled time scale of *The Tree of Life* is rich and rhetorical, mobilizing a wider argument about the contradictions of lived temporality.

Perhaps the most striking temporal leap occurs with the film's creation sequence, which presents a kind of unfathomable, cosmic time that precedes the O'Briens' existence by vast epochs and yet insists on a remote linkage. Then there is the final sequence and its abstract afterlife, bringing together the family's members in a communal space that is not so much outside of time as it is an intense condensation, showing us time in its effulgence and plenitude. The film's evident ambition here—its wish to operate unapologetically on a vast temporal scale—certainly attracted the attention of critics, motivating comparisons to Stanley Kubrick's *2001: A Space Odyssey* (1968).[20] But for my purposes, I prefer to think of Malick's strategies not just in terms of the projective mechanisms of science fiction but as something that reaches toward what is tangible; that is, as evocations of what is sometimes called "deep time."

A descriptor of geological processes, "deep time" marks an experience of temporality that is fundamentally fragmentary, making it necessary to reckon with events that are widely divergent—separated by millennia or more—in order to find the ways that they constitute the present. Whereas the density and interconnection of events in everyday temporal experience facilitates their explicability, allowing us to perceive causes and effects, in deep time such connections are sparse and more obscure. This is an experience of temporality where the usual rules don't apply; the challenge is to cope with vastly disparate elements that cannot be aligned into a familiar chronology, and to draw from these variances what is shared and potentially significant.[21]

With the dramatic temporal shifts of *The Tree of Life*, we encounter something comparable. Here is a narrative film that puts tremendous pressure on conventional storytelling coordinates, perhaps prompting us to question whether *narrative* is indeed the right word to categorize its emphases and effects.[22] Time, in Malick's film, proceeds as something holistic rather than incremental. It does not consistently assume the time of subjective willing and doing; instead, it generates alternative interpretations of temporality, showing us what time looks like as we belong to it, not just as we aggressively direct it. So the dilemma of deep time for Malick's film is one of epistemological vulnerability rather than ontological doubt: as viewers, we wrangle with a mode of temporal experience that is encompassing and secure, but that does not uniquely privilege our place within it. The film's whole aesthetic project operates in service to this idea, finding persistent articulation through its reversals, tensions, and sensuous logics.

Toward a Conclusion

Having traced the film's patterning at both micro- and macrolevels, I hope to recover two intertwined issues that have been implicit in this discussion but require a fuller place within it. The first is a technical point, and an important one: we should observe that the montage system that I have identified within *The Tree of Life* comprises multiple stylistic elements. Camera and figure movement, for example, consistently serve as complementary procedures: the dynamic quality of the shots, and the sense of propulsion from one to the next, is powerfully augmented by corresponding movements of the human form and by the action of the camera. Looking, for example, at the outdoor sequences of family interaction, we see that the precision of the editing both demands and motivates the forward-rush of the camera (a characteristic movement that energizes much of Malick's cinema) and also stipulates its finer gestures, such as the balletic half-rotations of the frame. Likewise, the actors' positioning and gestures serve as sympathetic extensions, so that a glance, or a sudden turn, carries the camera's movement across fragmented shots. Taken together, these tactics are constitutive components of the film's montage system that deliver, like the timing and quality of the cuts, the film's enfolded sense of drive and buoyancy.

Relatedly, it's useful to observe the degree to which these formal impulses are strongly aligned with feeling, translating the hypocrisies of paternal discipline, or the force of Jack's blunted energies, for instance, by a synergistic combination of moving camera and elliptical cuts. An exemplary instance spans several shots: across these images, the camera swerves suddenly, and violently, to convey the tensions of an escalating argument in ragged bursts. The shots are colored by subjectivity, though not constrained by it, always returning to more global issues of relation and interconnection. But it's worth remarking that this feeling of directness is new for Malick, and newly unpredictable, revising a cinematic style that has heretofore seemed more reserved.

Of course, a large contribution is made by the film's sound elements, which continually combine voiceover and elaborate musical scoring. If this chapter has dwelled more substantially on other formal elements, viewers of the film will attest to the decisive appeal of its sound design. Voiceover narration is a consistent feature of Malick's work, utilized in each of his films; arguably, the most distinctive aspect is his exclusive use of female voiceover as a framing device in *Badlands* and *Days of Heaven*—a choice that still feels slightly subversive in the contemporary context.[23] In *The Tree of Life*, the spoken narration is divided among the players (Mother, Father, Jack), in a way that complements the film's fragmented form. Relatedly, Malick's use of classical music within his films continues with *The Tree of Life*, which features extracts of thirty-seven individual pieces, blended with original music by French composer Alexandre Desplat.[24] As a particularly robust feature of the film, *The Tree of Life*'s score has received much attention from critics, who have sometimes construed it as a key to the film's workings. On this view, the film's elliptical form is explained in terms of an overarching "symphonic structure" that shifts impressionistically from dinosaurs to the desert. This approach is also said to reveal Malick's (closely guarded) aesthetic sensibility.[25] While there is no doubting the music's enormous impact on viewers, this focus tends to pass over the film's specificities, as though its complexity were not its own but a derivative of the score's meticulously assigned formal elements. Instead, the music is better conceived as the most prominent piece in a dynamic filmic system set to work on the sense perceptions of viewers. In this way, it makes its contribution to the formal possibilities raised this book's first chapter, serving a mode of horizontal montage that is adapted to the work of the fiction film, whose impact slides "from ear to eye."[26]

This brings us to a second issue that deserves a little more attention. I want to stress that *The Tree of Life*'s formal system, driven by montage and harnessed to other stylistic strategies, reflects the fragmentation and flow of temporal experience, mobilized specifically as a phenomenon of the body. It seeks to generate an experience of time as something *lived* and not merely theorized: perhaps the most persuasive evidence of this effort lies with the film's excesses, with their tendency to overwhelm rather than assure the viewer. This inclination speaks even to the epic time scales that the film formulates, foregrounding the vastness of time as it encompasses human experience over its more legible proximities.

In other words, the film sustains temporality as we live it, but fail to see it—not as logical progression but as a widened web of affinities. The task of apprehending these connections is sometimes difficult, and, as I believe Malick's film acknowledges, potentially foolish. The critical embarrassment that the film has occasionally inspired is precisely a measure of this risk. But the binding force of the film, bridging all its disparate structures, is a kind of tactile alignment, a shared flow of sensation that shows us temporal experience as something embracing—that surrounds us like music, or carries us forward in its dance. Again, a critical distinction is called for between Malick's method and any sort of scattered impressionism, the kind of half-formed aesthetic that might justify an imprecise claim for its poetry or profundity. These are plausible descriptors, but their suitability stems from the considered nature of the film's design and the depth of its arguments. The film does not only reflect the sensuous nature of temporal experience, or merely itemize its palpable contradictions: rather, it asks that we meet it halfway in an attitude of openness, acknowledging the way that we belong to temporality as we actively mediate it.

To develop this idea, we should review a curious episode that occurs midway through the film, during the long passage that charts Jack's adolescent rebellion. Despite its brevity (the episode lasts less than a minute), the impact of the sequence is intense, and its details are instructive. It begins with a close view of a book's page, lit by the restless beam of a flashlight. The light reveals the text and colored drawings of a boy's adventure book and then surveys Jack's room, while his brothers sleep. This gives way to a rapid-fire series of seven shots, focused on the menacing form of a garishly costumed clown. (See fig. 5.6.) He is framed both at close range and at a swaggering distance, squirting an onlooker with the flower in his lapel, and then plunged suddenly into the cloudy waters of a dunk tank. Eventually this shot is replaced with one of Jack, looking on. Two courses of movement are thus inscribed in this series: first, there is the surging movement of the camera, approaching and then pulling away from its subject; second, there is the sudden vertical movement of the clown's release into the water, told in four shattered perspectives like Eisenstein's broken plate(s). Like the strategies deployed elsewhere in *The Tree of Life*, the shots are double-edged, cutting along two affective axes simultaneously.

The sequence next shifts to a space that is familiar, but told differently: here is the attic presented earlier in the film with its small, squared window. This time the room is darker and contains the shadowed forms of Jack and his father. This is a younger Jack than before, a small child pictured in a rocking chair and then steering an oversized tricycle. His father stands above him, an exaggerated, looming figure barely containable by the space. There is something strongly Expressionist in these images, as though melding the tortured terrain of a Murnau film with the saturated hues of a 1950s comic book. At this odd intersection, the cinema of Stanley Kubrick comes to mind as well, particularly for *The Shining* (1980).

Figure 5.6. Immersion 1. From *The Tree of Life* (Terrence Malick, 2011).

But what else do these shots register, beyond the flickering associations of Jack's consciousness? A congruence of feeling ties one image to the next: from the cover of darkness, to the submerged clown, to the claustrophobic zone of the low-beamed attic, the series is strongly immersive, tied to experiences that are both pleasurable and grotesque. In retrospect, this is a persistent habit of Malick's film, as it continually enframes conditions that are fluent and enveloping. We need only think of the film's numerous images of water—ambivalently aligned with creation (the wonders of sea life; birth) and destruction (death and drowning). Immersion is pictured in other ways, too, as when the children lose themselves in imaginative play, or, with historical irony, are engulfed in clouds of toxic gas. In every case, what is pictured is a kind of sensuous involvement in the world that is dynamically multiplied from shot to shot.

This observation directs us to something fundamental in Malick's cinema. To understand what Malick's montage means for his films, we need to recognize that their core movement is not doubleness or equivocation but *inclusiveness*, an impulse toward the whole of experience, however much joy and suffering this entails. Moving outward from *The Tree of Life*, this idea finds prominent expression in Malick's next feature, *To The Wonder* (2013), again raising the ire of critics. In its often wordless telling of a passionate relationship between Neil and Marina (played by Ben Affleck and Olga Kurylenko), the film returns repeatedly to a particular type of image: the dizzying, whirling movements of Marina, a former dancer, whose balletic gestures sweep through each of the film's spaces, from the wide fields of Oklahoma to the cluttered aisles of a supermarket. Like many viewers, I wondered why the film kept returning to this kind of image, as though insisting on it. But its form and force make greater sense when we think back to the immersive emphasis that I have described above: this is as an iconic image for Malick that reverberates for all his cinema.

We find it, in variation, in *The Tree of Life* and all the films that precede it. It registers as a human or natural form animated by something greater than itself—lit up by it, standing open to it, overcome by it. As viewers, we encounter such images linked successively, elaborating a pathway or flow that moves from natural phenomena to the human form and back again, disclosing their shared energies across the shivering effects of montage. *The Tree of Life* clearly outlines the largest and most evident versions of this idea: human life in the service of god; the human body given over to childbirth. But Malick means that we should see the smallest versions of this idea, too, the ones that cinema is uniquely equipped to show us. So here is an image of green reeds swayed by water. Here are bodies held open to experience, caught up in dance, in the exuberance of play, or in the open-ended temporality of a game. Here is the human form in its pliancy and vulnerability, overcome by such things as old age, laughter, sleep, wonder, "the glory," in Malick's language—each swifly enumerated. (See fig. 5.7.)

This is an informing principle of Malick's cinema that attains special visibility in images like these, causing critics to sometimes question their overabundance. It also infuses the film's methods of montage, so far as these procedures enact a tension between the elliptical and the eternal, pulling the viewer into their permanence of flow. Thinking of the film's narrative premises, we might say that its temporal form shows us what Mr. O'Brien has trouble with: that the truth of life is not arrived at as an act of mastery, or by force of will; rather, it occurs in the in-between temporality of self and world, in yielding to it. The formal design of Malick's film traces this dynamic for us, repeatedly illuminating a thing and its opposite, to show us the generative tension that holds them together across time, in antagonism and affection.

One might still ask why a film like *The Tree of Life* should be composed via montage and not more holistically; surely its overarching concern with flow and connection would be better served by a contiguous formal method—for example, by the fluid movement and longer takes of Malick's earlier work. The answer to this question is a significant one, and justifies the film's place within this study: *The Tree of Life* particularly invites the mediating work of the viewer, sometimes pleasurable and sometimes difficult, to locate the fine correspondence of the film's

Figure 5.7. Immersion 2. From *The Tree of Life* (Terrence Malick, 2011).

pieces by their active synthesis. It might well have been an appealing instance of long take cinema—drawing nearer to critical expectations, perhaps—but the film's distinctive hermeneutic challenge is to draw us into the fray of its immersive operations, struggling to find their reciprocities of meaning.

In other words, the film seeks to animate *us* by its editing procedures and complementary camerawork, to catch us up in its movement, surrendering to its rigor and excesses. What *The Tree of Life* finally offers is not simply a form that mimics its content, but rather an effect that is visceral and generative. Put simply—possibly too simply—it teaches us that feeling something is already a way of knowing it. This is, I think, a critical valence of Bazin's concept of ambiguity, arising from experiences of long take and ellipses, and resonating powerfully for Merleau-Ponty. I take Malick's film as an attempt to render this idea concretely.

Conclusion

> What Saint Augustine said of time—that it is perfectly familiar to each, but that none of us can explain it to the others—must be said of the world.
>
> —Maurice Merleau-Ponty, *The Visible and the Invisible*

THROUGHOUT THESE PAGES, MY claim has been that cinematic time is productively conceived from the ground up, as it were, as an encounter mediated by films and viewers. This is to highlight, and to enter into account, the experience of temporality that arises from our active engagement with a film's temporal structures. My hope is that this book designates a space for thinking about cinematic time in new ways: namely, as an experience of film viewing that is dynamically charged and sensuous; as an incentive to phenomenological description and hermeneutical inquiry; and potentially, as a situation in which the ambiguities of time are held open for contemplation. These are the rich rewards for being open to a film's timeliness.

In an important sense, these arguments are motivated by the idea posed in the above epigraph, which asks us to consider a meaningful connection between temporality and our experience of the world. To stake this comparison for cinema—and more than that, to situate it with cinema's temporal devices, amid the cuts and pauses and lurches of time that a film generates—is to bring a big idea into contact with very particular matters. This is a proportionate claim for the cinema, perhaps, but a more ambitious one for the time we spend with it, which no longer appears inessential to thinking.

In another way, this book has sought to trace a dialogue between film analysis and filmic pleasure. These terms are commonly configured as opposites, on the assumption that one inevitably leads away from the other, or that analysis places us at a distance from the work that pleasure can never recuperate. A related question is to ask what counts as a scholarly response to a film, and whether our fondness for a work, or the pleasure we take in it, can ever be called generative—that is, whether it has any purchase for thinking seriously about cinema (or anything else). Yet I find the hermeneutical practice of attentiveness, as I have engaged it across this book's chapters for cinematic time, undercuts these assumptions, revealing ways that our analysis of a film is rooted in affection, borne out by patient strategies of looking, listening, and waiting. That is why a consideration of filmic temporality is especially suggestive hermeneutically: it shows us that the time given over to watching a film does not move only toward or away from pleasure, but may linger with it.

Let me refocus these premises to clarify how they pay off for our case studies, especially with respect to the issue of filmic ambiguity. With the benefit of hindsight, a few observations can be made about this group of films as they function here. In terms of broad narrative patterns, it's worth observing that all, or nearly all the films begin with a death. Certainly, this is true for Soderbergh, Tsai, and Malick's films: with Ozon's, the demise in question is a divorce, but it's harrowing enough. So opening sequences have proven to be critical for each of these titles, issuing an initial rupture that directs the narrative into a responsive patterning, forming a temporal frame that mobilizes deep concerns. Thus, the formal details that we engage in these instances—those stuttering, initiating repetitions of *The Limey*, or the drawn-out stillness into which Hsiao-Kang's father disappears in *What Time Is It There?*—are not arbitrary time structures, but ways of putting a question: How does time matter to us in our lives, especially in those situations when it is most at issue? Expressed another way, human pain and loss appear to have found formal equivalences here, or perhaps show us that with the cinema we have equated them already, as one of the meanings brought into alignment by a film's temporal syntax. Thus, the jump-cuts in Malick's film, registering the news contained in a telegram, are both searing and efficient, as though finding for the first time a way to disclose these truths of experience.

This draws nearer to the question of ambiguity. For the first two films, the prevailing uncertainties chiefly concern the way the past informs the present. While initially challenging us to make sense of an intricate temporal design that may hold the key to their meanings, both *The Limey* and *5x2* work to complicate this promise of clarity, eventually rescinding it. *The Limey* raises the possibility that we will not know the past until violently confronted with it, and even then stand powerless against it. Perhaps the projects we set for ourselves, like Wilson's, aren't really new at all, but instead reanimate old conflicts; in this sense, past and present are much closer than they first appear, and only vary, like Soderbergh's repetitions, in their minor inflections. Yet there is a certain optimism lurking within these operations, too: it surfaces in Wilson's wry expression, and in the tacit suggestion that the stranger we are to ourselves may be welcomed by others. With Ozon's film, these sentiments are blended differently. As viewers, we soon discover that a retrospective analysis may tend to deepen ambiguities, rather than dispel them. What dissolves a marriage, or preserves it, cannot be recovered after the fact, or objectively; instead, what we discern is a kind of luminous interval, a delicate interface between times, where the present pulls away from the past, however briefly, and is lit for the future.

The remaining case studies have much to say about the value of the present, but orchestrate their insights in nearly opposed ways. The slowed cadence of Tsai's film is a lesson in laconic humor, and enduring patience: it challenges us, as viewers, to accommodate the protracted temporality that it enframes, accepting the priorities of its players, with their obsessive routines and long silences. But what the film finally effects by its structuring of time is an intense dilation, highlighting the way a single action flowers for a wider context, and disclosing the shared fabric of our lives as a kind of comic revelation, presented as something that appears out of nothing (and also the reverse). Conversely, *The Tree of Life* approaches the time of our lives with a speed that is comparatively dizzying. Here, the technique of montage conveys a merged temporality of self and world: shots rise and descend in deliberate alternation, or move as a gale of sensuous sparks, vivid and immersive. Rapid cuts first accommodate and then shatter the wide paths of a circling camera to expose the generous movement that is internal to them. By this, Malick's film nearly reverses the strategies of slow cinema so far as its ambiguities are sustained by a temporal syntax that is comparative and elliptical. But in other respects, its way of understanding temporality is fully compatible, delivering an experience and an idea of time that is claimed only by yielding to it.

With these case studies, I have emphasized what is exemplary rather than representative, detailing the timeliness of representative titles rather than charting a broad, contextualizing landscape. In part, this is a methodological choice, trained on the peculiar temporal patterning of each film rather than its discursive life. It also serves as a counterbalance to the course of recent scholarship, which, for reasons I have touched on already, has deprioritized the tasks of film analysis and interpretation. But of course the larger landscape deserves consideration, too, as it reveals a common temporal syntax and also the ways these films may depart from it. So this approach to cinematic time can be productively extended to other films, to define the distinctive temporal cadences of contemporary cinema more comprehensively. This strikes me as a valuable extension of my arguments here and an exciting way forward for film-analytical and theoretical work.

After all, the work of interpretation is always unfinished; it is this temporal inflection and open-endedness to history that constitutes its ambiguity. This lends hermeneutical activity a quality of doubleness, especially as it reckons with experiences of time. On the one hand, there is the risk of interpretation, or the danger that a text will elude us, leaving us empty-handed. On the other, this is interpretation's intrinsic value: it tends to unsettle the familiar terrain that we inhabit, even just temporarily, to set us on fresh conceptual ground. This kind of duality also animates Heidegger's arguments concerning the constitutive tensions of the work of art, expressed in his fierce counterconcepts of "world" and "earth." Heidegger tells us that the work opens up a world *and* conceals it, framing an encounter with what is unfathomable, or with what cannot be put to use.[1] The question to take away from this concerns what it would mean to allow the work to *do* its work—or for this book's purposes, to take its own time.

This point deserves some additional support from a film, and one that has been mentioned only in passing. It's worth returning to Bela Tarr's most recent, and ostensibly final film, *The Turin Horse* (Hungary, 2012) as it consolidates the ideas that that underlie this study concerning time and interpretation, to show how they constitute each other. For those unfamiliar with it, *The Turin Horse* is an emphatic formal experiment, its delimited action developed in mesmerizing long takes. The film's 143-minute running time is molded into 30 long-lasting shots, charting, with patience and precision, the slow unmaking of a world.

The film's long takes assemble a kind of relentless, repetitive temporality, observing the attenuating routines of a farmer and his daughter across six days in their efforts to survive a desolate landscape. The film's temporality is grounded in their tangible tasks, unfolded in the work of getting dressed, of cooking potatoes, of harnessing and unharnessing a horse. Significantly, time doesn't disappear behind these tasks but seems intensified by their sameness, caught up in cycling rhythms like the raging winds outside, and in the redundancies of Mihály Víg's haunting score.

The section that especially interests me occurs in the first third of the film. The daughter stands at frame left, leaning over a sink basin;

she washes a shirt vigorously, lifting it and returning it to the steaming water, in a careful economy of movements. Her father moves about the space more freely, first dragging a tired basket toward the camera and then extracting a length of rope from it, which he secures to the wall. Now the daughter approaches, carrying a clean shirt to the line and adjusting its wet folds over it. Set in place, the white shirt obscures the frame entirely, and remains that way for longer than twenty seconds. Eventually, the shot terminates with a cut.

I admire this scene for its hermeneutical possibility, as condensed in the time we spend with the white shirt. The sudden blankness that registers in these moments creates an extended pause in our viewing experience, inviting us to contemplate its terms and limitations, like a slow-burning magician's trick. The drawn-out tenor of this pause is exactly in line with the film's temporal contours, but its reduction of the narrative action, already constrained, to nearly nothing is punctuating. Interpretation *matters* here: the challenge of it presses on us sharply, asking us to read the time as we endure it—or perhaps to endure the time by trying to read it.

Let me put things a little differently. This enforced pause is certainly a crucial aspect of the film's larger operations: the wall of white serves as an analogue, and an inversion, of the darkness that increasingly seeps into the film's spaces, threatening the players with an eventual eclipse. The film actually favors surprises like these, serving up occasional obstacles to vision in a manner that is stylized and yet also seems to extend from the mise-en-scène. This kind of obstacle is found, for example, in the hard, intrusive lines of certain compositions, like the vertical beam of a windowpane that appears later in the film, at first unseen and then rising up obstinately by the camera's repositioning, severing the lateral spread of landscape. There is also something comparable in the transitory masking that occurs when the house is later enveloped by clouds of dust, or lost in a spray of dark leaves, which fall like cinders. What is important about these moments is the way they locate, and then briefly center, the opacities of an environment, foregrounding, however briefly, the impediments to vision and understanding that form the quiet structures of this world. I think of cinematic time as offering an opportunity that is similar: it allows us to observe an ongoing interpretive process within occasions that are especially potent, or supersaturated. When we attend to it, cinematic time discloses a working out of temporality that is first filmic, but that opens up suggestively to wider experience.

My reading of this episode cannot reduce it to total transparency; it remains a little opaque—almost comically so—and this opacity means that this is not quite a level playing field. The film remains greater than me, carefully composed and enigmatic: *it knows more than I do*. My claim for this scene, and for this study as a whole, finds precise expression here; I think this experience of ambiguity, keenly felt as a temporal phenomenon, deserves acknowledgment for all the ways it is illuminating. It is necessary, and worthwhile, to remain with these shots, to notice how they make time for us, on the way to discerning their meaning. But the idea of timeliness also insists that we should hold that meaning up to our own experience, to see what is revealed by it. This is what this book's case studies have sought to elaborate.

So I take the temporal ambiguities that cinema offers to be richly instructive. They function not as a limit point for film interpretation, but rather, as a way of beginning again, of returning to a certain receptivity toward cinema, where film is always potentially more than we can say about it. One of cinema's profound capacities, as the contemporary films discussed here elucidate, is that cinema can lead us away from ourselves toward the world, to acknowledge how little we know about it. I understand this premise to be resonant for Bazin's commentaries, and also as a fair program for considering the experiences of time that cinema offers us. But it is through Merleau-Ponty's writings, and Heidegger's, and in the concept of filmic ambiguity most acutely, that this project is fully realized. Here phenomenological hermeneutics shapes an approach to cinematic time that treasures its timeliness, situating its significance in the lively interplay of film and viewer, and receiving the medium, in its continual evolution, as an occasion to reencounter a world immersed in meaning.

Notes

Introduction

1. I admire Noel Carroll's formulation of suspense as a "well-structured question." See "Toward a Theory of Film Suspense," in *Theorizing the Moving Image* (Cambridge: Cambridge University Press, 1996), p. 100.

2. See David Couzens Hoy's excellent study, *The Time of Our Lives: A Critical History of Temporality* (Cambridge MA: MIT Press, 2012).

3. *The World of Perception*, translated by Stéphanie Ménasé (London and New York: Routledge, 2004), p. 73.

4. Paul Ricoeur's way of understanding this overlap is to characterize phenomenology as the "unsurpassable presupposition" of hermeneutics, so far as both practices interrupt lived experience in order to signify it. See "Phenomenology and Hermeneutics," *From Text to Action: Essays in Hermeneutics, II*, trans. K. Blamey and John B. Thompson (Evanston: Northwestern University Press, 1991), especially 38, and 25–52.

5. New York: Oxford University Press, 1984.

6. On this discussion, see David Rodowick's essay, "An Elegy for Theory," in *October* 122 (Fall 2007): 91–109.

7. David Bordwell's long-standing arguments have tied a particular idea of hermeneutics to what he terms "Grand Theory." On this view, hermeneutics is a loose interpretive practice that facilitates neglectful theorization, advancing filmic meanings at the expense of textual and historical specificities. To the extent that Bordwell's critique is directed at a kind of interpretive work that positions films as mere demonstrations of theoretical concepts, this study is fully sympathetic. But of course film hermeneutics can be much more than this—and is not necessarily indifferent to the value of "practical interpretive reason," as Bordwell frames it. See *Making Meaning: Inference and Rhetoric in the Interpretation of Cinema* (Boston: Harvard University Press, 1989), p. 40. Likewise, hermeneutics potentially illuminates the kinds of film viewing experience that interests Noel Carroll; see, for example, "Art, Narrative, and Emotion," in *Beyond Aesthetics: Philosophical Essays* (Cambridge: Cambridge University Press, 2001), pp. 215–234.

8. See Merleau-Ponty's *Visible and Invisible*, edited by Claude Lefort, translated by Alphonso Lingis (Evanston: Northwestern University. Press, 1968), p. 13n7.

9. See Lewis Hyde's *Trickster Makes This World: Mischief, Myth and Art* (New York: North Point, 1998), 52.

10. Lesley Stern and George Kouvaros, *Falling For You: Essays on Film and Performance* (Sydney: Power Publications, 1999, 1999), p. 9.

11. Ibid, p. 9.

12. This concise explanation derives from J. W. Hefferman's *Museum of Words: The Poetics of Ekphrasis from Homer to Ashbery* (Chicago: University of Chicago Press, 2004), p. 3.

13. This formulation derives loosely from Hubert Dreyfus's idea of hermeneutics: see his *Being-in-the-world: A Commentary on Heidegger's Being and Time, Division I* (Cambridge, MA: MIT Press, 1991), p. 36.

14. Representative texts are *Closely Watched Films: An Introduction to the Art of Narrative Film Technique*, by Marilyn Fabe (Berkeley and Los Angeles: University of California Press, 2004); *Style and Meaning: Studies in the Detailed Analysis of Film*, edited by John Gibbs and Douglas Pye (Manchester, Manchester University Press, 2005), and, in different ways, Christian Keathey's *Cinephilia and History, or The Wind in the Trees* (Bloomington: Indiana University Press, 2006) and Girish Shambu's *The New Cinephilia* (Montreal: Caboose, 2014).

15. From Sobchack's *Carnal Thoughts: Embodiment and Moving Image Culture* (Berkeley and Los Angeles: University of California Press, 2004), p. 53.

16. See Sobchack's *Address of the Eye* (Princeton, NJ: Princeton University Press, 1992); Laura U. Marks, *The Skin of the Film: Intercultural Cinema, Embodiment, and the Senses* (Duke University Press,. 1999), and *Touch: Sensuous Theory and Multisensory Media.* (University of Minnesota Press, 2002); Jennifer M. Barker, *The Tactile Eye: Touch and the Cinematic Experience* (Berkeley and Los Angeles: University of California Press, 2009); *Phenomenology and the Future of Film: Rethinking Subjectivity Beyond French Cinema* (London: Palgrave Macmillan, 2012).

17. Sobchack, *Address of the Eye*, p. xvi.

18. See *Cinema 1: The Movement-Image*, translated by Hugh Tomlinson and Barbara Habberjam (Minneapolis: University of Minnesota Press, 1986); *Cinema 2: The Time-Image*, translated by Hugh Tomlinson and Robert Galeta (London: Athlone Press, 1989).

19. Deleuze's work, both independently and with Félix Guattari, has been enormously generative for scholars of film. An abridged sample of this literature is as follows: D. N. Rodowick, *Gilles Deleuze's Time Machine* (NC: Duke University Press, 1997); Barbara Kennedy, *Deleuze and Cinema: The Aesthetics of Sensation* (Edinburgh: Edinburgh University Press, 2000); Gregory Flaxman, ed., *The Brain Is the Screen: Deleuze and the Philosophy of Cinema* (Minneapolis: University of Minnesota Press, 2000); Ronald Bogue, *Deleuze on Cinema* (New York: Routledge, 2003); Patricia Pisters, *The Matrix of Visual Culture: Working with Deleuze in Film Theory* (Stanford: Stanford University Press, 2003); Elena del Río, *Deleuze and the Cinemas of Performance: Powers of Affection* (Edinburgh: Edinburgh University Press, 2008).

20. *Cinema 2: The Time-Image* (Minneapolis: University of Minnesota Press, 1989), p. 271.

21. Cinema's capacity to appropriate duration is a matter taken up in the philosophy of Henri Bergson, and subsequently, by Gilles Deleuze. For Bergson's objections, see *Creative Evolution*, tr., Arthur Mitchell, New York: Dover, 1998 [1911].

22. See Deleuze's critique of natural perception, *Cinema 1: The Movement-Image* (Minneapolis: University of Minnesota Press, 1986), p. 57.

23. Elena del Rio's essay, "Alchemies of Thought in Godard's Cinema: Deleuze and Merleau-Ponty" elaborates on this distinction. See *SubStance* 108, no. 34.3 (2005): 62–78.

24. See David Bordwell, "Intensified Continuity," *Film Quarterly* 55, no. 3(Spring 2002): 16–28.

25. On this point, see Jacques *Rancière, Bela Tarr, The Time After* (Minneapolis: Univocal, 2013), esp. pp. 63–81.

26. See Schoonover's acute essay, "Wastrels of Time: Slow Cinema's Laboring Body, the Political Spectator, and the Queer," *Framework* 53, no. 1 (Spring 2012): 65–78.

27. To this end, Dutch critic Dana Linssen has developed the term *slow criticism*, aimed particularly at the dialogue between filmmaker and critic. An early discussion appears here: http://www.filmkrant.nl/av/org/filmkran/slow/slow-lin.html.

28. Ira Jaffe, *Slow Cinema: Countering the Cinema of Action* (London and New York: Wallflower, 2014), pp. 7, 160.

29. Dudley Andrew, *What Cinema Is! Bazin's Quest and Its Charge* (West Sussex: Wiley-Blackwell, 2010), p. xvii.

30. It's worth noting that the films considered here need just this sort of focused attention. At this writing, neither Soderbergh's nor Ozon's film has received any sustained scholarly analysis, while the philosophical inflection of Malick's project has often tended to distract critics from its formal specificities. Only Tsai's film has inspired much scholarly assessment; valuable readings of his work are noted in chapter 4.

Chapter 1

1. This phrase derives from Jean Louis Schefer, "Ordinary Man of the Cinema," in *The Enigmatic Body: Essays on the Arts*, edited and translated by Paul Smith (Cambridge: Cambridge University Press, 1995).

2. This stands in contrast to the terms of Todd McGowan's analysis, *Out of Time: Desire in Atemporal Cinema* (Minneapolis, MN: University of Minnesota Press, 2011). McGowan's psychoanalytic framework regards the temporal distortions of recent cinema as a "turn away from chronology that is both broader and deeper than any historical antecedent," p. 7. Contextualized by a longer game of temporal experimentation, however, it becomes easier to see how contemporary examples belong to that history, and to temporality, rather than refusing it.

3. See Ricoeur's *Interpretation Theory: Discourse and the Surplus of Meaning* (Fort Worth: Texas Christian University Press, 1976), esp. pp. 71–95.

4. These ideas are developed across the three volumes of *Time and Narrative*, translated by Kathleen McLaughlin and David Pellauer (Chicago and London: University of Chicago Press, 1984–88). See especially Volume One, 52–90; Volume Three, 180–192.

5. Macquarrie and Robinson's authoritative translation of *Being and Time* renders *Zeitlichkeit* as "Temporality" and strongly cautions against any reading of this term as *timeliness* in the usual sense. Conversely, a recent reinterpretation of *Being and Time* (Carol J. White's *Time and Death: Heidegger's Analysis of Finitude*, edited by Mark Ralkowski [Burlington, VT: Ashgate Publishing Company, 2005]) proposes that *Zeitlichkeit* be translated as "Timeliness" rather than "Temporality" to render Heidegger's meaning more consistently across his text and with respect to his later writings. In any case, my use of the term within this book is a conscious revision, directed to very different ends: it aims to bring Heidegger's understanding of temporal experience (as active and profoundly immersive) into dialogue with the temporal dynamics we experience in film viewing.

6. To capture this sense, John Haugeland translates the term as *timeishness*; see *Dasein Disclosed* (Cambridge, MA: Harvard University Press, 2013). Michael Inwood's guide supplies this admirably clear explanation; see *A Heidegger Dictionary* (Malden, MA: Blackwell Publishers, 1999), p. 221.

7. Timeliness may be most familiar as it resonates for Nietzsche's thought. As a counterpoint to "the untimely," it mobilizes a distinction between what is appropriate to the time (in the sense of up to date, or fashionable) and what is discordant with it (as *zeitgemäss*). In different ways, this formulation has been taken up by both Jacques Derrida and Gilles Deleuze. A related distinction is made in Edward Said's elegant study, *On Late Style: Music and Literature Against the Grain*, where it develops a contrast between works that, when examined retrospectively, can be assimilated to a discernible pattern from which it is then possible to extrapolate meaning, and "late" works that refuse any expectation of accessibility, harmony, or reconciliation when examined in the same manner. Though the clarification is perhaps unnecessary, timeliness, as deployed in this study, has more than a little in common with the notion of the untimely outlined above, in so far as it seeks to illuminate what is underarticulated about cinematic time without reducing it to something fully companionable or predictable. On the above distinctions, see Nietzsche's *Untimely Meditations*, edited by Daniel Breazeale (Cambridge: Cambridge University Press, 1997), esp. pp. xliv–xlvii, and Said's *On Late Style: Music and Literature Against the Grain* (New York: Vintage, 2007).

8. Hans-Georg Gadamer, *Truth and Method*, 2nd ed., translated and revised by Joel Weinsheimer and David Marshall (New York: Continuum, 1997), pp. 102–110.

9. Significantly, this means acknowledging the kinds of (pre)understandings that we bring to the work; because all understanding is situated, it is achieved not by shutting out the world, but rather by recognizing one's (ever-shifting) place within it. On this point, see *Truth and Method*, pp. 302–307. These ideas are extended to matters of film history below.

10. André Bazin, "The Ontology of the Photographic Image." in *What Is Cinema?*, vol. 1, selected and translated by Hugh Gray (Berkeley and Los Angeles: University of California Press, 1967), pp. 9–16.

11. Ibid., pp. 14–15.

12. Ibid., p. 15.

13. Ibid, p. 38.

14. See *What Is Cinema?* vol. 2, selected and translated by Hugh Gray (Berkeley: University of California Press, 1972), p. 66.

15. See Bazin's review, "On John Huston's The Red Badge of Courage," in *Bazin on Global Cinema, 1948–1958*, edited by Bert Cardullo. Originally published in *Cahiers du cinema*, October 1953 (Austin: University of Texas Press, 2014), p. 126. Though praising the film, Bazin indicates that Huston's work in general lacks a "genuinely personal style." Indeed, the ambiguities that Bazin discerns spring from a style of editing that is "unoriginal," p. 125.

16. See Andrew's "Malraux, Bazin, and the Gesture of Picasso," in *Opening Bazin: Postwar Film Theory and Its Afterlife*, edited with Hervé Joubert-Laurencin (New York: Oxford University Press, 2011), p. 158.

17. Another title, Mary Ann Doane's *The Emergence of Cinematic Time: Modernity, Contingency, the Archive* (Cambridge: Harvard University Press, 2002) shares these concerns. These studies of cinematic time coincide with, and in important ways contribute to, a resurgence of interest in the work of André Bazin, spearheaded by Dudley Andrew. See also Andrew's recent anthology, which features a range of distinguished scholarship: *Opening Bazin: Postwar Film Theory and Its Afterlife* (New York: Oxford University Press, 2011).

18. Peirce's analyses also suggest that photographs are "iconic," insofar they have properties in common with the objects they represent. For an outline of the classificatory system, see "What Is a Sign?" in *The Essential Peirce: Selected Philosophical Writings, Volume 2, 1893–1913*, edited by the Peirce Edition Project (Bloomington, IN: Indiana University Press, 1998). Peter Wollen's influential text is *Signs and Meaning in the Cinema* (London: Secker & Warburg/BFI, 1969).

19. A clarifying essay on this issue is Tom Gunning's "What's the Point of an Index? Or, Faking Photographs," *Nordicom Review* 5, no. 1/2 (September 2004): 39–49.

20. See Rosen's *Change Mummified: Cinema, Historicity, Theory* (Minneapolis: University of Minnesota Press, 2001), p. 23.

21. See "The Ontology of the Photographic Image," in *What Is Cinema?*, vol. 1, selected and translated by Hugh Gray (Berkeley: University of California Press, 1967), p. 15.

22. Laura Mulvey, *Death 24x a Second: Stillness and the Moving Image* (London: Reaktion Books, 2006), pp. 52–53.

23. Building on her instrumental essay, "Visual Pleasure and Narrative Cinema" in *Screen* 16, no. 3 (Autumn 1975): 6–18, Mulvey's particular claim is that new technologies invite us to reclaim fetishism as a progressive viewing stance, producing "possessive" (fetishistic) spectators and a "feminized" film aesthetic. See Mulvey, *Death 24x a Second*, pp. 161–180.

24. Rosalind E. Krauss has characterized the workings of *The Clock* as exploiting an "extended dilation of the 'now effect,' transforming the reel time of film into the real time of waiting." See Krauss's "Clock Time," *October* 136, Spring (2011): 213–217.

25. An excellent dossier on Marclay's installation appeared in *Framework: The Journal of Cinema and Media* 54, no. 2 (Fall 2013): 161–176, edited by Catherine Russell. On this question of the work's intended accessibility, see Erika Balsom's "Around The Clock: Museum and Market," pp. 177–191. A recent assessment of Marclay's work is offered by Julie Levinson's essay, "Time and Time Again: Temporality, Narrativity, and Spectatorship in Christian Marclay's *The Clock*," *Cinema Journal* 54, no. 3 (Spring 2015): 88–109.

26. The art world comparison that Mulvey cites is an older work, Douglas Gordon's installation *24 Hour Psycho* (1993), which manipulates the time of Hitchcock's film so that every frame is slowed for exacting scrutiny. To my mind, Gordon's work is of considerably greater interest than *The Clock*; its disturbance of narrative time is generative, disclosing new ambiguities in its source material.

27. Dating back to an early essay in *Film Comment* 9, no. 2 (March/April 1973): 64–68, and the book-length study, *André Bazin* (Columbia University Press, 1978), Dudley Andrew has consistently argued for influence of thinkers in Bazin's milieu. A recent essay is focused on the significance of André Malraux for understanding Bazin, but also asserts Bazin's influence on Merleau-Ponty (and notably, not the reverse); see "Malraux, Bazin, and the Gesture of Picasso," in *Opening Bazin*, p. 158. Bazin also contributed to *Les Temps Modernes*, which was edited by Sartre and Merleau-Ponty. On these biographical details, see Donato Totaro's "Introduction to André Bazin, Part 2: Style as a Philosophical Idea," *Offscreen* 7, no. 7 (July 2003).

28. See S. F. Sapontzis, "A Note on Merleau-Ponty's Ambiguity," *Philosophy and Phenomenological Research* 38, no. 4 (June 1978): 538–543.

29. *The Phenomenology of Perception*, translated by Donald Landes (New York: Routledge, 2012), p. 11.

30. See Eran Dorfman's review of Landes's translation, *University of Notre Dame Philosophical Reviews* (April 18). Merleau-Ponty's point about the centering of subjectivity appears on page 87 of *The Phenomenology of Perception.*

31. *Phenomenology of Perception*, p. 195.

32. Ibid., p. 87.

33. Ibid., p. 362.

34. Ibid., p. 447.

35. Against the idea that Merleau-Ponty's analyses are aimed at a return to immediacy and unmediated experience, I take seriously his assertion that "description is not the return to immediate experience; one never returns to immediate experience. It is only a question of whether we are to try to understand it. I believe that to attempt to express immediate experience is not to betray reason, but, on the contrary, to work toward its aggrandizement." See *The Primacy of Perception*, p. 30. This follows from his insistence that the phenomenological reduction is impossible; instead, the tasks of philosophy are open-ended and

historically conditioned. See *The Primacy of Perception*, edited by James M. Edie (Evanston, IL: Northwestern University Press, 1964), esp. pp. 42–43.

36. See "The Film and the New Psychology," in *Sense and Non-Sense*, edited by James M. Edie, translated by Hubert L. Dreyfus and Patricia Allen Dreyfus (Evanston, IL: Northwestern University Press, 1964), p. 53–54.

37. Ibid., p. 52.

38. Ibid., p. 50.

39. Ibid., p. 54.

40. Ibid., p. 57.

41. Ibid., p. 57. Like Bazin, Merleau-Ponty locates ambiguity in these divergent possibilities, but here comes down more strongly on the side of stylization.

42. Ibid., pp. 56.

43. Ibid., pp. 53–44.

44. Timothy Barnard's discovery and translation of an essay written by Bazin in 1952, a germinal version of "The Evolution of Film Language," contributes much to our understanding of these issues, parsing fine distinctions between the terms editing, montage, and découpage. See Barnard's translation of Bazin's "Découpage" (Montreal: Caboose, 2015).

45. Both references appear in "William Wyler, or the Jansenist of Directing." See *Bazin at Work: Major Essays and Reviews from the Forties and Fifties* (New York. Routledge, 1997), pp. 8 and 20n8.

46. See Bazin's review, "Sur les routes de l'URSS et Dimanche à Pékin," *France Observateur* 372 (June 27, 1957), p. 19, my translation.

47. See "Bazin on Marker," in *Film Comment* 39.4 (Jul/Aug 2003): 44–45. The review originally appeared as "Lettre de Sibérie" in *France Observateur* 443 (October 30, 1958), and was subsequently included in Jean Narboni's 1983 anthology, Bazin's writing, *Le Cinéma français de la libération à la nouvelle vague* (1945–1958), 1983, pp. 179–181. A significant counterconcept is Sergei Eisenstein's notion of *vertical montage*. Emerging in Eisenstein's essays written July and August 1940, the term proposes a complex fusion of sound and image, and of meanings synthesized across perpendicular planes, generating an overall orchestration that sparks simultaneous, rather than successive, effects. Thus Bazin's conception of a montage that is horizontal in certain respects retraces tensions internal to Eisenstein's concept of the vertical. See "Vertical Montage" in *S.M Eisenstein Selected Works: Volume II: Toward a Theory of Montage*, edited by Michael Glenny and Richard Taylor, translated by Michael Glenny (London: BFI Publishing, 1991), 327–399.

48. Ibid., p. 45.

49. Bazin, "Sur les routes de l'URSS et Dimanche à Pékin," *France Observateur* 372 (June 1957), p. 19. See also "Encore la censure: les films meurent aussi," Paris: *France Observateur* 349 (January 17, 1957), 19–20.

50. See Mroz's *Temporality and Film Analysis* (Edinburgh: Edinburgh University Press, 2012), p. 41.

51. Garrett Stewart, *Framed Time: Toward a Postfilmic Cinema* (Chicago: University of Chicago Press, 2007), p. 2.

52. Ibid., p. 8.

53. Ibid., p. 85.

54. Concerning the different dimensions of film analysis, Dan Morgan has suggested that we try to get both experiential and analytical judgments "up and running" simultaneously, which strikes me as a salutary formulation. See 'No Trickery with Montage': On Reading a Sequence in Godard's *Pierrot le fou*," *Film Studies* (Winter 2004): 15.

55. See "The Paradox of Suspense," in *Beyond Aesthetics* (Cambridge: Cambridge University Press, 2001), pp. 254–270.

56. See Hans Robert Jauss's *Toward an Aesthetic of Reception* (Minneapolis: University of Minnesota Press, 1982). While the term originates with the phenomenology of Edmund Husserl, as Paul de Man's preface indicates (ibid., xii), Jauss's use of it clearly derives from Gadamer's hermeneutics. For Gadamer, "horizons" are shifting and overlapping structures that are never reducible to a monolithic foundation or a single standpoint for thinking; thus, understanding results from a fusion of one's own horizon with the historical horizon. See *Truth and Method*, esp. pp. 302–307.

57. *The Material Ghost: Films and Their Medium* (Baltimore, MD: Johns Hopkins University Press, 1998).

58. *Vertigo* is an interesting case for many reasons. See the details of the 2012 *Sight & Sound* poll, which placed it at the top of its all-time list: Ian Christie notes that Hitchcock only entered the top ten in 1982 (two years after his death), and rose steadily in esteem over the next thirty years. See: http://www.bfi.org.uk/news/50-greatest-films-all-time.

59. Jauss, *Toward an Aesthetic of Reception* (Minneapolis: University of Minnesota Press, 1982), p. 21.

60. On this aspect of Merleau-Ponty's thought, an illuminating recent account is Hubert L. Dreyfus's *Skillful Coping: Essays on the Phenomenology of Everyday Perception and Action* (New York: Oxford University Press, 2014).

61. See Bordwell's *Narration and the Fiction Film* (Madison: University of Wisconsin Press, 1985), p. 38.

Chapter 2

1. On Soderbergh's retirement, see "Matt Damon: Steven Soderbergh Really Does Plan to Retire from Filmmaking," *Los Angeles Times*, December 22, 2010.

2. *Eros* comprises three short films about erotic love, alongside filmmakers Wong Kar-Wai and Michelangelo Antonioni. Soderbergh wrote, directed, photographed, and edited his contribution, called *Equilibrium*. Though not a remake of the past in the way certain of Soderbergh's other films are, *Equilibrium* features black-and-white cinematography and an anxious 1950s setting. In resuscitating the form of the omnibus film, strongly associated with 1960s art cinema, it is clear that one of *Eros*'s ambitions was to merge the legendary figure of Antonioni with more contemporary film practice.

3. For a detailed account of Soderbergh's significance for independent cinema, see Jim Hillier's (ed.) *American Independent Cinema: A Sight and Sound Reader* (London: British Film Institute, 2001), pp. 261–268.

4. On the comparison to Boorman's film, Janet Maslin's review in the *New York Times* (October 22, 1999, E29) is representative, as is J. Hoberman's in the *Village Voice* (October 6–12, 1999).

5. Soderbergh's commentary about *The Limey* emphasizes the extent to which the generic contours of a "formula" were deliberately retained to permit formal experimentation: in other words, *The Limey*'s familiar, "straight as a die" narrative lends an essential cohesion to its otherwise splintered structure. On this issue, Soderbergh indicates that he did not arrive at the right balance of formal difficulty and legibility on the first edit. For a full account, see *Steven Soderbergh Interviews*, edited by Anthony Kaufman (Jackson: University Press of Mississippi, 2002), esp. p. 116.

6. See Elif Cercel's interview, "Soderbergh Brings Past, Present Together in *The Limey*," in *Directors World*, November 15, 1999.

7. Fredric Jameson's conception of the "nostalgia film" is probably the best-known critique of this kind. See "Postmodernism, or the Cultural Logic of Late Capitalism," *New Left Review* 146, July–August 1984, esp. 66–68. Although I do not take up Jameson's arguments directly here, I would maintain that his sense of the postmodern text as reliant on quotation and as therefore tending to displace authentic history is just the sort of assumption that *The Limey* complicates.

8. Victor Shklovsky, "Art as Technique," in *Russian Formalist Criticism: Four Essays*, eds. Lee T. Lemon and Marion J. Reis (Lincoln: University of Nebraska Press, 1965), p. 11.

9. These relations are lucidly developed by Kristin Thompson in *Breaking the Glass Armor: Neo-formalist Film Analysis* (Princeton, NJ: Princeton University Press, 1988). While Thompson's account offers a clear application to cinema, I have elected here to engage directly with Shklovsky's writings.

10. Shklovsky, p. 3.

11. Shklovsky, p. 13.

12. On this question of the formal self-consciousness of opening sequences, see David Bordwell's essay, "Authorship and Narration in Art Cinema," collected in Virginia Wright Wexman's *Film and Authorship* (New Brunswick, NJ: Rutgers University Press, 2003).

13. Soderbergh's more recent film, *Contagion* (2011) continues this characteristic use of color. Like *Traffic*, the film uses blue and yellow filters, underlighting the blue segments. Initially, the yellow tone situates narrative threads that are closer to the virus, while blue zones are more removed from it. As the film proceeds, color demarcations appear to diminish: the established palette remains, but the logic of "in" and "out" is no longer as remarkable.

14. Wilson's recitation is rendered through a range of medium-to-close framings of him as he speaks. These images are splintered by jump-cuts in a manner that recalls the French New Wave, and Godard, in particular.

15. Though originating earlier, Cockney rhyming slang is most often associated with the criminal gangs active in London's East End during the 1950s and '60s. In his research on language games, David Crystal characterizes it as "a form of 'speech disguise'—a way of systematically hiding what the real meaning of a message is. The expressions make sense to the insider, but are nonsense to the outsider." Significantly, the author also notes that while Cockney rhyming slang likely originated as a thieves jargon, "it soon came to be supplemented by a great deal of invention whose motivation was no more than innocent fun." This latter emphasis on inventiveness brings things rather closer to the terms of Shklovsky's riddle. See *Language Play* (Chicago: University of Chicago Press, 1998), p. 50. Rhyming slang resurfaces later in the film and also briefly in *Ocean's Eleven*, to comic effect.

16. Shklovsky, p. 20. The author here refers more specifically to the case of the erotic riddle; within this discussion, I deploy his formulation in general terms.

17. Ibid., p. 17.

18. Martin Heidegger, *Being and Time*, translated by John Macquarrie and Edward Robinson (London: SCM Press, 1962), 24–28.

19. Ibid., p. 264.

20. Ibid., p. 401.

21. This experiment is not entirely without precedent: John's Wayne's final film, *The Shootist* (Don Siegal, 1976) begins with a brief montage from *Red River*, *Hondo*, *Rio Bravo*, and *El Dorado*. This material supplies a background for Wayne's character before the narrative opens.

22. For a more detailed account of this process, see *Steven Soderbergh Interviews*, p. 117.

23. Roland Barthes, *Camera Lucida*, translated by Richard Howard (New York: Hill & Wang, 1981), p. 77. Barthes's text sets out an essential difference between photography and cinema that differs somewhat from my use of his thinking here; my point is simply that Loach's footage seems qualitatively different than the material that surrounds it, and is in this way set apart slightly from the ongoing movement of *The Limey*'s narrative. This tension between fragment and flow might remind us, in a certain sense, of *À la recherche du temps perdu*: though touched off by direct questions rather than by sensations, as in Proust's novel, the borrowed images are also memory fragments—brief enough to seem outside of time, yet finally meaningful within it.

24. *The Limey* even concludes "outside of itself," with an image and song lifted from Loach's film. Thus, the notions of "separation" and "deferral" that Barthes identifies are doubly figured: not only does Soderbergh's film end "elsewhere," but with a reference that gestures even further. In *The Limey*'s final moments, Wilson sings: "Freedom is a word I rarely use / without thinking / of the time / when I was loved."

25. We should note the extent to which the French New Wave was an influence on Lester's methods. In interviews, Lester specifically cites Truffaut in this capacity, but also suggests that Jacques Tati shaped his sense of mise-en-scène and comic staging. See Steven Soderbergh and Richard Lester, *Getting Away with*

It, Or: The Further Adventures of the Luckiest Bastard You Ever Saw (London: Faber and Faber Limited, 1999), 97–99.

26. See Steven Soderbergh and Richard Lester, *Getting Away with It, Or: The Further Adventures of the Luckiest Bastard You Ever Saw* (London: Faber and Faber Limited, 1999).

27. That Nicolas Roeg served as Lester's cinematographer on the film is not insignificant; in key respects, *Petulia*'s disorienting formal structures anticipate Roeg's directorial debut, *Performance* (1970). The influence of both Roeg and Lester is readily discerned in *The Limey*.

28. A relevant text in this context is Vivian Sobchack's essay, "What My Fingers Knew," in *Carnal Thoughts: Embodiment and Moving Image Culture*, pp. 53–84.

Chapter 3

1. See, for example, James Quandt, "Flesh and Blood: Sex and Violence in Recent French Cinema." *Artforum International* 42, no. 6 (February 2004); Martine Beugnet, *Cinema and Sensation: French Film and the Art of Transgression* (Edinburgh: Edinburgh University Press, 2007).

2. There are two book-length studies of Ozon in English: Andrew Asibong's *The Cinema of François Ozon* (Manchester, UK: Manchester University Press, 2008); and Thibaut Schilt's monograph, *Francois Ozon* (Urbana: University of Illinois Press, 2011), as well as René Prédal's surveys in French, *French Cinema of the 1990s: French Cinema since 2000*, which considers Ozon among other directors. In reference to "French Extremist Cinema," critics have called for a more concrete engagement with the formal specificities of the cycle. See Tim Palmer's "Style and Sensation in Contemporary French Cinema of the Body," *Journal of Film and Video* 58, no. 3 (Fall 2006): 22–32.

3. Ozon's films reveal a range of such influences. Having studied with Eric Rohmer at France's prestigious national film school, La Fémis, it is unsurprising that *5x2* should recall, in its setting and atmosphere, aspects of Rohmer's summer films, such as *La Collectionneuse* (1967), *Le genou de Claire* (1970), *Pauline à la plage* (1983), and *L'ami de mon amie* (1987). In terms of its narrative premise, *5x2* surely owes something to Ingmar Bergman's *Scener ur ett äktenskap* (*Scenes from a Marriage*, 1973). Further, Ozon's *Gouttes d'eau sur pierres brûlantes* (*Water Drops on Burning Rocks*, 2000) is a film adaptation of Rainer Werner Fassbinder's play of the same title. More recently, Ozon contributed a short film, *Quand la peur dévore l'âme* (2007) for the French release of a Douglas Sirk DVD box-set, recombining extracts from Sirk's *All That Heaven Allows* (1955) with Fassbinder's *Angst essen Seele auf* (*Ali: Fear Eats the Soul*, 1974).

4. Chronological experimentation has assumed special prominence within mainstream cinema, beginning with the exemplary *Pulp Fiction* (Quentin Tarantino, 1994). We might also think of *Memento* (Christopher Nolan, 2000), *Eternal Sunshine of the Spotless Mind* (Michel Gondry, 2004), *Crash* (Paul Haggis, 2004); *Babel* (Alejandro González Iñárritu, 2006); and more recently, Nolan's elaborate

Inception (2010). For the particular question of reverse chronology, *Bakha satang* (*Peppermint Candy*, Chang-dong Lee, 2000) and *Irréversible* (Gaspar Noé, 2002) are notable titles that deploy this device.

5. Interestingly, this comparison coheres with the *Washington Post*'s account of the film, which calls *5x2* "fascinating, like watching the collapse of a building in reverse." See Michael O'Sullivan's review, "An Intriguing Look Back At Love," Friday, July 1, 2005, p. WE32.

6. In this respect, McGuire's film recalls Cornell's *Rose Hobart* (USA, 1936) in its play of mechanisms related to optical point of view.

7. George Cukor's *The Marrying Kind* (1952) also deserves mention here. Like *5x2*, Cukor's film begins with a divorce hearing and then proceeds to recount episodes from the couple's marriage (in fact, these recollections constitute much of the film's narrative). Rather than deploying reverse chronology, however, *The Marrying Kind* operates more conventionally, presenting past events via flashback structures. A contemporary variation is Richard Linklater's film series, *Before Sunrise* (1995), *Before Sunset* (2004), and *Before Midnight* (2013), charting the course of a romantic relationship across temporal intervals, and the more recent project, *Boyhood* (2014), shot over twelve years.

8. Phil Powries's analysis of the film's score dovetails with this analysis in intriguing ways. See "The Haptic Moment: Sparring with Paolo Conte in Ozon's *5x2*," *Paragraph* 31, no. 2 (July 2008): 206–222.

9. These details significantly complicate Todd McGowan's dismissal of the film as generating "nothing but antagonism." See *Out of Time: Desire in Atemporal Cinema*, 85–86, 91–93.

10. This much is established by the dialogue and by the quality of light in evidence.

11. Critics have observed Buñuel's influence on Ozon's work, comparing *Sitcom*, for example, to Buñuel's *Discreet Charm of the Bourgeoisie* (1972). For the question of time, however, *Un chien andalou* (1929) is once again a salient title for the deliberate arbitrariness of its temporal markers.

12. In other words, these intricate arrangements evoke the sense that what is moving within this scene is *time*.

13. This much is promised by the film's title: *5x2* is an open equation, without a solution.

Chapter 4

1. Tsai's films observe stylistic trends that are well established in contemporary Taiwanese cinema, associated with influential directors Hou Hsiao-hsien and Edward Yang. Developing a broader analysis of Chinese cinema's place in a transnational culture of memory, Jean Ma characterizes Tsai's work as generating "uncanny temporalities of haunting and nostalgia." See her excellent study, *Melancholy Drift: Marking Time in Chinese Cinema* (Hong Kong University Press, 2010), 93.

2. The esplanade setting figures elsewhere in Tsai's work, specifically within the subsequent short, *Tian qiao bu jian le* (*The Skywalk Is Gone*, 2003).

3. As scholars have noted, *Rope* does not actually endeavor to mask all of the transitions in this way; certain transitions occur as unmasked, straight cuts where they would coincide with the changeover of reels in projection.

4. Tsai's films would seem to privilege this kind of situation, often expressing it in spatial terms. Consider, for example, the restrictive space presented in his 1998 film, *Dong* (*The Hole*) or the director's affection for the darkened cinematic space of film viewing, as in *Bu San* (*Goodbye Dragon Inn*, 2003).

5. See, for example, Mark Peranson's interview, "Cities and Loneliness: Tsai Ming-liang's *What Time Is It There?*" *Indiewire* (January 22, 2002), or "Scouting" by Jena-Pierre Rehm, Olivier Joyard, and Daniele Riviere, in *Tsai Ming-liang* (Paris: Editions Dis Voir, 2000).

6. An interesting account of Tsai's attachment to the French New Wave is offered in Nanouk Leopold's 2002 interview with the director, reprinted in *Senses of Cinema*. See "Confined Space: Interview with Tsai Ming-liang" at http://www.sensesofcinema.com/ contents/02/21/tsai_interview.html. This leads us back to André Bazin, whose influence on Truffaut as a quasi-paternal figure is well known.

7. This dynamic relates to cinema in still other ways: it should be noted that the Rotor's design strongly resembles the proto-cinematic optical device called the zoetrope (or the earlier phenakistoscope).

8. An important discussion of the Bazinian aesthetics of *Playtime* is offered by film critic Jonathan Rosenbaum. See "Tati's Democracy," in *Movies as Politics* (Berkeley and Los Angeles: University of California Press, 1997), pp. 37–40.

9. Representative of this tendency is J. Hoberman's excellent review, "Time (Clock of the Heart)," the *Village Voice*, January 9–15, 2002, which sees these scenes as leaving the characters "lonelier than before." Similarly, Lou Lumineck's review in the *New York Post* calls these scenes "devastating."

10. Linda Williams analysis of "body genres" points to the present-tense experience afforded by certain kinds of films, though her account is concerned with very different issues. See "Film Bodies: Gender, Genre, and Excess," in *Film Genre Reader II*, ed. Barry Keith Grant (Austin: University of Texas Press, 1995), pp. 140–158.

11. The film features several prominent Paris landmarks: here, the scene is set at the Tuileries Gardens; it is the Millennium Ferris wheel that appears in the distance. The wheel was built for the millennium festivities of 2000, and was dismantled as a permanent structure in 2002. (Appropriately enough, it reappears on occasion as a tourist attraction.)

12. Concerning the film's dedication, Tsai has offered this explanation: "When my father passed away I was scared to face it—I even said I would never make a movie about ghosts. But then in 1997, [the actor] Kang-Sheng's father passed away. We were very close to each other, and it felt like another father of mine had died. I started to think about death again. I could not pretend that it hadn't happened, so I decided to make this movie." See Mark Peranson's interview, "Cities and Loneliness: Tsai Ming-liang's *What Time Is It There?*" *Indiewire*, January 22, 2002.

13. Tsai's has expressed the regret, in interviews, that his father did not live to see his work. In this respect, *What Time Is It There?* formulates an interesting

response, leaving the death of Hsaio-Kang's father as "unseen" within the narrative (though reappearing later.)

Chapter 5

1. The version consulted here is the first draft, registered with the Director's Guild of America, June 5, 2007.

2. On Malick's extended break from filmmaking, see Michael Nordine's perspective in "Hollywood Bigfoot: Terrence Malick and the Twenty-Year Hiatus That Wasn't" (*Los Angeles Review of Books*, May 12, 2013). Michael Hill has suggested that Malick made a rare public appearance in Bartlesville, Oklahoma, in December 2005, previewing a version of *The New World*: see "Malick's Return to Bartlesville," *This Land Magazine*, posted August 12, 2010.

3. Arguably, Malick's intellectual biography encourages these tendencies. Before turning to filmmaking, Malick studied continental philosophy at Harvard with Stanley Cavell, eventually translating Heidegger's *Vom Wesen des Grundes* (*The Essence of Reasons*) and serving as a lecturer in philosophy at MIT. On the basis of these details, scholars have tended to read Malick's cinema exclusively in philosophical terms—as translations of philosophy-into-cinema. But this emphasis too often suppresses the rigorous cinematic character of the films themselves, situating them as extensions of a long-concluded philosophical practice rather than as instances of contemporary engagement with the film medium. As representative texts, see David Davies, *The Thin Red Line* (New York: Routledge, 2009); Stuart Kendall and Thomas Deane Tucker, *Terrence Malick: Film and Philosophy* (New York, Continuum, 2011); and Steven Rybin, *Terrence Malick and the Thought of Film* (Lanham, MD: Lexington Books, 2012).

4. Prominent examples of the acclaimed "slow" festival film include Alexander Sokurov's *Russian* Ark (2002); Jia Zhang-ke's *Still Life* (2006); Carlos Reygadas's *Silent Light* (2007); and Apichatpong Weerasethakul's *Uncle Boonmee Who Can Recall His Past Lives* (2010).

5. Robert Koehler, "Cannes: Ears to the Ground (2)," *Filmjourney.org*, May 18th, 2011.

6. J. Hoberman, "Cannes 2011: *The Tree of Life*," *Village Voice*, Monday, May 16, 2011. Hoberman's characterization of Brakhage as a modest artist, even just comparatively, deserves some scrutiny. As Hoberman surely realizes, Brakhage was never one to keep his "big ideas . . . to himself"; consider the cosmological epic *Dog Star Man* (1961–64), for example.

7. The very title of Amy Taubin's review of *The Tree of Life*—"Bible Camp"—aims at its perceived kitsch-factor: see *ArtForum*, May 27, 2011.

8. In the comments section that accompanies Koehler's review, Rosenbaum remarks: "I also agree with your verdict and analysis, having seen the film recently at a Chicago press show. Jim Hoberman calls it kitsch, and he's right as well." See "Cannes: Ear to the Ground (2)," *Filmjourney.org*, May 18, 2011.

9. The film's epigraph cites Job 38:4,7; I have looked back to Job 38:1,7. *The New Oxford Annotated Bible*, edited by Bruce M. Metzger and Roland E. Murphy (New York: Oxford University Press, 1994). Later in the film, the family

attends a sermon on Job, the text of which alludes to Augustine and Kierkegaard. On this interesting point, see http://anyeventuality.wordpress.com/2012/04/19/malicks-quotations-of-augustine-and-kirkegaard/.

10. On these complex tensions, see René Girard's study, *Job: The Victim and His People* (Stanford: Stanford University Press 1987).

11. A certain tension between sound and image registers in each of Malick's films, beginning with the ironizing voiceover of *Badlands* (1973). The issue of sound design is discussed at greater length below.

12. Wilfred died in 1968. Concerning Malick's appropriation of *Opus 161* (1965–66), see Gregory Zinman's informative piece, "Dept. of Optics: Lumia," appearing in *The New Yorker*, June 27, 2011, pp. 25–26.

13. See Johnston's "The Color of Prometheus: Thomas Wilfred's Lumia and the Projection of Transcendence," published in *Colour and the Moving Image: History, Theory, Aesthetics, Archive*, American Film Institute Series, edited by Simon Brown, Sarah Street, and Liz Watkins (New York, London: Routledge, 2012), pp. 67–78.

14. The perceptual situation that I am framing here deliberately recalls the thought of Maurice Merleau-Ponty, when he writes, "[H]e himself was never at the center of himself: nine days out of ten all he saw around him was the wretchedness of his empirical life and of his unsuccessful attempts, the debris of an unknown celebration. Yet it was in the world that he had to realize his freedom, with colors upon a canvas. It was from the approval of others that he had to await the proof of his worth. That is why he questioned the picture emerging beneath his hand, why he hung on the glances other people directed toward his canvas. That is why he never finished working. We never get away from our life. We never see ideas or freedom face to face." See "Cézanne's Doubt," in *Sense and Non-Sense*, translated by Hubert L. Dreyfus and Patricia Allen Dreyfus (Evanston: Northwestern University Press, 1964).

15. The film would seem to paraphrase a section of Thomas à Kempis's fifteenth-century text, *Imitation of Christ*; see book 3, chapter 51. The version I consulted was translated by Betty I. Knott (London: Collins, 1963).

16. Perez's essay is a standout assessment of the film that has proved prescient for thinking about Malick's later work. See "Film Chronicle: *Days of Heaven*," *Hudson Review* 32, no. 1 (Spring 1979): 97–104.

17. Richard Neer's essay, "Terrence Malick's New World," strikes an ideal balance of philosophical commentary and film-analytical precision: see *Nonsite.org* (issue 2, June 2011).

18. When the sunflower image recurs at the film's closing, has been reframed accordingly. It finally appears as a wide composition of innumerable flowers, as though to consummate the divided frames presented previously.

19. Sergei Eisenstein, *Nonindifferent Nature*, translated by Herbert Marshall (Cambridge: Cambridge University Press, 1987).

20. Additionally, that the film's personnel included special effects master Douglas Trumbull, Kubrick's collaborator on *2001* motivates such comparisons. As representative commentary, see John Patterson's "Is Terrence Malick Assuming Stanley Kubrick's Mantle?," the *Guardian*, July 2, 2011. Roger Ebert makes

this comparison, and very favorably, as well: see "The blink of a life, enclosed by time and space," June 2, 2011, rogerebert.suntimes.com. And finally, perhaps the most memorable comparison to Kubrick is this: "If the cosmic astronaut God-baby from the end of '*2001*' came back to earth and made a movie, this would be it." Andrew O'Hehir, "Terrence Malick's Gorgeous, Crazy '*Tree of Life*,'" Salon.com (May 26, 2011).

21. See Henry Gee's *In Search of Deep Time: Beyond the Fossil Record to a New History of Life* (Ithaca, NY: Cornell University Press, 2000).

22. I am grateful here to Bart Testa, who has argued this point eloquently and forcefully in our correspondence.

23. The literature on Malick includes assessments of individual sound elements. See, for example, Anna Latto, "Innocents Abroad: The Young Woman's Voice in *Badlands* and *Days of Heaven*"; Richard Power, "Listening to the Aquarium: the Symbolic Use of Music in *Days of Heaven*"; James Wierzbicki, "Sound as Music in the Films of Terrence Malick," collected in *The Cinema of Terrence Malick*, 2nd ed., edited by Hannah Patterson (London and New York: Wallflower Press, 2007).

24. A detailed account of the film's score is provided by Edward Davis in "Music List: All 37 Songs Featured In Terrence Malick's 'The Tree of Life,'" Indiewire.com, May 17, 2011. See also Roger Hillman's insightful discussion, "Malick's Music of the Spheres: *The Tree of Life*" *Screening the Past* http://www.screeningthepast.com/2012/12/malick%E2%80%99s-music-of-the-spheres-%E2%80%93-the-tree-of-life/ (no. 35). Concerning "flow," Alexandre Desplat indicates in the film's publicity materials that Malick wanted the music to flow "like a body of water throughout the film. So there was a river-like feeling to what I tried to achieve . . . The music had to be very organic and earthy so we used only live instruments and no electronics." *Tree of Life* press kit (USA: Twentieth Century Fox Film Corporation, 2011) pp. 14–15.

25. See, for example, Bob Mondello's piece, "A Symphonic Style Is What Roots *Tree of Life*" NPR.org (May 27, 2011), or Bilge Ebiri's review, http://ebiri.blogspot.ca/2011/05/at-violet-hour-first-stab-at-tree-of.html (May 18, 2011). Ebiri's claim for the film's symphonic form is premised on his interview with Paul Ryan, Malick's second unit photographer on *Days of Heaven*. Ryan's suggestion that Malick was interested in "the cinematic equivalent of how . . . Beethoven had structured his symphonies" is consistently cited in support of this idea. See Bilge Ebiri's "Thirty-Three Years of Principal Filming," nymag.com, May 15, 2011.

26. "Bazin on Marker" in *Film Comment* 39 (July/August 2003): 44.

Conclusion

1. See Heidegger's "The Origin of the Work of Art," in *Basic Writings* (London: Routledge, 1978). My understanding of this essay as a hermeneutical text is indebted to Gerald L. Bruns, in particular, his *Hermeneutics Ancient and Modern* (New Haven: Yale University Press, 1992).

Bibliography

Almendros, Nestor. "Photographing *Days of Heaven.*" *American Cinematographer* 60, no. 6 (1979): 562–465, 592–594, 626–632.

Andrew, Dudley. "André Bazin." *Film Comment* 9, no. 2 (March/April 1973); 9, 2, 64–68.

———. *André Bazin.* New York: Columbia University Press, 1978.

———. *Concepts in Film Theory.* New York: Oxford University Press, 1984.

———. *Opening Bazin: Postwar Film Theory and Its Afterlife.* New York: Oxford University Press, 2011.

———. *What Cinema Is! Bazin's Quest and Its Charge.* West Sussex, UK: Wiley-Blackwell, 2010.

Ashbery, John. *Houseboat Days.* New York: Penguin, 1977.

Attridge, David. *The Singularity of Literature.* London: Routledge, 2004.

Augustine, Saint, Bishop of Hippo. *Confessions.* Translated by Henry Chadwick. London: Oxford University Press, 1991.

Auerbach, Erich. *Mimesis: The Representation of Reality in Western Literature.* Translated by Willard R. Trask. Princeton: Princeton University Press, 1953.

Balsom, Erika. "Around the Clock: Museum and Market." *Framework: The Journal of Cinema and Media* 54, 195, no. 2 (Fall 2013): 161–176, edited by Catherine Russell, pp. 177–191.

Jennifer M. Barker, *The Tactile Eye: Touch and the Cinematic Experience.* Berkeley and Los Angeles: University of California Press, 2009.

Barthes, Roland. *Camera Lucida: Reflections on Photography.* Translated by Richard Howard. New York: Hill & Wang, 1981.

———. *Image, Music, Text.* Essays selected and translated by Stephen Heath. New York: Hill & Wang, 1977.

———. *The Rustle of Language.* Translated by Richard Howard. Berkeley: University of California Press, 1986.

Bazin, André. "Encore la censure: les films meurent aussi," *France Observateur* 349 (January 17, 1957): 19–20.

———. "Sur les routes de l'URSS et Dimanche à Pékin." *France Observateur* 372 (June 27, 1957): 19.

———. "Lettre de Sibérie." *France Observateur* 443 (October 30, 1958).
———. *Qu'est-ce que le cinéma?* (4 Vols.). Paris: Éditions du Cerf, 1958–62.
———. *What Is Cinema?* (2 Vols.). Essays selected and translated by Hugh Gray. Berkeley: University of California Press, 1967–71.
———. *Bazin at Work: Major Essays and Reviews From the Forties and Fifties*. Edited by Bert Cardullo. New York: Routledge, 1997.
———. "Bazin on Marker." *Film Comment* 39.4 (July/August 2003): 44–45.
———. *What Is Cinema?* Translated by Timothy Barnard. Montréal: Caboose, 2009.
———. *Découpage*. Translated by Timothy Barnard. Montréal: Caboose, 2015.
Bergson, Henri. *Matter and Memory*. Translated by Nancy Margaret Paul and W. Scott Palmer. New York: Zone (1911)1988.
———. *Creative Evolution*, tr., Arthur Mitchell, New York: Dover, 1998 [1911].
Bersani, Leo, and Ulysse Dutoit. *Forms of Being. Cinema, Aesthetics, Subjectivity*. London: BFI, 2004.
Bogue, Ronald. *Deleuze on Cinema*. New York: Routledge, 2003.
Bordwell, David. "Authorship and Narration in Art Cinema." In *Film and Authorship*, Virginia Wright Wexman, ed. New Brunswick, NJ: Rutgers University Press, 2003.
———. *Figures Traced in Light: On Cinematic Staging*. Berkeley and Los Angeles: University of California Press, 2005.
———. *Making Meaning: Inference and Rhetoric in the Interpretation of Cinema*. Cambridge: Harvard University Press, 1989.
———. *Narration and the Fiction Film*. Madison: University of Wisconsin Press, 1985.
———. *On the History of Film Style*. Cambridge: Harvard University Press, 1997.
Bresson, Robert. *Notes on Cinematography*. Translated by Jonathan Griffin. New York: Urizen Books, 1975.
Bruns, Gerald. *Heidegger's Estrangements: Language, Truth, and Poetry in the Later Writings*. New Haven: Yale University Press, 1989.
———. "The Hermeneutical Anarchist: Phronesis, Rhetoric, and the Experience of Art." In *Gadamer's Century: Essays in Honor of Hans-Georg Gadamer*, Jeff Malpas, Ulrich Arnswald, and Jens Kertscher, eds. Cambridge: MIT Press, 2002.
———. *Hermeneutics Ancient and Modern*. New Haven: Yale University Press, 1992.
———. *Modern Poetry and the Idea of Language: A Critical and Historical Study*. New Haven: Yale University Press, 1974.
Buckland, Warren (ed.). *Puzzle Films: Complex Storytelling in Contemporary Cinema*. Westchester, UK: Blackwell Publishing, 2007.
Carroll, Noel. *Beyond Aesthetics: Philosophical Essays*. Cambridge: Cambridge University Press, 2001.
Cavell, Stanley. *The World Viewed: Reflections on the Ontology of Film*, enlarged ed. Cambridge: Harvard University Press, 1971.
———. *Disowning Knowledge: In Seven Plays of Shakespeare*. Cambridge: Cambridge University Press, 2003.

Chamarette, Jenny. *Phenomenology and the Future of Film: Rethinking Subjectivity Beyond French Cinema*. London: Palgrave Macmillan, 2012.

Chion, Michel. *The Thin Red Line*. London: BFI, 2004.

Chow, Rey. *Sentimental Fabulations, Contemporary Chinese Films*. New York: Columbia University Press, 2007.

Ciment, Michel. "Entretien avec Terrence Malick." *Positif* 170 (June 1975): 30–34.

Cook, G. Richardson. "The Filming of *Badlands*: An Interview with Terry Malick." *Filmmakers Newsletter* 7, no. 8 (June 1974): 30–32.

Davies, David. *The Thin Red Line*. New York: Routledge, 2009.

Deleuze, Gilles. *Cinema 1: The Movement-Image*. Translated by Hugh Tomlinson and Barbara Habberjam. Minneapolis: University of Minnesota Press, 1986.

———. *Cinema 2: The Time-Image*. Translated by Hugh Tomlinson and Robert Galeta. Minneapolis: University of Minnesota Press, 1989.

Del Rio, Elena. "Alchemies of Thought in Godard's Cinema: Deleuze and Merleau-Ponty." *SubStance* 108, no. 34.3 (2005): 62–78.

Dilthey, Wilhelm. *Selected Writings*. Edited and translated by H. P. Rickman. Cambridge: Cambridge University Press, 1976.

Doane, Mary Ann. *The Emergence of Cinematic Time: Modernity, Contingency, the Archive*. Cambridge: Harvard University Press, 2002.

Dreyfus, H. L. *Being-in-the-World: A Commentary on Heidegger's Being and Time, Division I*. Cambridge: MIT Press, 1990.

———. *Skillful Coping: Essays on the Phenomenology of Everyday Perception and Action*. New York: Oxford University Press, 2014.

Eisenstein, Sergei. *Film Form*. Translated by Jay Leyda. Orlando, Florida: Harcourt, Brace & Company, 1977.

———. *Non-Indifferent Nature*. Translated by Herbert Marshall. Cambridge: Cambridge University Press, 1987.

———. *S.M. Eisenstein: Selected Works Volume II. Towards a Theory of Montage*. Edited by Michael Glenny and Richard Taylor, translated by Michael Glenny. London: BFI Publishing, 1991.

Fabe, Marilyn. *Closely Watched Films: An Introduction to the Art of Narrative Film Technique*. Berkeley and Los Angeles: University of California Press, 2004.

Flaxman, Gregory (ed.). *The Brain Is the Screen: Deleuze and the Philosophy of Cinema*. Minneapolis: University of Minnesota Press, 2000.

Gadamer, Hans Georg. *The Relevance of the Beautiful and Other Essays*. Translated by Nicholas Walker; edited by Robert Bernasconi. Cambridge: Cambridge University Press, 1986.

———. *Truth and Method* (2nd rev. ed.). Translation revised by Joel Weinsheimer and Donald G. Marshall. New York: Continuum, 1994.

Gaudrault, André, and Tom Gunning. "Early Cinema as a Challenge to Film History." In *The Cinema of Attractions Reloaded*, Wanda Strauven, ed. Amsterdam: Amsterdam University Press, 2006.

Gibbs, John and Douglas Pye (eds.). *Style and Meaning: Studies In the Detailed Analysis of Film*. Manchester: Manchester University Press, 2005.

Grosz, Elizabeth. *The Nick of Time: Politics, Evolution, and the Untimely*. Durham and London: Duke University Press, 2004.

Gunning, Tom. "What's the Point of an Index? Or, Faking Photographs." *Nordicom Review* 5, no. 1/2 (September 2004): 39–49.

Hammond, Paul (ed.). *The Shadow and Its Shadow*. San Francisco, CA: City Lights Publishers, 2001.

Haugeland, John. *Dasein Disclosed*. Cambridge: Harvard University Press, 2013.

Hefferman, J. W. *Museum of Words: The Poetics of Ekphrasis from Homer to Ashbery*. Chicago: University of Chicago Press, 2004.

Heidegger, Martin. *Being and Time*. Translated by John Macquarrie and Edward Robinson. London: SCM Press, 1962.

———. *Being and Time*. Translated by Joan Stambaugh. Albany: State University of New York Press, 1996.

———. *Basic Writings*, revised and expanded edition, London: Routledge, 1993.

———. *Country Path Conversations*, translated by Bret W. Davis. Bloomington: Indiana University Press, 2010.

———. *Poetry, Language, Thought*. New York: Harper & Row, 1971.

Hoberman, J. "Film Review" [*The Limey*]. *Village Voice*, October 6–12, 1999.

———. "Cannes 2011: *The Tree of Life*," *Village Voice*, Monday, May 16, 2011.

———. "Time (Clock of the Heart)." *Village Voice*, January 9–15, 2002.

Hoy, David Couzens. *The Critical Circle: Literature, History, and Philosophical Hermeneutics*. Berkeley: University of California Press, 1978.

———. *The Time of Our Lives: A Critical History of Temporality*. Cambridge: MIT Press, 2012.

Inwood, Michael. *A Heidegger Dictionary*. Malden, MA: Blackwell Publishers, 1999.

Jaffee, Ira. *Slow Movies: Countering the Cinema of Action*. New York: Wallflower Press, 2014.

Jauss, Hans Robert. *Toward an Aesthetic of Reception*. Translated by Timothy Bahti. Minneapolis: University of Minnesota Press, 1982.

Kaufman, Anthony (ed.). *Steven Soderbergh: Interviews*. Jackson: University of Mississippi Press, 2002.

Keathley, Christian. *Cinephilia and History, or The Wind in the Trees*. Bloomington: Indiana University Press, 2006.

Kendall, Stuart, and Thomas Deane Tucker. *Terrence Malick: Film and Philosophy*. New York, Continuum, 2011.

Kennedy, Barbara. *Deleuze and Cinema: The Aesthetics of Sensation*. Edinburgh: Edinburgh University Press, 2000.

Kierkegaard, Søren. *Fear and Trembling*, edited by C. Stephen Evans and Sylvia Walsh. Cambridge: Cambridge University Press, 2006.

Kinslake, Rudolf. *A History of the Photographic Lens*. San Diego, CA: Academic Press, 1989.

Krauss, Rosalind. "Clock Time," *October* 136, (Spring 2011): 213–17.

Lehman, Peter (ed.). *Close Viewings: An Anthology of New Film Criticism*. Tallahassee: Florida State University Press, 1990.

Leopold, Nanouk. "Confined Space: Interview with Tsai Ming-liang." *Senses of Cinema* (www.sensesofcinema.com), May 2002.

Levinson, Julie. "Time and Time Again: Temporality, Narrativity, and Spectatorship in Christian Marclay's *The Clock*." *Cinema Journal* 54, no. 3 (Spring 2015): 88–109.

Lim, Bliss Qua. *Translating Time: Cinema, the Fantastic, and Temporal Critique.* Durham: Duke University Press, 2009.

Linssen, Dana. "Introducting: Slow Criticism." *Filmkrant* 307 (February 2009) (http://www.filmkrant.nl/slowcriticism_2009/6795).

Livingston, Paisley, and Carl Plantinga (eds.), *The Routledge Companion to Philosophy and Film.* New York: Routledge, 2009.

Lumineck, Lou. "It's Timely." *New York Post.* January 11, 2002, 042.

Ma, Jean. *Melancholy Drift: Marking Time in Chinese Cinema.* Hong Kong: Hong Kong University Press, 2010.

Malick, Terrence. *The Tree of Life* (screenplay). Los Angeles: Registered with the Writer's Guild of America, 2007.

Marks, Laura U. *The Skin of the Film: Intercultural Cinema, Embodiment, and the Senses.* Durham, North Carolina: Duke University Press, 1999.

———. *Touch: Sensuous Theory and Multisensory Media.* Minneapolis: University of Minnesota Press, 2002.

Maslin, Janet. "Film Review" [*The Limey*]. *New York Times*, October 22, 1999: E29.

McGowan, Todd. *Out of Time: Desire in Atemporal Cinema.* Minneapolis: University Minnesota Press, 2011.

Merleau-Ponty, Maurice. *Phenomenology of Perception.* Translated by Colin Smith. London: Routledge, 2002.

———. *Sense and Non-Sense.* Translated by Hubert L. Dreyfus and Patricia Allen Dreyfus. Evanston: Northwestern University Press, 1964.

———. *The Visible and Invisible.* Edited by Claude Lefort; translated by Alphonso Lingis. Evanston: Northwestern University Press, 1964.

———. *The World of Perception.* Translated by Oliver Davis. London and New York: Routledge, 2002.

Michaels, Lloyd. *Terrence Malick.* Champaign, IL: University of Illinois Press, 2008.

Moretti, Franco. *Signs Taken for Wonders: Essays in the Sociology of Literary Forms.* Translated by Susan Fischer, David Forgacs, and David Miller. London: Verso, 1988.

Morgan, Dan. "No Trickery with Montage": On Reading a Sequence in Godard's *Pierrot le fou.*" *Film Studies* (Winter 2004), 8–29.

Morin, Edgar. *The Cinema, or the Imaginary Man.* Translated by Lorraine Mortimer. Minneapolis: University of Minnesota Press, 2005.

Morrison, James, and Thomas Schur. *The Films of Terrence Malick.* Westport, CT: Praeger Publishers, 2003.

Mroz, Matilda. *Temporality and Film Analysis.* Edinburgh: Edinburgh University Press, 2012.

Mulvey, Laura. *Death 24x a Second: Stillness and the Moving Image.* London: Reaktion Books, 2006.

———. "Visual Pleasure and Narrative Cinema." *Screen* 16, no. 3 (Autumn 1975): 6–18.

Neer, Richard. "Terrence Malick's New World." *Nonsite.org* (issue #2), June 2011.

Neupert, Richard. *The End: Narration and Closure in the Cinema*. Detroit: Wayne State University Press, 1995.

Ng, Maria N., and Philip Holden, eds. *Reading Chinese Transnationalisms: Society, Literature, Film*. Hong Kong: Hong Kong University Press, 2006.

Nietzsche. Friedrich. *Untimely Meditations*. Edited by Daniel Breazeale. Cambridge: Cambridge University Press, 1997.

O'Sullivan, Michael. "An Intriguing Look Back at Love." *Washington Post*, Friday, July 1, 2005, p. WE32.

Patterson, Hannah (ed.). *The Cinema of Terrence Malick: Poetic Visions of America*, 2nd ed. New York: Wallflower Press, 2007.

Peranson, Mark. "Cities and Loneliness: Tsai-Ming-liang's 'What Time Is It There?'" indieWIRE.com, January 22, 2002.

Peirce, C. S. "What Is a Sign?" In *The Essential Peirce: Selected Philosophical Writings, Volume 2, 1893–1913*, Peirce Edition Project, ed. Bloomington: Indiana University Press, 1998.

Perez, Gilberto. "Film Chronicle: *Days of Heaven*." *Hudson Review* 32, no. 1 (Spring 1979): 97.

———. *The Material Ghost: Films and Their Medium*. Baltimore, MD: Johns Hopkins University Press, 2000.

Perkins, V. F. *Film as Film*. London: Penguin, 1972.

Pisters, Patricia. *The Matrix of Visual Culture: Working with Deleuze in Film Theory*. Stanford: Stanford University Press, 2003.

Proust, Marcel. *Remembrance of Things Past* (3 Vols.). Translated by C. K. Scott Moncrieff and Terence Kilmartin. London: Penguin, 1981.

Rancière, Jacques. *Béla Tarr, The Time After*. Translated by Erik Beranek. Minneapolis: Univocal Publishing, 2013.

Ricoeur, Paul. *Freud and Philosophy: An Essay on Interpretation*. New Haven: Yale University Press, 1970.

———. *From Text to Action*. Translated by Kathleen Blamey and John B. Thompson. Evanston: Northwestern University Press, 1991.

———. *Interpretation Theory: Discourse and the Surplus of Meaning*. Fort Worth: Texas Christian University Press, 1976.

———. *Time and Narrative* (3 Vols.). Translated by Kathleen McLaughlin and David Pellauer. Chicago: University of Chicago Press, 1984–1988.

Rivière, Danièle. "Scouting." In *Tsai Ming-liang*, Jean-Pierre Rehm, Olivier Joyard, and Danièle Rivière, eds. Paris: Éditions Dis Voir, 2000.

Rodowick, D. N. *Gilles Deleuze's Time Machine*. Durham: Duke University Press, 1997.

Rosen, Philip. *Change Mummified: Cinema, Historicity, Theory*. Minneapolis: University of Minnesota Press, 2001.

Rosenbaum, Jonathan. "Tati's Democracy." *Movies as Politics*. Berkeley: University of California Press, 1997.

Rothman, William. *Hitchcock: The Murderous Gaze*. Cambridge: Harvard University Press, 1984.

———. *The 'I' of the Camera: Essays in Film Criticism, History, and Aesthetics*. Cambridge: Cambridge University Press, 1988.

Rhym, John. "The Paradigmatic Shift in the Critical Reception of Terrence Malick's *Badlands* and the Emergence of a Heideggerian Cinema." *Quarterly Review of Film and Video* 27 (2010): 255–266.

Russell, Catherine (ed.). *Framework: The Journal of Cinema and Media* 54, no. 2 (Fall 2013): 161–176.

Rybin, Steven. *Terrence Malick and the Thought of Film*. Lanham, MD: Lexington Books, 2012.

Said, Edward. *On Late Style: Music and Literature Against the Grain*. New York: Random House, 2006.

Sapontzis, S. F. "A Note on Merleau-Ponty's Ambiguity." *Philosophy and Phenomenological Research* 38, no. 4 (June 1978), 538–543.

Schefer, Jean Louis. "Ordinary Man of the Cinema." In *The Enigmatic Body: Essays on the Arts*, Paul Smith, ed. and trans. Cambridge: Cambridge University Press, 1995.

Schleiermacher, Friedrich. *Hermeneutics and Criticism and Other Writings*. Translated and edited by Andrew Bowie. Cambridge: Cambridge University Press, 1998.

Seid, Steve. "Strain Andromeda, The." Pacific Film Archives Film Programs, www.bampfa.berkeley.edu/search/film, May 27, 1993.

Shambu, Girish, *The New Cinephilia*. Montreal: Caboose, 2014.

Sisario, Ben. "John Randolph, 88, an Actor On Broadway and in the Movies." *New York Times*, February 28, 2004, p. C15.

Sobchack, Vivian. *The Address of the Eye: A Phenomenology of Film Experience*. Princeton: Princeton University Press, 1992.

———. *Carnal Thoughts: Embodiment and Moving Image Culture*. Berkeley and Los Angeles: University of California Press, 2004.

Shklovsky, Victor. "Art as Technique." In *Russian Formalist Criticism: Four Essays*, Lee T. Lemon and Marion J. Reis, trans. Lincoln: University of Nebraska Press, 1965.

Stern, Lesley, and George Kouvaros. *Falling for You: Essays on Film and Performance*. Sydney: University of Sydney, 1999, p. 9.

Sterrit, David. "Days of Heaven and Waco: Terrence Malick's *The Tree of Life*," *Film Quarterly* 65, no. 1 (Fall 2011): 52–57.

Stewart, Garrett. *Framed Time: Toward a Postfilmic Cinema*. Chicago: University of Chicago Press, 2007.

Stiegler, Bernard. *Technics and Time, 1: The Fault of Epithemeus*. Translated by Richard Beardsworth and George Collins. Stanford: Stanford University Press, 1998.

Tarkovsky, Andrey. *Sculpting in Time: Reflections on the Cinema*. Translated by Kitty Hunter-Blair. Austin: University of Texas Press, 1986.

Thomas à Kempis, *The Imitation of Christ*. London & Glasgow: Collins, 1963.

Thompson, Kristin. *Breaking the Glass Armor: Neo-Formalist Film Analysis*. Princeton: Princeton University Press, 1988.

Totaro, Donato. "Introduction to André Bazin, Part 2: Style as a Philosophical Idea." *Offscreen* 7, no. 7 (July 2003).

Turim, Maureen. *Flashbacks in Film: Memory and History*. London: Routledge, 1989.

Weil, Simone. *Lectures on Philosophy*. Translated by H. Price. Cambridge: Cambridge University Press.

White, Carol J. *Time and Death: Heidegger's Analysis of Finitude*. Edited by Mark Ralkowski. Burlington, VT: Ashgate Publishing Company, 2005.

Williams, Linda. "Film Bodies: Gender, Genre, Excess." In *Film Genre Reader II*, Barry Keith Grant, ed. Austin: University of Texas Press, 1995.

Woessner, Martin. "What Is Heideggerian Cinema? Film, Philosophy, and Cultural Mobility." *New German Critique* 113, no. 38.2 (Summer 2011): 129–257.

Wollen, Peter. *Signs and Meaning in the Cinema*. London: Secker & Warburg/BFI, 1969.

Index